RESURRECTION SONG

The Bishop Henry McNeal Turner/Sojourner Truth Series in Black Religion

Editor: Dwight N. Hopkins
  The University of Chicago, The Divinity School

Associate Editors:
  James H. Cone, Union Theological Seminary, New York
  Katie G. Cannon, Temple University
  Cain Hope Felder, Howard University, School of Divinity
  Jacquelyn Grant, The Interdenominational Theological Center
  Delores S. Williams, Union Theological Seminary, New York

The purpose of this series is to encourage the development of biblical, historical, theological, ethical, and pastoral works that analyze the role of the churches and other religious movements in the liberation struggles of black women and men in the United States, particularly the poor, and their relationship to struggles in the Third World.

Named after Bishop Henry McNeal Turner (1843-1915) and Sojourner Truth (1797?-1883), the series reflects the spirit of these two visionaries and witnesses for the black struggle for liberation. Bishop Turner was a churchman, a political figure, a missionary, and a pan-Africanist. Sojourner Truth was an illiterate former slave who championed black emancipation, women's rights, and the liberating spirit of the gospel.

Previously published in the Turner Series:

In the Turner/Truth Series:

The Bishop Henry McNeal Turner/Sojourner Truth Series
in Black Religion, Volume XVI

RESURRECTION SONG

African-American Spirituality

Flora Wilson Bridges

ORBIS BOOKS

Maryknoll, New York 10545

The Catholic Foreign Mission Society of America (Maryknoll) recruits and trains people for overseas missionary service. Through Orbis Books, Maryknoll aims to foster the international dialogue that is essential to mission. The books published, however, reflect the opinions of their authors and are not meant to represent the official position of the Society. To obtain more information about Maryknoll and Orbis Books, please visit our website at www.maryknoll.org.

Queries regarding rights and permissions should be addressed to Orbis Books, P. O. Box 308, Maryknoll, New York 10545-0308.

Published by Orbis Books, Maryknoll, NY 10545-0308
Manufactured in the United States of America
Manuscript editing and typesetting by Joan Weber Laflamme

Library of Congress Cataloging-in-Publication Data

Bridges, Flora Wilson, 1948–
    Resurrection song : African-American spirituality / Flora Wilson Bridges.
        p. cm. – (The Bishop Henry McNeal Turner/Sojourner Truth series in
        Black religion; v. 16)
    Originally presented as the author's thesis–Vanderbilt University
    Includes bibliographical references (p.) and index.
    ISBN 1-57075-359-8 (pbk.)
    1. African Americans–Religion. 2. Spirituality–United States. I. Title. II. Series.

BR563.N4 B67 2001
200'.89'96073–dc21

00-068808

To the Ancestors

One ever feels his two-ness—an American, a Negro; two souls, two thoughts, two unreconciled strivings; two warring ideals in one dark body, whose dogged strength alone keeps it from being torn asunder. The history of the American Negro is the history of this strife—this longing to attain self-conscious manhood to merge his double self into a better and truer self. In this merging he wishes neither of the older selves to be lost. He would not Africanize America, for America has too much to teach the world and Africa. He would not bleach his Negro soul in a flood of white Americanism, for he knows that Negro blood has a message for the world. He simply wishes to make it possible for a man to be both a Negro and an American, without being cursed and spit upon by his fellows, without having the doors of Opportunity closed roughly in his face. This, then, is the end of his striving: to be a co-worker in the kingdom of culture, to husband and use his best powers and latent genius. Those powers of body and mind have in the past been strangely wasted, dispersed, or forgotten. The shadow of a mighty Negro past flits through the tale of Ethiopia the Shadowy and of Egypt the Sphinx.

—W. E. B. Du Bois, *The Souls of Black Folk*

Contents

Preface

When I was a graduate student, I sat in class one afternoon and listened in dismay when the professor claimed that the African-American worldview was no different from the European-American worldview. As a deeply spiritual and somewhat religious African-American woman, I knew this statement was far less than accurate. This book is based upon a conviction that I now hold more deeply at the conclusion of my work than I did at its beginning. This conviction is that the scholarly articulation of African-American theology has heretofore neglected or ignored the African-based spirituality that is the foundation of the culture of African Americans, their religion, and their struggle for freedom in the United States. Thus this work concerns itself with two major questions: What is African-American spirituality? What were its effects upon African-American culture—particularly in its religion and its quest for freedom?

The study of African-American spirituality is of crucial importance because it was this underlying spiritual matrix that helped African Americans to forge their own worldview. This, in turn, helped them to be more resilient; less malleable to racial, social, and economic exploitation; and able to live with some sense of dignity and cultural cohesion as a community. African-American spirituality was the "sorcerer's stone" upon which black people in America birthed and nurtured a new-old culture: they created a new kinship network, raised and socialized children in their own way, built a new-old religion, and continued creatively and effectively to articulate and struggle to achieve their high hopes and dreams in the face of the horrifying and spirit-numbing conditions of American racism.

In this quest of "tracking" African-American spirituality, it has been necessary to examine the folk sources without which it is impossible to understand the culture and religion of African Americans. In light of this, I substantially departed from doing theology in the usual manner of basing it on intellectual constructs. I have utilized the folk materials, as fully as possible, because they reveal the truest spiritual imagination, perceptions, and complex imagery of the minds and souls of black folks.

Therefore, my focus has been to illustrate the continuance of spiritual "patterns" historically present in African-American culture and religion rather than to detail the emergence of new lines of theological thought. The folk materials I analyze are not only relevant to but are the very origins of African-American spirituality and culture; they have helped to create black consciousness with reference to and often in opposition to the dominant culture of the United States. This entire body of sources, until very recently, has been substantially ignored by many black theologians. Yet these materials are necessary as a vehicle for purveying an analysis of black spirituality. Since I have found it necessary to illustrate spiritual patterns in black culture, the reader should assume some redundancy; I repeat these patterns over and over in whatever variations they frequently appear in African-American culture. Hopefully, in the end, the reader will have a comprehension of this elusive spirituality.

It would not have been possible to complete this work without the past and present work of scholars in the fields of African and African-American studies, folklore, music, art, literature, film, philosophy, history, theology, spirituality, and religion. I thank them for shedding light upon the vast network of African and African-American thought, culture, spirituality, and religion. Though my aims have been different from theirs, I would not have been able to confront the scholarly challenge of exploring African-American spirituality without them. My debt of gratitude to them is incalculable. Unfortunately, the work of many of these fine scholars predates the concern for gender-inclusive language. In the interest of clarity I have left quotations from their works as I found them, but my own views are firmly womanist and I am personally dedicated to using inclusive language.

I am also deeply grateful to Professor Peter C. Hodgson and Professor Lewis V. Baldwin of Vanderbilt University, who helped to birth this work by reading my earliest drafts when it was originally submitted in dissertation form to complete my graduate degree. The subsequent acts of nursing and mothering were skillfully performed by the kind and experienced editors of Orbis Books, including Editor-in-Chief Robert Ellsberg, who graciously agreed to allow me to submit it to him for his review; my editor, Susan Perry, who gently helped me to transform it into a book; and finally, Dwight Hopkins, the able scholar and general editor for the Bishop Henry McNeal Turner/Sojourner Truth Series of Orbis Books, who approved its inclusion in this wonderful and prestigious series.

Yet before I researched and wrote about African-American spirituality, I lived it in my own family. I am profoundly grateful to my mother, Mrs. Agnes Harris, and my daughter, Mrs. Tracey Bridges Mason, who demonstrated this spirituality in their encouragement and support of just about whatever I have chosen to do in life, even when they did not fully understand what it was I was about or why. I thank them for the meals they cooked for me and delivered to my door while I was writing; for the bills they paid; for my beautiful grandchildren, Imani, Ireti, and Itabari; and for the holy space they helped to create and protect in my life so that I could have proper room to think my own thoughts, pray my own prayers, and pay homage to my own people. I thank my son, David Lee Bridges Jr., for helping to take care of his grandmother and getting good grades throughout this endeavor so that I did not have to worry about him for one single moment.

I also thank the people of my home church, Grace Baptist Church of Mount Vernon, New York, and the members of the church I pastored, Amistad United Church of Christ of Atlanta, Georgia, for continuing the good work of nurturing me spiritually that my family began. My gratitude is humbly extended to the students I taught for many years at Fisk University and Spelman College who filled my classroom for the course "African-American Spirituality" to overflowing as we struggled together to understand and articulate our spirituality.

Finally, I am eternally grateful to my people—Africans and African Americans—who lived their spirituality, quite consciously, to gain psychological, emotional, spiritual, and physical release from the cruel limitations of their societies and their situations. I am grateful for the most ancient tales of flying Africans, to the ring shout, to the Negro spirituals, to black theologians, to the religious expression of the black church. I thank the Africans and African Americans, the living and the "living dead," for giving me great reason to be proud to be who I am because of who we are. I thank God for making me an African-American woman. For, as my colleague of many years at Spelman College Dr. Norman Rates once remarked to a professor who suggested that the answer to the challenge of being black in North America was to become more white, "You must not know how exciting it is to be black!"

Introduction

African-American spirituality is the essence of African-American culture and religion and the impetus for the struggle for freedom of the African-American community in America. This study uncovers the distinctive aspects of what black church historian C. Eric Lincoln called the black sacred cosmos or the religious worldview of African Americans in order to work toward a definition of African-American spirituality.[1] African Americans, like their African ancestors, are not monolithic in terms of their religious expression, even though most of the enslaved who became Christian embraced Protestantism. Yet it is possible to sketch a common thread "beneath" the diversity. This common thread is African-American spirituality or the peculiar spiritual temperament that was born from the enslaved Africans and preserved and transformed by their children in succeeding generations.

African-American spirituality is of more than historical interest. Contemporary black theologians have been criticized for ignoring spirituality in their strongly sociological descriptions of black religion and the black church. Critic Calvin E. Bruce writes that any workable theological system addressing African Americans should posit the importance of the African-American spiritual temperament as an indispensable starting point.[2] For, he suggests, intrinsic to African-American spirituality are proper ingredients that help to shape and frame the black American cultural context. This spirituality influenced the African-American community to conceive of freedom as a *cultural tendency* or *direction* that resisted European culture and religion in its hostile attitudes toward the African-based African-American culture that began to emerge from chattel slavery. For African-American spirituality, in its very essence, is African-based, against white racism and the source of inspiration for the black community's struggle toward freedom.

Bruce also emphasizes that African-American spirituality and African-American religion are quite often used interchangeably when discussion focuses on the faith of the African-American community.[3] Yet, he contends, spirituality (black or otherwise) is not synonymous with religion. They may be related, but they are not identical. Religion essentially involves the institutionalization of rites, rituals, and dogmas. It is therefore quite possible for human beings to be "religious" without experiencing God and responding to God's call to participate in community. The black community expresses this reality when it speaks about the religious rite of baptism. The people say, "You can go down a dry devil and come up a wet devil." In other words, whether or not a person is "saved" and truly spiritual is not essentially defined through the arena of observing religious rites, creeds, dogmas, and so forth. It is defined by whether one "knows Jesus." By this black people mean whether one has actually encountered God and been transformed by God in that existential encounter in such a way that one knows how to, and begins to, in the words of the Negro spiritual, "treat everybody right."

Spiritual identity, in this sense, is the result of an actual encounter with the Divine wherein the human being cannot bypass participation in what Bruce calls a "transpersonal ultimacy" that requires the person to live out cultural values that foster true community.[4] Religion teaches humankind to appreciate God's love; but spirituality challenges human beings to directly experience the transformative power of God's love. Religion is a belief system or reflection on the nature of ultimate reality. Spirituality is the method and manner by which the ultimately real actually touches the depth of being of the human personality, transforms it, and causes it to long for true community. Religion may enlighten the mind, but spirituality converts the entire existence.

African-American spirituality, with an inherited African unified worldview, does not divide the human personality into distinctly separate spheres of mind, body, and soul. The self is an inextricable whole. In this view, religion can be a form of knowing, while spirituality, in a far more holistic sense, is a way of being. To talk about African-American spirituality is to talk about African Americans' ways of being—mind, body, and soul—in American society. Therefore, African-American spirituality is rooted in the totality of black culture in America, not just in black religion. The result is, Bruce claims, that religion edifies while spirituality actually sanctifies. Religion may help to inform the soul's journey toward God, but spirituality itself *is* the soul's journey.[5]

Given the above, in order to define African-American spirituality, the discussion cannot be confined simply to black religion and the black church. Black religion and the black church play a crucial part in and must be included in African-American spirituality, but this spirituality is a far more enormous and comprehensive phenomenon within black life and culture in America. In an African-based spiritual sensibility (or unified worldview), it arises from within many aspects of the entire culture of African Americans and is by no means compartmentalized or limited to black religious expression, whether within or without the black church. For black people, traditional Africans and African Americans, understand themselves to encounter God everywhere and in everything.

I've heard as many sermons preached and the Bible as passionately and thoroughly expounded upon in the "juke joints" (tiny bars in the Deep South) as in the black church. African Americans often claim that God helped them to dream the "number" to win the lottery. It is not at all uncommon to hear African-American athletes, movie stars, singers, and other celebrities accept awards on television and state, "First, I want to give honor to God for helping me to win this award." They then thank their family, their community, and their peers. African-American spirituality may be found (as theologian James Cone wrote) in the spirituals as well as the blues,[6] the beauty shop and the barber shop as well as the prayer meeting, the bar and the street corner as well as the choir rehearsal, the hoodoo prophet's silver trailer and the spiritual adviser's parlor as well as the preacher's pulpit, and the prison cell as well as the pew.

The locus of black religious expression helps us to see African-American spirituality in a "distilled" way within the enormity of black culture in America. But we must remain ever aware that the African-American community, with its cultural tendency toward a unified worldview, does not confine spirituality to religion, a building, or an institution. African-American religion and African-American spirituality are not identical, though the latter certainly includes the former; African-American spirituality permeates all of black culture.

This spiritual temperament emerged from the impact of three sources: (1) It was built from pieces of an African past (African retentions) that were reconstructed to address the issue of survival in a hostile and threatening new world. (2) It was also formed from the experiences of the enslaved and included their strong sense of involuntary presence in America. (3) Finally, it was constructed in part from Africanized elements of the European-Christian tradition. These three sources provide the distinctive loci for studying African-American spirituality.[7]

Given the above, this book enters the debate among African-American theologians at two points. First, there may be consensus in the black scholarly community as to the need for a black theology that uses the experiences of the African American as a point of departure. Yet there is no consensus as to precisely what principle should organize black theology. Second, there has been no serious theological attempt to integrate the rich and varied spiritual expression of African Americans into African-American theology. One may suggest the task for the contemporary African-American theologian is not to create some "new" theory or express some old theological concept in a new way. It may be a more profoundly radical task of speaking about spirituality as it has always existed in the African-American community in a way that, in and of itself, will integrate into black theology that which has been neglected and left out by black theologians doing theology in the essentially European manner of confining it to European Protestantism.

Black theologian Cecil Cone seriously criticizes black theology for ignoring the intrinsic uniqueness of black religion as derived from African retentions, and he says that black theology tends to make black religion identical with the ideology of the Black Power era and Christian orthodoxy. As a result, he concludes, black theology has essentially failed to distinguish adequately between black religion and white religion (as it is rooted in Judaism, Catholicism, and Protestantism) and has reduced black religion to politics by not recognizing black religion's roots in its own unique spirituality.

African-American scholar of religion Joseph R. Washington Jr. emphasizes that there is a "gulf of intimacy" that "continues to divide Negro and white Americans" in their commonly Protestant religious communions.[8] His assumption is that this is a bad thing, and that it is rooted in the lack of theological sophistication on the part of black religion (which he defines solely as black Protestantism rooted in European Protestantism) in America. He states that it is not helpful to speak of black Protestants in the same historical and theological sense as white Protestants. While he is correct in this assertion, he is less than accurate in his claim that this gulf is centered in the "vacuum," defined as the absence of a theological center, in black religion.[9] There is definitely a significant difference between Negro and white Protestants. But this difference is not based, as Washington asserts, in African-American religion's lack of theology or understanding of the Christian faith.

The difference lies in the fact that the Christian faith is essentially different in African-American cultural and religious expression than it is in white Protestantism because the essence of black religion is African-American spirituality. It is this factor that accounts for the fact that African-American religion is not now nor necessarily ever has been strictly imitative of white religion. And, in direct challenge to Washington's claim of black religion's inability to critique its drive toward crass materialism and assimilation into the American middle class, this peculiar spirituality allows for the possibility for black religious expression in America to be characterized by an "internal alertness,"[10] to use C. Eric Lincoln's term, that can judge black religion's response in the sphere of culture in a way that white Protestantism has conspicuously failed to address American greed disguised as religion.

This book seriously addresses these criticisms by unifying the powerful strands of black religious expression under the organizing principle of African-American spirituality. It is this underlying dynamic that fuels black religion as it emerges from the three essential contexts of African retentions, slave religion, and the Africanized appropriation of European-Christian language. This, I believe, will reconnect black theology to its essence—black religion as it is shaped by black spirituality. In addition, the concept of spirituality has the potential to reconcile the tension between the universal and the particular that surrounds liberation theologies. In the notion of spirituality, the experience of the African American has the potential to be connected into that of the total human community.

This spirituality is discussed around the themes of (1) a unified worldview; (2) black people's self-definition of human identity; (3) spirituality embodied as the call to protest; and (4) the quest for community as these themes are undergirded by the motif of freedom. These are the materials, lifted out from and justified by their preponderance in black history and culture, needed to build a picture of a comprehensive African-American spirituality.

The African-American spiritual sensibility most clearly reveals itself in the people's longing and struggle for the freedom to be in community in the midst of an alien and racist surrounding culture that sought to destroy their culture. Black culture attests to black consciousness expressing itself as Jonah trapped in the belly of a fish—or North American culture as a vicious shark—struggling to be free. This freedom is sought by means of African-American "cultural self-containment." Historian Lawrence Levine describes this as the ability of black people in America to retain, remold, and reshape aspects of black culture that could be used as resistance by the people in a "culturally marginal situation."[11] Levine states that emancipation and cultural marginality were parallel developments for the bulk of black people in the United States. Tension arose from the people's need or urge to continue to identify with many of their own central cultural traditions and the demand of the wider racist society for black people to absorb and emulate white culture.

African-American spirituality essentially addressed this tension. It empowered black people to form their own sense of identity, to protest the racism that sought to force upon them a false identity, and to create authentic community. Thus, for African Americans, salvation has been about living out, in day-to-day existence, their own unique cultural ideals of community. Evil is to forget or neglect those ideals and to betray the community by embracing the life-threatening values of the dominant culture. Salvation, for the individual self in community, is to embrace those values that strengthen the health and vitality of the community.

This book suggests that within African-American spirituality (1) the African past acts as a true source of authority as well as scriptures (predominantly Christian but marginally the Qur'an) and the tradition of Protestantism for black religion and the black church; and (2) the protest tradition of black religion and the black church and their struggle for the freedom of the African-American community were not solely or even primarily based on the external stimuli of white racism; more fundamentally, the struggle for freedom occurred because of an internal agency that, in and of itself, resists oppression and strives for freedom because it is essentially liberative; and (3) this internal agency is African-American spirituality, and it has persisted among African Americans even into the twenty-first century. This spirituality has empowered black religion, the black church, and the black community, within its unified worldview, in the struggle to define a truer sense of identity, to protest when that sense of identity is maligned, and to heed the "urge" toward the end of true human community and harmony in all of creation.

The unified worldview, in a relationship of causality, led the people toward a spiritual definition of the self as self-in-community. This, in turn, led the individual to protest any barrier to self-definition in community. And community came to be generously and expansively defined as a radical inclusiveness that was culturally expressed as a "oneness" or an "interrelatedness" with God and all of creation. Thus the task for each successive generation of African Americans has historically revealed itself to be essentially a religious one in the concrete struggle for the freedom to be in community. African Americans are not concerned about freedom as a concept or an idea. They are compelled by the spiritual and religious necessity to "live freedom" in their everyday existence—in their culture.

The first derivative of African-American spirituality is a unified worldview. Chapter 1 concerns itself with the African legacy of a unified worldview that was "inherited" by African Americans. Enough revisionist scholarship exists to disprove E. Franklin Frazier and other early theorists who claimed a total break with the African past caused by the brutalities Africans encountered in the Middle Passage in the Atlantic slave trade. Scholars have more than adequately shown that African Americans retained many customs and practices from West Africa.[12] But they kept more than just externals. More fundamentally, they were able to preserve parts of a worldview or internal way of ordering life in terms of a blend of the ordinary and extraordinary worlds. They brought together, like the West Africans, the sacred and the secular in a way that saw divine participation in ordinary life. Therefore the sacred colored the everyday events of life.

This unified worldview, in turn, had serious implications for the African American's understanding of the individual self and the self's relationship to community. Chapter 2 discusses the African-American quest for identity in the midst of American racism. Calvin E. Bruce writes that for black Christians, this African-based temperament of a unified worldview recognizes the human family as "one branch of the cosmological Tree of Life."[13] In such a view, spirituality informs all understandings of self, reality, and divinity. As a result, human beings understand themselves to share a part of divinity (therefore divinity's struggle) and relate to one another in terms of spiritual identity. The vocation of the self, as we will see demonstrated in the lives of black religious leaders in Chapters 3 and 4, is profoundly linked with the community. This is true identity. This view of identity, defined as the vocation of the self toward the building of community, demonstrates a central continuity between West Africa and African-American religion and spirituality that helps to uncover the organizing key that unifies and interprets African-American culture and its freedom struggle. The quest for identity is explored from the perspectives of (1) African retentions; (2) the worldview of the enslaved; (3) the black church and the enslaved; and (4) the values of the enslaved.

Chapter 3 discusses the call to protest defined as spirituality embodied in the third dimension in this movement toward freedom. It arose from the internal "pressure" of a spirituality that resisted anything that would act as a barrier to the African American's sense of identity as it is discovered in community. The protest tradition of black America, in light of this necessity, may be defined as the perpetual movement of black persons and the collective people toward the end of community. This chapter, in examining the phenomenon of protest in the black community, focuses on certain figures whose lives show evidence of a spirituality that compelled them toward the freedom to be in community: Harriet Tubman, William Edmondson, Fannie Lou Hamer, and Ruby Bridges. These individuals are not examined exhaustively or in and of themselves. They are analyzed in order to lift up their life experiences and vocations as occasions for illuminating the peculiar spirituality that they share. These people all illustrate what Septima Clark called a "readiness from within."[14] They are discussed because the life of each reveals clear evidence of all six aspects of black spirituality as it is embodied in apprenticeship, the experience of alienation, rejection of the societal norm, personal sacrifice versus self-interest, solidarity with the despised poor, and joy in community.

Chapter 4 is a study of the vision of community as it is guided by African-American spirituality rooted in the African legacy of a unified worldview. This chapter looks at an actual African-American community—Bainbridge, Georgia—that reveals strong African retentions that guide the people's value system. This discussion allows the reader to see the effect of African-American spirituality in an actual community.

Chapter 5 discusses the vision of community from the perspectives of three famous African-American spiritual leaders: Howard Thurman, Martin Luther King Jr., and Malcolm X. One discovers common theological visions of community between the Africans and their African-American descendants well into the twentieth century based on the ideals of justice, love, and harmony and reconciliation in creation.

Howard Thurman, who was in living touch with the enslaved generation through the grandmother who brought him up, figures prominently
in this chapter. His ideal of community shows a marked continuity with
the African legacy in its unified worldview that extended to nature as
well as human society. Martin Luther King Jr. spoke, in his last sermon
before he was assassinated, from a similar base of spirituality about the
radical interrelatedness or "oneness" of all of human society, and his
ideal is discussed from this perspective. Finally, Malcolm X is examined as his vision of the ideal of the community continues in the tradition of African-American spirituality. His vision includes the marginalized
within the African-American community itself, as well as the African-
American community as a whole, Africa, and the poor all over the world.

Chapter 6 explores the theological vision of three black film makers.
It looks at the films *Sankofa, The Piano Lesson,* and *Daughters of the Dust*
from the perspective of the film makers' ideals of black spirituality. The
chapter also reviews the implications those ideals contain for shaping a
contemporary vision of African-American spirituality as it continues to
define and protect the African-American community.

Finally, Chapter 7 focuses on findings and conclusions as it attempts
to build a definition of African-American spirituality from the building
blocks of the preceding discussion. This chapter suggests that African-
American spirituality can continue to heal, cure, protect, and make whole
or "holy" the cultural brokenness of the African-American community,
whether it stems from internal or external causes, just as it has done
throughout the history of the Africans in America.

Chapter 1

The African Legacy—
A Unified Worldview

This chapter analyzes the mystique of what African scholar of religion Laurenti Magesa in *African Religion* calls the "life force" of African religion in the African-American context.[1] Magesa claims it is the main principle behind African religiosity and identity, the source and basis of African religious meaning. The transmission of this same life force from the enslaved Africans to their descendants helped black people in America to forge their own worldview, fight the enemies of its life, and restore the life force of generation after generation. As John Mary Waliggo wrote of this life force, no sane society voluntarily chooses to build its future on foreign (and antagonistic) cultures, values, or systems. Neither did the African Americans. In order to survive, African Americans built their culture on the life force of an African-based unified worldview. It is the foundation upon which their values, development, identity, and liberation were built. As Waliggo surmises, for any people to do less is "nothing less than communal suicide."[2]

Thus there is a cultural precedent to black religion and black spirituality—namely African traditional religion—that influenced and informed the framework of social norms and values by which the people ordered their lives and their relationship to others. African traditional culture and religion will not be explored in an exhaustive or comprehensive manner as they support this thesis; rather, they will be looked at in a circular, counterclockwise fashion, through African retentions found in how the oral and religious traditions of the North American enslaved transmitted and reinforced essentially African values, social norms, and religious beliefs. These values, social norms, and religious beliefs were literally *recalled, remembered,* and, finally, *remolded* to function as a powerful and consistent source of identity for the enslaved that was stronger than the conflicting values, social norms, and religious beliefs of chattel slavery and American racism.

9

This chapter first focuses on a certain key aspect of the religio-cultural tradition of pre-colonial Africa that is based on African cosmology. The interpretive principle that governs and shapes that cosmology is a *unified worldview*. In other words, African cosmology contains a deep, underlying, unified, structural content that serves as the foundation for the African worldview; it acknowledges a culture whose major reference points are taken from within the culture itself. The theme of a unified worldview is a reflection of this positive apprehension. It is the root of what the African scholar of religion Temba J. Mafico calls "a fundamental difference between Western people and traditional Africans" that stems from a difference in worldview.[3] This unified worldview is the undergirding principle or normative "regulator" of what would become the African religio-cultural legacy of the Africans to their African-American descendants.

Second, using Mafico's seven categories of the context for understanding African theology, this chapter discusses how the African unified worldview both informs and is built upon

- African conception of time
- African community structure and the place of the ancestors
- the role of the grandparents
- African approach to God
- the African community and social concerns
- attitudes toward strangers
- belief in witchcraft[4]

These categories clearly constitute a useful "showcase of culture" through which we can more easily see the lasting vigor of the African influence in America. As Mary A. Twining and Keith E. Baird write in their work on the African presence in the antebellum South of the Carolinas and Georgia:

African American families have customs which are reminiscent of the various areas of Africa from which they came...The cultural, societal and family behavior of Africans forcibly transplanted in the United States through the institution of slavery was, inevitably, profoundly disrupted by the violent impact of that experience. Their modes of conduct, their moral and aesthetic values, and their sense of psychosocial integrity were not, however, completely extinguished. On the contrary, the Africans reacted to the life situations imposed upon them in America by taking recourse to their ancestral patterns of social and cultural conduct to the extent that these modes of behavior could be re-enacted in the new environment.[5]

These ancestral patterns of social and cultural conduct formed the basis of what Mafico calls the "dichotomy between African traditional culture and Western civilization and Christianity."[6] Employing these categories will somewhat isolate the nature of this dichotomy and, at the same time, demonstrate several of the important philosophical and theological links between the Africans and the African Americans across the bridge of the African legacy. Finally, these categories that point to a unified African worldview are helpful in examining African worship practices and values as they relate to and influence African-American worship practices and values. The theoretical objective of this chapter, therefore, is contained entirely in this problematic of the relationship between African and African-American spirituality, although it is not possible within the scope of this necessarily limited discussion to provide a systematic reconstruction of the complete religious worldview of African peoples.

Finally, this chapter, building upon the discussion of the "building blocks" of the African unified worldview and African traditional religion, will highlight characteristic African morals and values.

As the African theologian Kwesi A. Dickson asserts, African culture has its own religious traditions; "the theologian's working materials inevitably lead to the awareness of the need to give culture a meaningful role in...theology in Africa."[7] Dickson then cites Christopher Dawson's book *Religion and Culture* as describing culture as a theogamy or a coming together of the divine and the human within the limits of a sacred tradition. He states that in so doing, Dawson provided an accurate characterization of African life and thought:

> African culture and religion are bound up together, so much so that the term culture is in the context of this [theological] inquiry properly used as an umbrella description which subsumes religion...Religion informs the African's life in its totality.[8]

Dickson goes on to state that in the African theologizing process, culture must be considered an important informative factor of theology. He describes it as an "inescapable nature of the need to theologise in and through" African cultural particularities. In the light of this necessity, he writes, theologizing in the African context must take account of traditional African religion which includes much that the West would consider as "unsavoury ritualism, polytheistic excesses," and so forth.[9]

It is necessary to take seriously Dickson's question about the place of African culture as a source of theology. While this book is not intended to provide inquiry into the relation between Christianity and other religions in a comparative sense, an exploration of African traditional

religion may challenge the Christian theologian to gain a broader understanding of religion and theology in order to better understand the
nature of African-American religion and spirituality that resulted from
the contact between African traditional religion and European-Christianity. African religion has traditionally been viewed by the West as a
"species of 'primitive' or 'nature' religion," but as Dickson emphasizes:

> It is clear that African religion is not about to disappear, either
> before the Christian Church's advance (and the Church has been
> making very rapid progress in Africa), or in the face of advancing
> technology, industrialisation and urbanisation. Herskovits' study
> of the Blacks in America and the life-styles among Black popula-
> tions in the West Indies and Brazil and elsewhere, have demon-
> strated the resilience of African life and thought.[10]

African philosopher Paulin J. Hountondji attacks the popular myth (popu-
larized by African ethno-philosophers) that an indigenous, collective
African philosophy has been articulated as distinct from the Western
philosophical tradition. Even though the philosophical status of African
worldviews and value systems is a subject of considerable debate,
Hountondji contends that a genuine discussion of African philosophy
must transcend even the theoretical heritage of Western philosophy. In
other words, a question must be raised about the possibility of developing a distinctive approach to philosophical activity "in an African register, if not in African languages," in order to prevent the construction of
an African philosophy that "is nothing but a revamped version of Levy-
Bruhl's 'primitive mentality.'"[11] He calls for an "unshackling of the discourse."[12] He accuses many theoretical attempts to systematize African
philosophy of being fueled with the "ideological problematic of trium-
phant imperialism" precisely because the ideological debate "is centred
elsewhere—in the ruling classes of the dominant society."[13]

This study also concerns itself with the purpose and functions of the
various cosmologies and thought systems produced within the framework of pre-colonial African societies and cultures. But, unlike the pre-
occupations of European philosophers and African philosophers such
as Hountondji, Diop, Senghor, Kagame, and others, it remains outside
of the double problematic (Hountondji's description) of philosophical
discourse that aims either to present African thought in a better light for
Europe or to present it as superior (morally or otherwise) to European
philosophical discourse.

The aim of this chapter is to use a circular, double movement *between*
(for lack of an appropriate English preposition) African theology and
African-American theology both (1) at the intersection of the evidence
of their commonality; and (2) as they can be seen to be separate and

distinct from the Western philosophical and theological traditions as these two conditions meet in the concrete history of the Africans and their descendants in America. So, although this discussion must also broadly concern itself with genuine African philosophy and theology from outside of Africa, it can possibly transcend the oppressive theoretical heritage of the West toward African discourse by conducting its argument solely from the point of departure of the effect of the common spiritual heritage between pre-colonial Africans and African Americans as it is evidenced within African retentions in African-American culture.

The essential problem inherent in this discussion is nothing new. But it is no longer solely the problem of adequately and authoritatively documenting what genuinely constitutes African theology and philosophy as distinctive from the West or whether an African influence persisted among African Americans in North America. Revisionist scholarship has now thoroughly addressed and continues to speak to these problems to the extent that we now know that much of Africa's culture is definitely its own, and there are cultural antecedents now in the form of African retentions in African-American culture. The problem now is more one of describing the spirituality of a "hyphenated" people whose experience emerges from the influence of at least two different cultural contexts. Even from the vantage point of a life that encountered two centuries and spanned both the continents of Africa and America (he was born in Massachusetts in 1868 and died in Ghana in 1963), the great African-American sociologist W. E. B. Du Bois struggled to describe and define African-American spirituality. In 1903 he poignantly wrote:

> I have sought here to sketch, in vague, uncertain outline, the spiritual world in which ten thousand thousand Americans live and strive...I have sketched in swift outline the two worlds within and without the Veil, and thus have come to the central problem of training men for life...Leaving, then, the white world, I have stepped within the Veil, raising it that you may view faintly its deeper recesses,–the meaning of its religion, the passion of its human sorrow, and the struggles of its greater souls.[14]

Du Bois articulates the "peculiar sensation" of the African American as a "double-consciousness" wherein the person ever feels his or her "twoness—an American, a Negro; two souls, two thoughts, two unreconciled strivings; two warring ideals in one dark body."[15] Thus he describes the psychology and the spirituality of the African American as "strife." This "warring" on both the physical and metaphysical planes is experienced in the conflict between racism in the outer world of Africans and their descendants in America and a prior inner disposition as a spirituality influenced by African values that produces a fundamental tension at the heart of their contemporary African-American experience. It is a strange paradox that this "twoness" produces a tension that is itself the bridge to the next cultural step of the Africans in America: becoming a "new-old" people in succeeding generations. The categories in the following section help to explain the nature of the new-old dual spiritual heritage of African Americans.

THE BUILDING BLOCKS
OF A UNIFIED AFRICAN WORLDVIEW

African Conception of Time

African scholars make it abundantly clear that Africans do not regard traditional religion as a separable element of their culture. The people's social life and spiritual formation are integral parts of their culture. God, or the Divine, is the beginning of everything, radically relates to everything, and binds everything together. This theology influences the African concept of time, which, in turn, affects every other aspect of the people's theological view. Therefore, to discuss African theology, one cannot simply discuss theoretical formulas. In the light of this, the descriptive task may be more adequately undertaken by also discussing Africa's social values as they are concretely lived within African culture. Mafico states, in this regard, that it is even difficult for Africans to grasp a theological lesson illustrated solely by theories because the people value actions more than words. This chapter, employing Mafico's method of doing theology, must therefore focus on certain key aspects of African culture that in and of themselves speak directly to African theology as it is revealed in its cultural context.

In his discussion of African philosophy, Hountondji criticizes the great Senegalese thinker and physicist Cheikh Anta Diop for "postulating an essential affinity between the forms of social organization and the cosmology of the ancient Egyptians and...the traditional world of black Africa."[16] His hostility towards Diop's assertions is largely based in his assertion that Diop appeals only to the African past. Instead, Hountondji suggests, one must look toward the philosophy of Frantz Fanon for a more legitimate conclusion. He quotes Fanon: "African culture will take concrete shape around the struggle of the people, not around songs, poems or folklore."[17] He writes that cultural expression, for Fanon, refers "not to a predetermined model offered by the past but to a reality that lies in the future as a perpetual creation: for him culture is not a *state* but a *becoming*."[18]

African-American spirituality, as influenced by the African past, does not raise this question of either/or–either the African past or the contemporary struggle. Hountondji essentially views the notion of the past from a Western philosophy of time. He understands the African past as a static time in pre-colonial African history that presupposes a collective cultural personality of the black race that is objectified in the forms of articulation of the traditional culture. In this sense he believes that it is an "ideological veil thrown over the interests of the new African bourgeoisie."[19] Yet this is in conflict with the traditional African conception of time.

To understand the cosmology of the traditional Africans, Mafico writes, is to understand that the African's conception of time is "qualitative and concrete–not qualitative and abstract."[20] Time is "not uniform duration, nor is it a succession of qualitatively different moments."[21] Time is circular instead of linear in nature. The universe is considered to be permanent, eternal, and unending; as John Mbiti writes, "In many places, circles are used as symbols of the continuity of the universe."[22] In this African view, the universe–both visible and invisible–is an unending circle without limits or discrete moments. As a result of this concept of circularity, "African ideas of time concern mainly the present and the past, and have little to say about the future, which in any case is expected to go on without end."[23]

Although there will be no end, there *was* a beginning. This beginning is God. Mbiti writes:

> The belief in God is found everywhere in Africa. When people explain the universe as having been created by God, they are automatically looking at the universe in a religious way. We can say, therefore, that the African view of the universe is profoundly religious. Africans see it as a religious universe, and treat it as such.[24]

This circular view of time creates the possibility for a worldview that sees all of the ordinary and the extraordinary as radically interrelated or linked; indeed, it is difficult, from a traditional African worldview, to compartmentalize the two as separate and distinct. As many scholars have already noted, in the African worldview there is no real separation between the sacred and the secular–everything is sacred. (Therefore the word *religion* is used in a qualified manner in this discussion.) The awareness of the African view of the universe as profoundly "uni" or "one" results in the African view of all of the universe as religious. Not only is there a link between all that is created, as Mbiti states, there is also a vital link between earth and heaven. Though in many African societies it is believed that the universe is divisible into two (heaven and earth) or sometimes three (heavens, earth, and underworld), "African peoples do not think of these divisions as separate but see them as linked together."[25] God is the beginning, and God is radically related to all of existence and binds existence together in a circular relationship of con- nectedness and interrelatedness.

Therefore, in the African conception of time, there is no "graveyard" of "dead time" that is in the past; nor are past actions static or irrevo- cable. By way of contrast, a linear, Western philosophy of time views time as progressing in a straight, relentless, forward movement from past to present to future. There is no possibility of time moving back- ward from future to present to past or of it leapfrogging from past to future. In the West we speak of someone or something as being "dead and gone" or an event as "water under the bridge." We are told not to "cry over spilled milk." In the African circular conception of time, what is "dead and gone" is never dead and gone, and the past can continually and eternally speak to and either wreak havoc in or empower both the present and the future.

The Nigerian writer Wole Soyinka expresses this circular view of time as explicitly within the temporal concepts of the Yoruba worldview.[26] Soyinka writes:

> Traditional thought operates, not a linear conception of time but a cyclic reality. One does not suggest for a moment that this is pecu- liar to the Yoruba or African world-view…But the degree of inte- grated acceptance of this temporal sense in the life-rhythm, mores and social organisation of Yoruba society is certainly worth em- phasizing, being a reflection of that same reality which denies pe- riodicity to the existences of the dead, the living and the unborn.[27]

More will be said about this in the following sections on the place of the ancestors and the roles of the grandparents in African traditional societ- ies.

The circular conception of time influences the African visual ideal.[28] There is a clear connection between the cosmographic signs of spiritual symbolism in the African visual tradition and this circular worldview. For example, the Ashanti people created a wooden representation of a bird whose feet are pointed forward but whose head faces backward. What this symbol represents is the traditional African conception of time as circular. In other word, the past (the bird's head facing back- wards) vitally informs both the present (the bird itself) and the direction of the future (the feet facing forward).[29] In both Ashanti and Yoruba terms, *ashe* (the power to make things happen), the key to futurity and self-realization, is informed by the past. This philosophy of time, fused with new elements overseas, shaped and defined the black Atlantic visual tradition and black life in general as it is shaped and defined by African spirituality.[30]

Each of the building blocks of a unified worldview discussed below demonstrates how African culture and society are radically interrelated and interlocking. Beginning with the notion of God as the Supreme Being who is radically related to creation, this same theology guides the practice of community structure as it links together the ancestors (as the "living dead" in the spirit-world) with the living, first with the grandparents and then the parents, who through marriage are the link or bond with the future as the unborn.

African Community Structure and the Place of the Ancestors

Mafico states that "the traditional African philosophy of life is based on the community. This community comprises the living and those who are long dead."[31] God is the beginning, and all that is created, the dead as well as the living, are connected to God and to each other. In this unified worldview Mbiti writes that the dead are viewed as present in their "spiritual form" among the living. It is in the light of this belief that scholar of religion Joseph Omosade Awolalu discusses Yoruba beliefs in ancestors: "No one can hope to appreciate the thoughts and feelings of the black man who does not realise that to him the dead are not dead but living."[32] It is helpful to look closely at the beliefs of the Yoruba people, because African Americans are thought to have derived mainly from these West African people.

Awolalu writes:

> The Yoruba, like any other Africans, believe in the active existence of the deceased ancestors. They know that death does not write *finis* to human life but the earthly life has been extended into the life beyond.[33]

For the Yoruba, as in many other cultures, an ancestor is one from whom a person descends, either from the mother's family or the father's family, at a distance in time. The difference may lie in the fact that when the Yoruba refer to the ancestors, they also think of the departed spirits of their forebears with whom the living maintain relationship. This is not true of every dead person.

> To qualify, such men and women must have lived well, attained an enviable old age before dying, must have left behind good children and good memory...all who die a "bad" death are excluded from this group...The father is seen as the one who links the

individual lineage to the lineage ancestors. But all the lineage of past generations who are in the spirit world are ancestors of the individual and he is linked to all of them.[34]

Male ancestors are far more important than female ancestors, although females are included. To become what the Yoruba call a "welcome ancestor," a person has to "live well, die well, and leave behind good children who will accord him proper funeral rites and continue to keep in touch with him by means of offerings and prayer."[35]

The treatment of the corpse for burial was thus of considerable importance in Yoruba tradition. The Yoruba, like the ancient Egyptians, had discovered from ancient times a way to process a dead body so that it would not putrefy or stink, because Yoruba funeral rituals—especially for those of venerable age and social status who died a "good" death—required that the dead lie in state two or more days. For each of these days the corpse, after being ritually washed and the hair dressed for women and often shaved for men, was dressed in a different set of beautiful and dignified clothing from the fine to the finer to the finest as the days progressed. In ancient times a royal personage was accompanied by servants and attendants who were put to death at the time of the burial as well as possessions for the person's immediate needs. Relatives and friends came from near and far, and there would be great feasting. In summary, it was of extreme importance to bury the dead in the proper ritual and ceremonial way, because it was believed that if they were buried improperly, they could not enter the "abode of the ancestors" and mediate between the living and the dead.

Awolalu states that the ancestors are included in the religious system of the Yoruba as "immediate intermediaries" between the living and the supersensible world. Therefore there is a difference in the "tone" of prayers addressed to the ancestors and those addressed to God (Olodumare), the Supreme Being. Although the ancestor is accorded honor and respect because of his or her crucial role as an intermediary to the Supreme Being, the ancestor is not the Supreme Being.

There is also a Yoruba belief in the hereafter, but the difficult problem, according to Awolalu, "is to state precisely where the hereafter is located."[36] The elders of Yoruba society give different answers. Some say that they are gone on a long journey. Others say that they are under the earth. Still others say that they go to certain ancient villages and markets in Yorubaland. Others maintain "that the departed are in an invisible world which is separated from the living only by a very thin partition, and that they are very close to the living."[37]

In addition to the above, the Yoruba also have a strong belief in reincarnation as a way for the departed to return to the living. "One of the commonest ways of doing this is for the soul to be reincarnated and to be born as a grandchild to a child of the departed parents."[38] For example, a daughter born after the death of a mother or grandmother is called Iyabo or Yetunde (mother has returned). A boy is called Babatunde (father has returned). These names reflect the assumption that if a child is born soon after the death of a parent or grandparent, "it is the soul of the immediately deceased that is back."[39] In this sense,

> Neither "child" nor "father" is a closed or chronological concept...The expression "the child is father of the man" becomes, within the context of this time-structure, not merely a metaphor of development, one that is rooted in a system of representative individuation, but a proverb of human continuity which is not uni-directional...The world of the unborn, in the Yoruba world-view is as evidently older than the world of the living as the world of the living is older than the ancestor-world. And, of course, the other way around.[40]

These ideas go, as Soyinka emphasizes, beyond notions of sequential time. What results is an affective social principle that "intertwines multiple existences so absolutely" that an old man would call a child Baba (father, or elder) "if the circumstances of his birth made his actual entry into the living world retrospective."[41]

> The deities exist in the same relation with humanity as these multiple worlds and are an expression of its cyclic nature...a further affirmation of the principle of continuity inherent in myths of origin, secular or cosmic.[42]

In this relationship between the living and the ancestors, the ancestors are keenly interested in the well-being of their living descendants. They function as both protective and disciplinary influences on their children. "They are the guardians of family affairs, traditions, ethics, and activities. Offences in these matters [are] ultimately an offence against the forefathers who, in that capacity, act as the invisible police of the families and communities."[43] There is a cause-and-effect relationship between the attitude of the living toward the ancestors and the living's temporal welfare.

> It is, therefore, believed that the ancestors can be of tremendous benefit to the children who keep them happy and who observe the family taboos; but can be detrimental to the disobedient and negligent children.[44]

The ancestors are believed to be close both to the divinities and to their living children so that they can readily mediate on behalf of their children if they are erring or suffering.

Finally, "the spirit of a particular ancestor may be invoked to assume a material form and to appear singly and speak to the living children and widows, bringing them assurance of the spiritual care and blessings which they desire."[45] This may be done collectively in the form of an annual festival.

The Role of the Grandparents

The grandparents are the next link in the interrelated "circle" after God and the ancestors. In the traditional African family organization "the role of the grandparents was to play with the grandchildren."[46] In this capacity they proved to be of inestimable importance to the continuance of the cultural legacy of the community as they "spent time with the youths telling them stories of ancient times, teaching them heroic songs and tales."[47] Not only did the grandparents tell the grandchildren about their own lives and the lives of the family members before them, the grandparents were also very eager to hear what the grandchildren had to say about their own lives. In this way the grandparents played a crucial advisory role in the lives of their grandchildren. Mafico states that in this traditional African family structure, "Africans did not require a psychiatrist's services because the traditional family structure had a way of dealing with stress, loneliness, sickness and death."[48] This family structure provided several things: "a structure for worshipping God, personnel for dealing with youth, old age, and related social problems."[49] Thus, he writes, in traditional African culture there was no need either for daycare centers or babysitters for the grandchildren or for senior-citizen facilities for the grandparents. The grandparents cared for the grandchildren because they loved them and, in a dual, reciprocal relationship between the very old and very young, a very important relational bond was formed between the generations that fostered a great sense of respect for the elders and their invaluable role in the society. Their job was ultimately the most important in the community: the day-to-day loving care and education–through play, listening, advising and storytelling–of the community's most valuable resource: the very young.

African Approach to God

Mbiti describes God, in African traditional thought, as the Creator of the universe, as outside and beyond it. Yet, at the same time, God is also the sustainer and upholder of the universe and "very close" to it.[50] In Western theology the words *immanence* and *transcendence* are used more or less as metaphors in an attempt to express both the nearness or indwelling of God in the Creation and the way in which God "surpasses" or "goes beyond" Creation in God's "otherness." African traditional religions also express both metaphors, though even in stating this I must be careful not to suggest that language or concepts about God in the two cultures function in precisely the same manner. It is enough to say that there is an affinity. Yet upon closer examination of the way in which God is "immanent" (not an African concept per se) in African thought, God may be considered to be far more immanent or radically immanent in the African understanding of *God-as-member-of-the-community.*

In African myths of creation, as Mbiti emphasizes, humanity sees itself at the center and consequently sees the universe from that perspective.[51] In the African "structure" for worshiping God, God is regarded as "the patron of the family."[52] God then must be respected "as the most senior member or guardian of the community."[53] Again, the divine is radically interwoven into the entire structure of the family and the community.   *Supreme being*

As Mafico points out, God is radically in community through the African concept of family as embracing both the worlds of the ordinary and the extraordinary: *God is member of community*

> Therefore to approach Him by any form of worship, one must follow the family procedure. In other words, the ancestral spirits cannot be by-passed because they are intermediaries between God and human beings.[54]

did not worship ancestors, worshipped god through ancestral spirits.

It is to be noted that African scholars Awolalu, Mbiti, and Mafico, who are all Christian, use the English masculine pronoun *him* for God, though other African scholars, religionists, writers, and artists tend to use actual names of God. This reveals a certain internal coherence in African traditional thought about God, because male ancestors are often considered more important as intermediaries between God and the living.

There is a consistent concern in the work of most African scholars that people of the West tend to see the African approach to God as gross superstition, and ancestor worship as the religion of Africa. Awolalu, who is Yoruba, cautions against this view:

> The fact of the matter is that the Yoruba, like the other ethnic groups in Africa, employ [the African approach] as a means of protesting against death. And we share Edwin Smith's view that "the cult (of the ancestors) answers to what lies deep in human nature—the desire for survival, the refusal to acknowledge that death ends all."[55]

Awolalu believes:

> There is nothing wrong in employing different avenues of reaching the Supreme Being…The essential fact to emphasise is that the Yoruba, like other Africans, believe in the Supreme Being and have the strong desire to have constant contact with Him; they, therefore, employ the ancestors (who are the closest and most familiar to them in the spirit-world), the divinities and spirits as a means of reaching Him who is the Source of life and whose biddings never go unfulfilled.[56]

Mafico, in the same vein, cautions against the ignorance of the West concerning this approach to God:

> Failure by the missionary church to understand and appreciate the role of the ancestral spirits led to the condemnation of what has been labelled African ancestral worship. African Christian scholars have begun scrutinizing African worship and are finding evidence that traditional Africans did not, in actual fact, worship ancestors, but they worshipped God *through* ancestral spirits, in accordance with their highest degree of reverence to Him who is the supreme head of the family circle.[57]

African Community and Social Concerns

A major traditional African social concern, Mafico emphasizes, included the care of aging parents. African people were required to observe this necessity in order to please God.

> In traditional Africa there was no pension plan and life insurance. The parents were ensured of health care, subsistence and a decent burial by the children they reared. The Shonas have a saying, *"Yakakura ika amwa mwana"* ("It grew old and lived on the milk of its child").[58]

He states that the reason why it was so important for wives not to be barren among traditional Africans (as in the Hebrew Bible and other texts of the Ancient Near East) was because children were required to play a crucial role in caring for aging parents. In this community organization the responsibility for the aging parents was undertaken by male children. The daughters, once married, no longer belonged to their family of origin but to their husband's family. Mafico states that this is why traditional Africans (again like the attitude prevalent in the Hebrew Bible and other texts of the Ancient Near East) preferred sons to daughters.

It was also important that there be children to bury the parents properly because, as discussed earlier, the Yoruba understand the deceased as truly members of the families on earth (though no longer of the same fleshly order) who have crossed the "border" between this world and the supersensible world. They now invisibly and spiritually (or as spirits) abide with their families on earth to aid or hinder them or bring them prosperity or adversity according to how well they are honored and remembered.

Attitudes toward Strangers

In African traditional beliefs, courtesy and hospitality were to be extended to the poor, including widows, orphans, people with disabilities, and strangers. Traditional Africa had no commercial lodging places; traditional ethics required that the stranger must be offered shelter and food.

The traditional welfare system required that when crops were harvested, "one must deliberately leave some ears of corn, some grain, beans, and so on, for the poor."[59] This (like the attitudes toward barren women and the importance of male children) is again very much like the Hebrew Bible. Even when planning a festive gathering such as a wedding or a party, more food was prepared than was necessary for the family and the invited guests so that if the uninvited poor attended the festivities, there would be enough for them to eat. Mafico quotes the Shona saying, *Mupfumi ndimambo* (the rich person is a king). In traditional Africa it was the king's responsibility to feed the poor of his land and protect them from exploitation. Helping and caring for the poor were seen as virtues.

If the society refused to take care of the poor, "God was expected to intervene for them and punish the evil doers."[60] The people believed that the ancestral spirits would see this injustice and report it to God, who would then "immediately execute justice by punishing the guilty person in his life time, and not in the world to come."[61] Divine punishment could take several forms: (1) God could take the wealth away from the rich people who were unjust and give it to the poor victims of injustice; (2) the ancestors could withdraw their protection from the wicked; (3) the wicked would be thrown out of the family circle; and (4) become immediately exposed to the dangers of evil spirits and witches.[62]

Belief in Witchcraft

Belief in witchcraft is strong and persistent in African culture and exists simultaneously with belief in Christianity. The people find it possible to hold these two highly divergent points of belief and practice in an apparently harmonious relationship. We will see the same phenom-enon evidenced in a strikingly similar way in the discussion of African retentions in African-American religion.

Mbiti states that in the African worldview "the universe is composed of visible and invisible parts."[63] We have already discussed the ances-tors as being a part of the spirit-world, but the spirit-world is far more complex in African traditional religions and is not comprised solely of recently or long-departed human beings. It is sometimes believed that besides God and human beings, there are also other beings called spir-its who are a part of the universe. These spirits, according to Mbiti, are not identical either with God or humanity and have a status "between" God and humankind, but because they are created by God, they are subordinate to and dependent upon God. God may even use some of these spirits as "agents" to do God's bidding. Mbiti classifies these spir-its into two categories: nature spirits, which include sky spirits and earth spirits; and human spirits, which include both the "long dead" (ghosts) and the recently dead (living dead).[64]

Some African societies believe that certain of these spirits are respon-sible for evil. But because all are under the control of God, the people may appeal to God for help in order to get rid of these evil spirits. There are also certain people within African society whom others may em-ploy to help them by means of interaction and consultation with the spirit-world. Diviners, mediums, oracles, and medicine men and women are believed to be able to consult the spirits in their work. As Mbiti points out, the spirits are more or less the "tools" of this class of workers with the supernatural. On the other hand, there are also people called witches, sorcerers, and bad magicians who consult the spirits that cause misfortune, sickness, and even death (often regarded, itself, as a spirit). These people use evil spirits to do harm to other human beings and are greatly feared in African society.

In African traditional religions witches are seen as the personifica-tion of evil, as innately wicked people who work harm against others.[65] E. B. Idowu, quoted by Awolalu, describes them in this way:

> Witches are human beings of very strong determined wills with diabolical bent…[They] are the veritably wicked ones who derive sadistic satisfaction from bringing misfortune upon other people.[66]

Awolalu also quotes Margaret Field in her careful study and research of religion and medicine in Ghana. She describes witchcraft as being dif-ferent from the work of other craftspeople of the spirit because not only is it used destructively against other people, but "there is no palpable appa-ratus connected with it, no rites, ceremonies, incantations, or invocations that the witch has to perform."[67] Sorcerers, on the other hand, may use all of these methods and materials.

> Witchcraft is a part of an individual's being, a part of his innermost self while sorcery is merely a technique which a person utilizes. Thus, in some societies, a person's witchcraft can operate at times without his being consciously aware of the fact that it is doing so. This can never be the case with sorcery; recourse to it must always be on a deliberate, conscious voluntary basis.[68]

Awolalu states that the sorcerer makes magic to kill; a witch, on the other hand, has an "inherent and intangible power for harming others."[69] The witch, it seems, may project evil thoughts directly, without cursing and invoking, while a sorcerer must manipulate some tangible materials.

Western culture may concern itself with the question of whether witchcraft is real. Yet, in African traditional religions this question appears to be meaningless. Awolalu writes:

> In the mental and social attitudes of the Yoruba, and of the Africans in general, there is no belief more profoundly ingrained than that of the existence of witches *(aje)*. All strange diseases, accidents, untimely death, inability to gain promotions in office, failure in examinations and business enterprise, disappointment in love, barrenness in women, impotence in men, failure of crops and a thousand other evils are attributed to witchcraft.[70]

Witchcraft is a reality to Africans. Awolalu states that it is a belief very prevalent among "literates and illiterates, among the high and the low in the society."[71]

Mafico, a theologian who worked for many years as a pastor in the United Church of Christ in Zimbabwe, states that even Africans who "passionately confess Christ as their Lord and Savior" still believe in witchcraft.[72] Thus, these two divergent conceptualizations of the universe, European Christianity and witchcraft, are often merged in the African lifestyle without one subordinating or obliterating the other.

> They live two contradicting lives: one as Christians only on Sunday mornings, and the other as ardent followers of their traditional religion for six and a half days a week; one as Christians when life is going well, and the other as observers of traditional superstitious practices whenever they are faced with life's predicaments. It should be unequivocally stated that to the Africans both God

the Creator of the world, and forces of evil which defy God's authority co-exist. Therefore, many Africans superficially affirm belief in the Christian God in order to look civilized according to
Western custom, while at the same time secretly observing all the
traditional customs which they publicly and hypocritically claim
to have discarded.[73]

Mafico goes on to state that they do this in order to "ensure that family
ancestors are happy" and to keep witches and others who may wish
them harm at bay, "a role which Christianity fails to perform,"[74] but one
the people believe the ancestors and their traditional religions *can* perform.

For traditional Africans, religion was not a set of rules, regulations,
and laws observed to please God. Instead, it was a way of life intimately
woven or integrated into all aspects of life.

AFRICAN TRADITIONAL RELIGION

Africa is a vast continent with more than eight hundred ethnic groups
with many differences in culture and language. Yet African scholars of
religion maintain that there are common elements that run through all
African traditional religion (just as there are common elements in Christianity in its multiplicity of expressions) that allow one to speak of "thematic features."[75] These thematic features may help one to understand
more clearly the basic African worship beliefs and practices that have
been passed on from one generation of Africans to another and—of ut-
most importance to this discussion—their influence upon African-American religion and spirituality. Consistent attention will be paid primarily
to Nigerian traditional religion and, even more specifically, Yoruba religion because of the historical connection between these people and
African Americans through the Atlantic slave trade.

Chancellor Williams and many other scholars emphasize that the
conquest of black people in Africa by means of the Christian religion
was far more than a concern to convert black people to Christianity. He
asserts that it was meant to change the black Africans into the white
man's image, ideas, and value system.

But what happened in the process of converting the blacks to Islam and Christianity was the supreme triumph of the white world
over the black. Millions of Africans became non-Africans. Africans who were neither Muslims nor Christians were classed as
"pagans" and therefore required to disavow their whole culture

and to regard practically all African institutions as "backward" or savage.[76]

The Christian religion was often used as a way to destroy African culture and conquer African peoples. Many black scholars have cited how the Christian religion was used to subordinate the African peoples. Yet many aspects of African traditional religion that differed from European-Christianity helped the people to maintain their own cultural heritage and worldview as a defense against the cultural imperialism, religious and otherwise, of the West.

These same elements or characteristics of traditional religion were transmitted by the Africans to African Americans in the form of African retentions. Preserved in African-American religion and spirituality, they helped African Americans to forge an identity separate from the identity forced upon them by American racism. This self-identification, in turn, helped the Africans and their descendants to survive and struggle for freedom in the hostile culture of America. In addition, the African retentions enabled the Africans in America and their African-American descendants to Africanize the Christianity that they would eventually create so that this "new-old" religion would serve to protect them in America rather than poison them to death in the form of racial genocide and/or suicide.

Mbiti states that African religion is found in *all* aspects of African life: rituals, ceremonies, festivals, art and symbols, music and dance, proverbs, riddles and wise sayings, people and places, myths and legends, and beliefs and customs. To speak of African religion is to speak of all of African culture. Two categories, "Religion and Community" and "Religion and Meeting the Uncertainties of Life," are useful in describing the traditional African concept of the world and in understanding the influence of the Africans on their African-American descendants.

Religion and Community

An exploration of the crucial role of rites of passage in African traditional religion provides a path to understanding the traditional African circular worldview of the linked or interlocking relationships among humankind, the Creation, spiritual beings within the physical environment, and God. Osadolor Imasogie examines some rituals of the most common rites of passage in African traditional religion, including birth and child-naming ceremonies (initiation into human community), puberty rites (initiation into adulthood and its responsibilities), marriage, and death and funeral ceremonies (initiation into the ancestral spirit-world). These rites of passage include the entire human cycle from birth to death and even beyond death; therefore, one may suggest, they ritually and ceremonially include the total notion of *community* in African traditional religion, for they provide for all of human experience. The term *rite of passage* is defined as "a religious form, ritual, or ceremony used in traditional religion in which an individual and his or her community—either in the form of the family unit or the clan—marks each stage of life with a religious rite." Mbiti writes that African religion "tries to make the journey of life worthwhile for both the individual and the community"[77] by helping it to be meaningful, happy, safe, and satisfied; therefore, key points in life's journey are marked out and celebrated by African peoples. These rituals are for purification, protection, and thanksgiving.

Birth and child-naming ceremonies—initiation into human community

Pre-birth rituals. In African traditional life, the ritual of birth begins during pregnancy, as soon as the wife announces the conception to her husband and parents. Mbiti states that there is "great joy when a wife finds out that she is expecting a baby."[78] A new child is considered to be one of the greatest blessings of life in African culture. Everything is done to protect the mother and baby, and she must be treated with respect by all: "If it is the first pregnancy for her, it assures everyone that she is able to bear children. Once that is known, her marriage is largely secure, and the relatives treat her with greater respect than before."[79] In traditional African societies time is calculated in lunar months; therefore, the pregnancy is completed around ten months or less. Certain regulations and taboos have to be observed so there will be a safe birth for the mother and the child. Customs vary, but some are consistent. Mbiti cites the following:

1. In some countries the expectant mother has to return to her parents to give birth at their home.
2. Midwives are always called upon to assist during the time of delivery.
3. All over Africa, men may not be present in the house when the delivery is taking place.
4. After the baby has been born, the placenta, in some societies, is thrown into a running stream or dried up and kept for later rituals, or sometimes buried nearby or in fields because people look upon the placenta as a religious link between the infant and the mother. The umbilical cord is sometimes seen in a like manner and in some areas it is dried up and kept for a long period of time with great care.[80]

Introduction to society. Initially the mother and baby (or just the baby) are kept for a period of time in seclusion. This is done to give the mother time to recover and also to allow time for preparations for the various ceremonies and festivals that occur after the birth of the child when a large number of relatives, friends, and neighbors gather to share in this time of great jubilation.

> This is like *a social birth for them*: they now come out into the open to be received by society. In some places it is believed that even the living dead are also present for the occasion. In other areas the baby is introduced to the moon, to the sun or to God, in a short ceremony...At the occasion of introducing the child to society, the baby's hair is often shaved...It...shows that the baby is now separated from the mother's womb, so from that moment onwards it belongs to the whole family and the whole community...The whole occasion is a renewal of the life of the community.[81]

The naming of the child. An elaborate naming ceremony takes place on the seventh or eighth day after birth. A name must be given in order ritually to incorporate the child into the community.

> The initiation process follows the threefold pattern of "separation, transition and re-incorporation" in the sense that the spiritual community is also involved. The child is a gift from the spiritual community represented by God, divinities and ancestral spirits. The naming ceremony, therefore, involves acceptance of the baby which, from the standpoint of the spirit-community, symbolizes separation from their community. "Transition" is represented by the duration of the ceremony while "re-incorporation" is symbolized by the giving of a name that identifies him as a member of the family in the community. The community in the larger sense includes the living and the spiritual members.[82]

The concept of community is emphasized by the fact that the naming ceremony is performed by either the oldest member of the family or a priest. The oldest member of the family symbolizes the link between the living and the dead, while the priest symbolizes (by virtue of calling) the link or bridge between the temporal and spiritual realms.[83]

In some places in Africa the name of the baby may be chosen before the baby's birth. Names are chosen with much consideration and care because in African societies the name is often considered to be a part of the personality of the person. Or a child may be named the name of the day of the week on which he or she was born. Mbiti cites a multitude of sources for names, including names that reflect the parents' feelings, names given when it is expected that the child will die, and special names given to twins and triplets. The following is a naming prayer given by the one officiating:

> "In the names of our forefathers and of the family and those gathered here, I welcome you to our family and to the community. In our world...people are identified by names; hence, we have come to give you a name by which you will be identified."[84]

Puberty rites–initiation into adulthood and its responsibilities

The second major point in the religious and ceremonial life of the traditional African comes when a young person goes through the initiation period that marks his or her transition from childhood to adolescence to adulthood. Important initiation rites include circumcision for boys and clitoridectomy for girls. In some African societies, until this rite of passage is observed, a person is still considered to be a child, no matter how old he or she becomes.

Some of the major refugee camps in present-day Kenya for internally displaced persons have large groups of young men popularly called "the lost boys." In order to survive, they have lived in the refugee camps for many years. Faced in early childhood with the necessity to flee their families, clans, and homelands because of ethnic wars and post-colonial land disputes, these young men (many of them now in their twenties) have no possibility of observing the rite of passage out of childhood and adolescence that would mark their official recognition by the community into manhood. This, in turn, affects their ability to marry. They cannot marry because they are seen, in African traditional society, as perpetual "boys." These young men are depressed by a sense of living in a condition of continual "limbo" from which they see no possibility of escape until and unless they can return to their homelands, where their transition into adulthood can be enacted and recognized by the community. Girls are still being circumcised (albeit covertly because the international organizations that support the refugee camps uniformly consider this custom as life-threatening and barbaric) in the camps by elderly women who know the procedure and rituals. They are thus able to marry.

It is believed that the blood shed during the circumcision of boys and clitoridectomies of girls "binds the person to the land and consequently to the departed members of his society."[85] The blood is viewed as the making of a covenant, a solemn agreement, between the individual and his or her people. Until the operation, the individual is considered to be an outsider; once the person's blood is shed, that individual joins "the stream of his people, he [or she] becomes truly one with them."[86] Above all, this rite of passage is, as Mbiti states, "a mark of unity with the people" that brings the initiate together with the entire people: the departed, the living, and those yet to be born. Thus it is understood by the people as a profoundly religious act.

During this period of initiation into adulthood, the young people also experience an important period of seclusion, during which they are "taught many things concerning the life of their people, its history, its traditions, its beliefs and above all how to raise a family." Mbiti states that this rite of passage serves as the "gateway to marriage."[87]

Marriage

Marriage is the sequel to the puberty rites. While the process by which marriages are contracted may differ from one ethnic group to another, Imasogie writes, "common to all is the fact that marriage is not so much seen as a union of two individuals as it is a union of two families or two ethnic groups if the marriage is exogamic."[88] This, he contends, heightens both the religious and social aspects of marriage in the traditional African understanding.

Marriage and the raising of a family are considered to be the most responsible phase of life. After young people have gone through the rite of passage, they are considered to be under a solemn obligation to get married. Mbiti expresses this view in the following manner:

> It is believed in many African societies that from the very beginning of human life, God commanded or taught people to get married and bear children. Therefore marriage is looked upon as a sacred duty which every normal person must perform. Failure to do so means in effect stopping the flow of life through the individual, and hence the diminishing of mankind on the earth.[89]

According to African traditional religion, Mbiti explains, marriage is the "meeting-point" for the three layers of human life: "the departed, the living and those to be born."

> The departed come into the picture because they are the roots on whom the living stand. The living are the link between death and life. Those to be born are the buds in the loins of the living, and marriage makes it possible for them to germinate and sprout. If one deliberately refuses to get married it means, therefore, that one is cutting off the vital link between death and life, and destroying the buds which otherwise would sprout and grow on the human tree of life.[90]

In this profoundly unified worldview, African traditional religion sees marriage, which creates the environment for childbearing and family, as able to "reduce and neutralize the effects of death...Marriage and childbearing are the medicines against death."[91] Therefore, willfully not to marry is considered a major offense against society, for the obligation to get married is the only means of human survival.

It is important to note that although the actual marriage ceremonies may differ from one ethnic group to the next, usually when the marriage proposal is made, either through an intermediary or directly by the parents of the would-be-husband, the would-be-wife's parents do not immediately agree to or reject the proposal:

> They begin the religious activity by going to a diviner to find out the wishes of the ancestral spirits and in addition (in some areas) the wishes of the divinity in charge of fertility...They also launch an intensive investigation into the social history, the character and the health history of the suitor. No affirmative answer will be given to the proposal until the results of these investigations are considered positive...The parents of the suitor must have carried out the same investigation prior to the making of the proposal.[92]

If everything is in proper order, a date is fixed for the wedding; during this period sacrifices are made to both the ancestral spirits and fertility divinity to protect the union with the assurance of children, good health, and the permanence of the marriage. A bride price, which symbolizes a binding covenant between the two families, is then paid.

Among some ethnic groups the bride is lifted over the threshold to symbolize her entry into a new relationship from which she can be separated only by death. This underscores the permanence of marital union. Once inside the house, the bride is escorted to the father of the bridegroom, who, in turn, gives the bride to his son:

> Thus, the fact that the union is more than that between two individuals is emphasized. Marital union involves two families...In fact, it may be said that in Africa you do not marry an individual; you are married into a family because the individual is not human apart from his community. This does not mean that the individual is not important, but, rather, it means a recognition of the stabilizing role of a community in a healthy human existence.[93]

In this vein, Mbiti states, marriage in African traditional religion signifies the following:

1. the obligation to bear children
2. uniting link in the rhythm of life

3. the building of a family
4. new relationships between families
5. remembrance of parents after death
6. regaining a lost immortality
7. bringing people together
8. giving a status in society
9. giving a person "completeness"
10. creation of good personal qualities
11. multiple marriages. This may warrant some additional discussion. The custom of marrying additional wives in traditional Africa occurred by the following means: inheriting the wife of a deceased brother (or husband of a deceased sister), arranging for a dead son to be married in absence, arranging for the wives of impotent or long-absent husbands to have children by close relatives or friends and so on. These means were designed to insure two things: (1) that nobody would be left out of marriage; and (2) that children would be produced for each family involved.[94]

Death and funeral ceremonies–initiation into the ancestral spirit-world

African traditional religion does not have a clearly developed eschatology when all the dead will be judged collectively, as does Western Christianity. According to the theological analysis of African scholars of African traditional religion, however, it is clear that there is an afterlife and that each deceased spirit will be judged on the basis of his or her earthly character. There is also a strong belief that the deceased person may become an ancestral spirit–provided that he or she has lived a good earthly existence and that the proper funeral rites have been observed by the children and next of kin. Traditional African religion incorporates the belief that at death the person's spirit immediately leaves the body and hovers around nearby (the house), waiting for the funeral rites that will enable the spirit to go to the spirit-world.

The first phase of the rituals involves the corpse lying in state. The second phase usually begins a few days after the burial. This phase may last from seven to forty days:

It must not be [postponed] too long; otherwise, the ghost of the deceased, unable to gain admission into the community of the departed members of the family in the absence of a proper funeral ceremony, may haunt the family.[95]

The deceased, by means of proper funerary rites and ritual interment, then goes to the spirit-world. The deceased is then, "by the elevation or divinification ritual,"[96] reincorporated into the community of the living as an ancestral spirit who, though invisible, is symbolized on an ancestral shrine. In this manner the communion between the living and the deceased members of the family is ritually maintained.

This emphasizes, again, the great importance that Africans place on childbearing. Africans believe in an indissoluble relationship between the living person and the members of his or her family, both dead and living. They even use the phrase "the living dead" for the deceased because of the strong belief in the unbroken tie between the dead and the living. Death does not dissolve the union, but if the deceased is not given a proper burial as a rite of passage and, as a result, is not incorporated into the ancestral spirit-community, he or she becomes a ghost and can come back and haunt the family. Imasogie writes, "To be a ghost is to be cut off from one's family as a ghost cannot be invoked at the ancestral shrine."[97]

As discussed, entry into the ancestral community is dependent on the person's character and proper funeral rites. The former, however, may not be as important as the latter because, as Imasogie points out, "everyone thinks his character is good enough to gain him membership."

> Proper funeral rites are crucial partly because the individual at death does not have any control over it and yet so much depends on it. For one without children, the thought that no one may care about one's destiny as much as one's children becomes unbearable. Seen from this perspective, it is easy to understand why the African regards childlessness as a tragedy. Only those who are able to accept that their relatives will care enough to give them appropriate funerary ceremonies can look forward to death with some family hope of continuity in the nexus of family solidarity.[98]

Thus the funeral rite of passage from the earthly mode of existence to the spiritual mode has serious implications for continuity of the family interaction.

Religion and Meeting the Uncertainties of Life

The rites of passage create

> a bond between temporal processes and archetypal patterns in order to give form and meaning to human events...The specific object of rituals of passage is to create fixed and meaningful transformations in the life cycle (birth, puberty, marriage, death), in the ecological and temporal cycle (planting, harvest, seasonal changes, New Year), and in the ascension of individuals to high office.[99]

The general survey outlined above discussed the major rites of passage (birth, puberty, marriage, death) to demonstrate how crucial it is in African traditional life and religion to observe the sacred responsibility of honoring before both the visible and invisible communities the individual's formal and official integration into the community by way of religious rites. This is essentially done to ensure the survival and continuance of the community as a response in meeting the exigencies of life.

A second important mode of response to human anxiety about the uncertainties of life with important theological implications is found in three expressions of African traditional religion: divination, sacrifices, and the use of protective charms or amulets. In the traditional African worldview "there is no event without a spiritual/metaphysical cause,"[100] so human beings must look beyond physical events to their spiritual beginning. The earth is seen as an essentially mysterious place ruled by spiritual forces of good and evil. In African theodicy "God may intervene, but not always, and in any case he has made provision by means of which one may deal with life's problems."[101] This may be done by consulting religious leaders (medicine men and women, diviners, mediums, seers, ritual elders, rainmakers, priests) who, by various means of divination that may require the use of sacrifices and protective medicines, charms or amulets, lead the people in religious activities. A few of these religious leaders and their work in the community are discussed below.

Divination

Diviners, who can be either men or women, deal with "the question of finding out why something has gone wrong"[102] in the lives of individuals, families, or the community. Divination is usually an inherited "gift" from a parent, or the person is specially chosen by the divinity of divination to become its medium for solving the secrets and riddles of life. No one enters the profession unless he or she is divinely chosen to do so. Once it is known that a person is destined to become a diviner, he or she is apprenticed (for as long as three to twelve years) to an expert. This training may begin as early as seven years of age if it is known from birth (usually by revelation) that the child will be a diviner. The apprentice must learn a vast amount of material. For example, in the Yoruba divination tradition of *Ifa*, the diviner has a total of 4,096 stories to memorize before becoming a master of the art.[103] Diviners are considered to be "intelligent people with uncanny insights into human nature and its social expression."[104] This is not to deny that there may also be a mystical element in their divination.

Mbiti also includes among this genre of religious leaders medicine men and women, mediums, and seers. He states that medicine men and women are found in every African society. In addition to being counselors, they "carry out the work of healing the sick and putting things right when they go wrong [through] knowledge and skill [that] have been acquired and passed down through the centuries."[105] Medicine men and women may use medicine to bring good or bad fortune. Mediums, often women, are people who get in touch with the spirit-world. They, too, must be trained from several months to several years (Nigeria has medium schools). Seers are said to be able to foresee events before they take place. They have no special training but are people who have "a sharp capacity for both foresight and insight into things."[106] All of these types of religious leaders, according to Mbiti, are highly respected in African society as "wise, intelligent and talented people, often with outstanding abilities and personalities."[107] Some are professionals. Others perform only when a need arises in the community.

Sacrifices

Sacrifices play an important part in the religious activities of African traditional religionists. Imasogie states, "Every divination consultation is followed by sacrifices."[108] They (among many other life occasions) are made to expiate for sins committed, or to show gratitude for blessings received or for permission to use certain natural resources, such as farming or fishing. But sacrifices are most significantly and most often employed to ward off evil spirits and for spiritual guidance and protection.

Diviners ask their clients to make sacrifices to their ancestral spirits for protection against evil spirits. Divinities are also given sacrifices to placate them because of sins committed by the individual. The devil (as a "trickster-messenger of the gods who brings irrationality and confusion into the world"[109]) is another spiritual being to whom sacrifices for protection are often made.

Protective charms or amulets

It has already been implied that, in an African worldview, the earth is seen as ruled by forces that make life unsafe. These evil forces are believed to work through people, namely sorcerers and witches, who are in alliance with them. They may harm people by evil and magical means. Therefore, charms and amulets are used to arm one's self and one's family against the attack of nefarious powers:

> This is why people spend a lot of money in acquiring charms which they wear in [the] form of finger-rings, arm-bands and waist-bands. Some are worn on the wrists and ankles. Besides the ones worn on the body, others are hung on door lintels while others are buried under the threshold of the entrance to the house to protect people against invading spirits.[110]

Imasogie writes that the worldview that calls for this reaction is "so entrenched" in the lives of the people that "neither intellectual sophistication nor over a century of Christianity has made a decisive inroad into the [ancient] practice."[111] The people firmly believe these practices have crucial existential implications for their survival in an unfriendly environment. Often a negative side of these beliefs in both African and African-American culture is that they may be rooted in fear–and fearful people can often be manipulated and exploited.

AFRICAN TRADITIONAL MORALS AND VALUES

Traditional Morals

African societies believe that God gave them morals, in the beginning, to know what is right and what is wrong. Mbiti describes two types of morals: (1) *personal*-conduct morals regarding the individual, and (2) *social*-conduct morals, which regard the life of society at large.

> But the greater number of morals has to do with social conduct...the conduct of the individual within the group or community or nation. African morals lay a great emphasis on social conduct, since a basic African view is that the individual exists only because others exist.[112]

Thus morals, in the African view, guide people in doing what is considered right and good for their own sake and for that of the community. Morals are taught both within the larger society and the family.

People belong to a larger group of common origin, customs, and traditions (tribe) and to a family (including children, parents, grandparents, uncles, aunts, various relatives on the father's and mother's sides, and the departed). "The family is the most basic unit of life which represents in miniature the life of the entire people."[113] African family life is structured in a hierarchy based on age and degree of kinship from oldest to youngest. Within these familial and community hierarchies, according to Mbiti, the following morals must be observed.

Obligations of parents and children

1. *Parents* have a duty to protect, educate, discipline, and clothe their children and bring them up to be well behaved and integrated within the family and larger community.

2. *Children* have to obey their parents, work at home and in the fields, respect those who are older, and be humble in the presence of their parents and older people.

3. *Children* must look after their parents when they become old or sick.

4. *Children* cannot take their parents' property without the parents' knowledge and consent.

Obligations of husbands and wives

1. They should care for each other.

2. They should be faithful to each other (unless custom permits some other arrangement).

3. Each should do his or her duty for the welfare of the family without arguing and fighting.

Community morals

Community morals govern the welfare of the whole community. Whatever is regarded as strengthening the community is viewed as good and right; but whatever is regarded as weakening the community is viewed as evil and wrong. Taboos are instituted to protect the community. Breaking them is considered to be a violation of morals within the community.

Morals of hospitality

To deny hospitality, even to strangers, is considered evil. "When people travel they may stop anywhere for the night and receive hospitality in that homestead."[114]

Punishment for breaking the moral laws

Each individual in the community must participate in the above. Those who break the moral laws of personal or social conduct will be punished in any or all of the following ways:

1. The departed and the spirits, who keep watch over people and make sure they observe these moral laws, insure that they are punished by God if they break them.

2. *Adults* may be ostracized by the community.

3. *Children* may be punished by their parents or have things taken away from them.

Traditional Values

We have seen above that traditional African religion emphasizes the importance of the practice of morals in everyday life and insists that they extend into all areas of life for the well-being of the individual and the society. These morals are undergirded by traditional religious values directed toward strengthening the moral life. Mbiti and other African scholars point out that though certain morals may differ according to different African ethnic groups, the underlying values are basically the same. These values may be seen implicitly within African traditional religion as guiding cultural expressions of African life and practice as a sort of "grid" through which the traditional African sees the world.

Ultimate respect and reverence for the Creator–for the greatness of God

The traditional Yoruba name *Osadolo-agbonyi* adequately summarizes the view of God as Supreme Being. It may be literally rendered, "It is God who sustains and renews the universe."[115] God, as Mbiti emphasizes, is seen as the beginning and the cause of Creation. God, as expressed in some of the people's given (as opposed to baptismal) names, takes providential responsibility for Creation. God is a good God who provides for the sustenance and renewal of God's Creation through giving one a good harvest, family, and protection from hurt, harm, and danger.

The value guiding the society is that people must honor, give praise, and offer thanks to God as the Good Creator and Sustainer of life. This value is expressed in two important ways. First, people's religion is lived out as a part of all of life–not separated or compartmentalized (in African traditional culture, there is no word for religion). *All* actions must revere the sacredness of God. Second, there is ultimate trust in God to guide, protect, and provide for one's life and needs.

Respect and reverence for Creation

This is inherent in the respect for God as the Creator. Since God created Creation, love for God entails love for all of life, which is God's own Creation. For God expresses God's self through Creation.

The value derived from this view is that people must honor and respect the earth (nature) and all that is upon the earth, because all is of God. This value is expressed in several ways. Children are to be honored and respected, because children are the people's greatest wealth and God's greatest gift. Children (as the renewal of the community) are the guarantee of the survival and continuance of God through Creation. Marriage is to be honored and respected as the cultural institution that ensures the creation and protection of children. Mothers and fathers are to be honored and respected because they bear and provide for children. Finally, the individual should also be honored and respected because he or she will one day become a parent.

Respect and reverence for community

The individual cannot be "human" apart from his or her community. The community is of ultimate importance for the possibility of healthy individual existence. God expresses God's self through community.

This leads to the cultural value "I am because we are."[116] This value is expressed as unity, responsibility, and interdependence for each person as a unit in the link for the cooperation and success of the whole community which includes God, the living, the living dead, and the dead from the beginning through all eternity. People can possess a keen, clear, and true sense of individual purpose and identity as it is derived from within this community, a sense that is not easily overcome by difficulties. The community must demonstrate honor and respect for the indissoluble union existing between the living members and the dead members of the community. Honor and respect is also extended to the elderly, leaders, and those in authority.

Respect and reverence for the stranger

Ultimately, no one is a stranger because God is in everyone. But God especially "appears" or has, as stated in Western terms, a "preferential option for the poor" who are widows, orphans, the disabled, strangers, or those who are at any societal disadvantage. People must honor, respect, welcome, and help strangers and never mistreat them.

This value is expressed in the creation of a welfare system for the poor. People must always be hospitable to and honor and respect the alien or anyone who is different or "other."

Respect and reverence for justice

God desires fair play and freedom between human beings and throughout all Creation for God is just and God judges us in this life and the one to come. Thus it is necessary for each person to live his or her earthly life fully conscious of God's impending day of judgment—whether it appears in this life or in the one to come. As the Yoruba say:

> Lying does not debar one from becoming rich, covenant-breaking does not debar one from reaching old-age; but the day of sleeping (death) there awaits trouble.[117]

God is not ignorant of each person's life on earth, and there will be a day of reckoning.

The underlying value is the belief that what people sow, they also shall reap, or, "What goes around comes around." This value is expressed in treating all people justly and fairly. Do not lie to them, steal from them, murder them, commit adultery with their husbands or wives, slander them, use witchcraft against them, or do any evil against them, because the nature of the universe is essentially moral and circular, and one's own actions—for good or for evil—will return to one. God, the ultimate Judge, can be "told" if anyone is treated unjustly or unfairly, and God will "hear" and "answer."

CONCLUSION

This chapter has emphasized how the traditional African worldview is *unified*. This unity informs all forms of traditional cultural expression, including traditional religion and the morals and values it inspires. It shows a culture highly invested in the moral domain by ideals of peace, justice, goodness, and optimism, because God, who is good and just, is radically related to and cares about Creation. Human beings are, therefore, interrelated and indispensably a part of each other and all that is.

The building blocks of this unified worldview–conception of time, community structure, the place of the ancestors, the role of the grandparents, approach to God, community and social concerns, attitudes toward strangers, belief in witchcraft–form a cosmology and a social order that has an internal coherence stemming from the central belief that God is radically related to everything and binds everything together. Each building block, guided by this central tenet, implicitly reveals the framework of social norms and values by which the people order their lives and–most important–their relationships to others. The result is a cultural style or theological style that is characterized by *relationality*. The implications of this conceptualization of the universe lead to a communal spiritual temperament characterized, as Asa Hilliard notes, by the following:

1. African people and their descendants tend to respond to things in terms of the whole picture instead of its parts. In an African-based worldview, there is little tendency to compartmentalize or divorce God and religion (a word that has dubious value in African and African-American culture) from all aspects of everyday life. To discuss God and religion is to see how God is closely related to the whole functioning of culture. One cannot legitimately discuss God in an African theological sensibility apart from culture or the people living out their ideas of God in their everyday existence. There is no separate, technical "God language."

2. Individual "rights" or "wrongs" are not critical concerns. Cultural values and the norms adhered to allow for these details to be somewhat "blurred" or modified with a greater concern for "fit" or "harmony" in community. Individual nuances of human behavior have little meaning in and of themselves. Meaning is dependent upon context.

3. African-based culture is characterized by *circular* organization with heavy emphasis on the group. This conceptualization of the universe fosters a relational worldview.

4. The result of the above is that African people and their descendants tend to focus on people and their activities rather than things; have

a keen sense of justice and are quick to analyze and perceive injustice; lean toward altruism and a concern for their fellow human beings.[118]

This unified worldview is crucially important to all African diasporans, for recent investigations into African culture in the diaspora show, as Hilliard contends, "varying degrees of cultural retentions at the deep structural levels"[119] of the cultures of the descendants of black Africa. Since a fundamentally indigenous African value system continues as an enduring heritage to African Americans, these African cultural antecedents are the cornerstone in the structure of mental and physical liberation for black people in America. Only a real consideration of the African past can keep in the African American's consciousness a truer understanding of the historical continuity of Africa and its influence in the struggle for liberation of its children in America.

Chapter 2

The Quest for Identity

The complexion of African-American spirituality inherits its distinctive hue not only from the experience of the enslaved in America. An intricate symbiosis of African and American cultures also threads its way through various dimensions of black American culture, perhaps most vividly through black American religion. African traditional culture and religion influenced black religion and spirituality in North America and helped the enslaved Africans not to conform when the European church attempted to rationalize the exploitation of the enslaved. In other words, many of the Africans and their descendants were not converted to the racist anti-Christ who was presented to them by the church and culture of the Western world; instead, they continued to look to Africa and African values in order to define their selves *for* themselves. The African forms were kept alive through the desperate need of the Africans for "humanness," which the slave system forcibly sought to strip away from them.

African retentions were essentially employed to allow the slave community *to name itself* in ways that were truer than the false name given to them in America, where President Thomas Jefferson and many others described African slaves as less than fully human. A first step toward liberation through self-determination for the enslaved in America (as for any oppressed person or people) was to name one's experience for one's self and—within that life context—to name one's self. The enslaved knew that their name was not *nigger*. Howard Thurman writes of how his grandmother remembered the sermons of the slave preachers who were allowed to come once or twice a year to preach to them on the plantation. Their message was: "You are not niggers! You are not slaves! You are God's children!"

The slaves knew this before they touched Western shores, for this was the first and most important theological premise of African traditional religion upon which every other religious belief rested. The enslaved community, as in Africa, named itself (when and where possible) as individuals with names that held meaning. For example, there were names that were common to the slave community, like Iona, which the parents used to mean "I own her" in order to contradict the slave owners who said they owned the black child.[1] Other popular names given to girls included Queen Esther and Princess. Boys were commonly named King, Prince, and Royal. Some boys were even named Doctor (like my own great uncle who was born in the 1800s) and Mister. These last two names were fully conscious attempts on the part of black parents to make white people use respectful names toward their children. The titles Miss and Mrs. were combined, first in slave culture and then well into the twentieth century, to form the single word Misra, so that no black woman who had a child without a husband would be humiliated. In this way every mother in the community was valued and respected (as in Africa) by virtue of the fact that she brought another precious child into the community. The matter of how the child arrived there was left between the mother and God.

The enslaved community also struggled collectively to name and define itself. This essentially involved retaining and redefining its identity by looking "back" to Africa in order to survive in the present. The great Kenyan writer Ngugi Wa Thiong'O writes of this:

> For what has been...is intimately bound up with what might be: our vision of the future, of diverse possibilities of life and human potential has roots in our experience of the past.[2]

In this African view, history is a continuum in which the past, present, and future are inextricably tied together, each helping to mirror, justify, or condemn the others.

AFRICAN RETENTIONS

African writers and scholars equate the coming of Christianity to pre-colonial Africa with the setting in motion of a process of social change that involved the rapid disintegration of "the tribal set-up and framework of social norms and values by which people had formerly ordered their lives and their relationship to others."

> The evidence that you were saved was not whether you were a believer in and follower of Christ, and accepted all men as equal: the measure of your Christian love and charity was in preserving the outer signs and symbols of a European way of life...Thus acceptance of the Christian Church meant the outright rejection of

all the African customs. It meant rejection of those values and rituals that held us together: it meant adopting what in effect was a debased European middle-class mode of living and behaviour.[3]

Thiong'O asserts that early African converts had to prove how Christian they were by the rejection of their "past and roots":

In Kenya, while the European settler robbed people of their land and the products of their sweat, the missionary robbed people of their soul. Thus was the African body and soul bartered for thirty pieces of silver and the promise of a European heaven.[4]

The European colonialists emphasized the same Christian values that had refused to condemn—and indeed had helped—the exploitation of the African body and mind by the European colonizer. The colonists manipulated the Bible in such a way that instead of Christian values being used to enhance love and mutual respect among all people, as they were originally intended, they were distorted and used to dominate and oppress the African people.

In their research of Christianity and the black slave trade many African-American scholars have also highlighted the contradiction between Christianity, whose basic doctrine is love and equality between people, and how it was used as an integral part of that social force—chattel slavery—that was built on the inequality and hatred between people and the consequent subjugation of the black race by the white race. Thus the Africans in America, as in Africa, continued to suffer from European mercenary greed under the guise of Christianity. Africans in America, in many instances, came to see European-Christianity as something to blind the black race while the white race stole everything from them. African retentions became a way for the Africans in America to survive with their own way of life and identity. In this worldview the "measure" of how much one knew and loved God was not so much invested in European-Christianity as in the opposite—how much one was able to *resist* European-Christianity and its "gospel of inequality" by recalling, remembering, and remolding African spirituality. It is in this light that certain important African retentions are explored and analyzed below in order to provide a greater understanding of the role of African retentions in influencing and informing the emerging African-American spirituality.

Black Folktales

Sterling Stuckey writes that the "final gift" of African tribalism in nineteenth-century America was its life as a lingering memory in the minds of American slaves...That memory enabled them to go back to the sense of community in the traditional African setting and to include all Africans in their common experience of oppression in North America...African ethnicity...was in this way the principal avenue to black unity in antebellum America. Whether free black or slave, whether in the North or in the South, the ultimate impact of that development was profound.[5]

Remnants of the African past were, as Stuckey emphasizes, retained in the "folk memory" of black people. One of the most important forms of memory—Stuckey claims *the* most important—was slave folktales.

The folktale, in the culture of the enslaved, was a means by which the African worldview was retained, reshaped, and then transmitted from generation to generation. These folktales did not reflect New World religious concepts but rather African ones. The storytellers, Stuckey states, "told tales in which the dominant spiritual configuration provided the means by which Africans, whatever their ethnic differences, found values proper to them" when the institution of slavery tore them away from their land and culture. These tales became what Stuckey calls "the common property of the community":

> Listeners in the slave community who had previously been unexposed to those tales immediately understood what was being related, irrespective of the section of Africa from which their parents came. Moreover, those who told or listened to one set of tales also listened to and told others, all the common property of the community...Slave folklore was not created to be transcribed or even to be heard by whites.[6]

Rather, this folklore was created to teach the slave community how to survive through the transmission of African values in simple yet complex stories, stories that were childlike but not childish, rich and replete with sophisticated multiple meanings, used as a tool of survival by the enslaved elders in the midst of a hostile and threatening New World.

Whites unwittingly provided the means for the transmission of African folktales in the American slave community. Slave culture was predominantly a "youth culture" (as stated by E. Franklin Frazier and Sterling Stuckey) because slaveholders preferred African males aged sixteen or under. Yet, on the part of the enslaved themselves, slave culture was centered upon the elders and ancestors; the youth had been taught in Africa and by their parents to honor and revere the elders. Enslaved adults were used, most often irrespective of whether or not they had young children, as a part of the household or plantation work force.

Often a slave who was too old to work was given the task of looking after all of the slave community's children from, in the dialect of the black enslaved, "cain't see to cain't see"–from predawn to dusk–when the mothers returned to the slave quarters. Thus the elders in the slave community, in continuity with the role of the grandparent in traditional African society, played with the children, and told them stories, but these stories were not primarily about play. They used play to teach the children, in a way that they could easily appropriate and understand, the wisdom of Africa that would help them to survive. One may even claim (unlike Stuckey) that the Uncle Remus stories collected by Joel Chandler Harris (who did not have a clue as to what they meant) were also used by the elderly in the slave community to teach white children how to be human from an African worldview. White narratives from the antebellum period and well into the twentieth century speak with yearning and nostalgia about the tenderness of black elders (both men and women) toward white children. This, too, is an African worldview of the value of the young. All children were treasured and loved. This did not mean, as will be demonstrated below, that black children were not disciplined by the elders. When and if they endangered the welfare of the community by adopting white behavior that threatened either themselves as individuals or the community as a whole (much the same thing), they were severely punished.

In African culture, the storytellers, called *griots,* were elders in the community who remembered the history and wisdom of the tribe. The African *griot* tradition was continued in the slave community with the important role of the elder as slave storyteller. The slave storyteller's responsibility was to remember and transmit the people's African cultural heritage by means of stories. Storytellers were also required to remember all the children born to the slave community and what parents the children were born to in order to prevent incest to the degree possible within the confines of chattel slavery.

The content of black folktales

Black folktales were, first, about *racial memory*. For example, the following story comes from the life experience of Sojourner Truth, who was born in the 1700s. In the *Narrative of Sojourner Truth,* one finds a clear example of the content of black storytelling as employed by the enslaved. Sojourner Truth, at the time the *Narrative* was written, distinctly recalled the following incident from her childhood as a slave and the daughter of slaves:

> In the evening, when her mother's work was done, she would sit down under the sparkling vault of heaven, and calling her children to her, would talk to them of the only Being that could effectually

aid or protect them. Her teachings, translated in English, ran nearly as follows: "My children, there is a God, who hears and sees you." "A *God,* mau-mau! Where does he live?" asked the children. "He lives in the sky," she replied; "and when you are beaten, or cruelly treated, or fall into any trouble, you must ask help of him, and he will always hear and help you."[7]

In this way, the African-born Mau-Mau Bett, Sojourner Truth's mother, used simple storytelling to teach her children about a God who would protect them in their perilous condition. In Mau-Mau Bett's worldview or theology, when her children asked, "Who and where is God?" she spoke of a transcendent God-in-the-sky who was "above" or "over" human misery but who was immanent in the human condition as a caring God who saw, heard, and would protect them when compelled by the cries of human suffering and humiliation.

Second, folktales were used to *teach the children how to survive* with dignity and grace—how to be human from an African perspective. This included treating everyone (even oppressors) justly and fairly because God was a just and fair God. Sojourner Truth relates that Mau-Mau Bett taught her children a sense of morality that was in keeping with an African worldview. In the *Narrative* the recorder writes, "She entreated them to refrain from lying and stealing, and to strive to obey their masters." At first glance, from a twenty-first century perspective, one may see this injunction from the slave mother to the slave child as counterproductive to her children's welfare. Upon closer examination, however, it may be that the true definition of genuine dignity and character involves carrying one's self with dignity even when others treat one with less than dignity. Perhaps African-born Mau-Mau Bett refused to react to her oppressors with hatred, deceit, and violence because her African values were stronger and more deeply ingrained than her horror of slavery in America.

It is true that many slave owners emphasized those sections of the Bible that eschewed lying and stealing so that they could keep the enslaved community docile and passive. But it also may be that the enslaved community, for the most part (there were very few known violent revolts and/or poisonings or otherwise murdering of whites on the part of the enslaved), believed in African-based ethics that said that God would be displeased with retaliation in the form of lying, stealing, and/or murdering, and that if they did engage in this kind of immoral behavior, it would come back to them. In any event, Sojourner, with the slave child's utter respect and reverence for elders, obeyed her mother's injunction explicitly. Ironically, this respect for truth and honesty inculcated by her African mother eventually led to her freedom.

For when the slave master promised her freedom at a certain point in time and then refused to honor it, his dishonesty led her to feel free to walk away down the road and never return! One of her most famous sayings became, "Truth burns up error."

In the light of the above, antebellum figures such as Uncle Tom and Aunt Jane may need to be revisited by perspectives more insightful than that of Harriet Beecher Stowe or various voices of contemporary black militancy. This notion will be discussed further in chapter 3 in terms of the spirituality of Martin Luther King Jr. and Howard Thurman. Their ancestors may have taught them a form of resistance other than force and violence. Like the African rites of passage of circumcisions and clitoridectomies, this way may have been an extremely painful moral code calling for significant forbearance and self-control on the part of the young. But precisely in its most painful aspect of being required to refrain from fighting against evil with evil (or refraining from acting less than human in an African worldview) it may have taught them what it truly cost to become an adult.

Third, the content of the slave folktale was about *giving the people hope for freedom and liberation.* The following folktale runs pervasively through almost all of the oral testimonies of the slaves, ex-slaves, and their children who were interviewed in the famous Georgia Writers' Project sponsored by the government's Work Projects Administration in the late 1930s and published by the University of Georgia Press in 1940 (and many other collections of slave narratives as well). This compilation of interviews is entitled *Drums and Shadows: Survival Studies among the Georgia Coastal Negroes.* At a later period this story would emerge as the *High John the Conqueror* tale discussed below. Nearly all of those interviewed related having been told this tale in childhood:

> ### The People Could Fly
> *Prince proved to be an interesting talker, much of his knowledge having been gleaned from conversations by the fireside with his grandfather. The following narrative was still fresh in his memory: "Muh gran say ole man Waldburg down on St. Catherine own some slabes wut wuzn climatize an he wuk um hahd an one day dey wuz hoein in duh fiel an duh dribuh come out an two ub um wuz unhuh a tree in duh shade, an duh hoes wuz wukin by demsef. Duh dribuh say 'Wut dis?' an dey say, 'Kum buba yali dum buba tambe, Kum kunka yali kum kunka tambe,' quick like. Den dey rise off duh groun an fly away. Nobody ebuh see um no mo. Some say dey fly back tuh Africa. Muh gran see dat wid he own eye."*[8]

Another storyteller within this same study relates: "Anytime dey want tuh dey would fly back tuh Africa...Dey come back cuz dey hab some

chillun wut didn hab duh powuh tuh fly an hab tuh stay on duh plantation."

This folktale, as an African retention, reflects several important aspects. The storyteller says the slaves that had the power to fly had not
been "climatize." In other words, they were still African–not American.
They had not been acculturated to American slavery. This meant that
the power to fly–or the power to survive, transcend, and abolish slavery–came from staying African or preserving African values and beliefs.

Many of their children, as the second storyteller relates, did not have
the power to fly, that is, over time they had become more American
than African. To become more American than African meant a loss of
the power to become free. In order to overcome one's bondage through
transcending it (the imagery of flying away), one had to preserve the
memory of Africa (fly back to Africa). The second storyteller also spoke
of the flying Africans returning to the plantation because they had children who did not know how to fly. In other words, the further the generations were removed from Africa by birth, the less power they had to
transcend slavery by behaving or remembering an African-based spirituality.

The flying Africans, in a radically communal worldview, came back
for their children, who were permanently grounded (this may remind
one of Harriet Tubman, a conductor of the Underground Railroad).
They could not enjoy freedom without the community, without their
children. In the end, the freedom of the individual meant next to nothing without the freedom of the whole community. Historians of folklore
write that the later black folklore hero High John the Conqueror emerges
from this older folktale after the Christianization of the enslaved. One
of the most popular subjects of slave folklore, he is thought by folklorists to be an African-American synthesis of Africa, Jesus Christ, and
John the Baptist.

Like Bur Rabbit, High John the Conqueror was a black folk hero in
the storytelling tradition of slavery times. Unlike Bur Rabbit, High John
was not a character whom white people–especially the slave owners–
often heard about. John was a man for the slaves, a bold and witty figure who through his cleverness and vision always managed to outwit,
out-guess, and out-distance the slave master. Evolving from the early
tale of African ancestors who were able to fly away back to Africa and
disappear, High John reflects a Christianized version of the older tale.
He, too, functioned as a *hope-bringer figure* who helped the people to
have the will to dream of a better day–a day of freedom. High John had
the power to fly and, like Bur Rabbit, always outwitted the slave masters.

The elders, then, assumed the responsibility of preserving the racial memory and honoring the spirits of the ancestors by telling their children, as soon as they were able to understand, simple stories that would communicate an African-based African-American worldview—their heritage—as a means to survive and resist slavery. Sterling Stuckey asserts that "African religious culture is expressed more faithfully and with greater power in the tale than in other sources."[9] He claims that even the spirituals must be understood from the perspective of the folktales.

The structure of black folktales

The structure of many important folktales of the slave community continued the use of the counterclockwise, circular movement of African notions of time as the means of "unlocking" the meaning of the slave stories with their encoded, secret language that spoke of racial survival. In West African culture the circle was the principal African metaphor for life. Stuckey writes that a key example is the use of dancing in a circle among the Mende and Temne secret societies of Sierra Leone:

> Dancing in a circle with people in the center is a common practice on sacred occasions, for example, during rites of passage for young girls. When they are eligible to be selected for marriage by young men, they go through rites in "the secret house, usually in the bush...A couple of days are set aside, or one big day, when they are brought out into the open for all to see as they participate in final ceremonies."...The women stand around the girls, who are generally teenagers, clapping and singing as the girls sit in the middle of the circle.[10]

The circle is the main symbol of the ceremony, which leads to marriage and the renewal of the life process with the birth of children.

Melville and Frances Herskovits wrote that many of the enslaved who came to the New World were African priests. Indeed, some became the first slave preachers.[11] These priests helped tremendously to preserve African values in slavery. The counterclockwise dance continued in America through the people and the priests, though it came to be used primarily as a religious activity because slave marriage was forbidden in America. Yet its association with the institution of marriage preparation in the secret house, Stuckey writes, survived even in slavery.

This is abundant evidence of the importance of the ancestral function of the circle as a symbol in the religion of the enslaved. "The use of the circle for religious purposes in slavery was so consistent and profound that...it was what gave form and meaning to black religion and art."[12] The symbolism of the circle repeatedly appears with crucial meaning and importance as an African retention in slave religion. The circle was also linked to the most important of all African ceremonies–the burial ceremony.

Given the spiritual context of the circle in slave life, it is important to look more closely at the use of the circle in the structure of slave folktales. The slave folktale *Bur Rabbit in Red Hill Churchyard*, cited by Stuckey, clearly demonstrates how the slave tales were structured to serve as the main context in which the Africans and their children recognized and preserved values common to them.

Bur Rabbit in Red Hill Churchyard

De ground was kiver all over wid snow, an' de palin's on de graveyard fence was cracklin'; it been so cold...An' I look an' listen...an' I see a rabbit settin' on top of a grave playin' a fiddle, for God's sake...Den [Bur Rabbit]gave some sort er sign to de little birds and beasts, an' dey form dey self into a circle 'round de grave...All kind 'er beasts been runnin' round, dancin'...An dere' was wood rats an' squirrels cuttin' capers wid dey fancy self, and diff'ent kind er birds an' owl. Even dem ole Owl was sachayin' 'round look like dey was enjoyin' dey self. Well, I watch an' I see [Bur] Rabbit take he fiddle from under he arm an' start to fiddlin' some more, and he were doin' some fiddlin' out dere in dat snow...Dat mockin' bird an' dat rabbit–Lord, dey had chunes floatin' all 'round on de night air. Dey could stand a chune on end, grab it up an' throw it away an' ketch it an' bring it back an' hold it; an' make dem chunes sound like dey was strugglin' to get away one minute, an' de next dey sound like sump'n gittin' up close an' whisperin'. An' as I watch, I see Bur Rabbit lower he fiddle, wipe he face an' stick he han'k'ch'er in he pocket, an' tak off he hat an' bow mighty nigh to de ground...De snow on de grave crack an' rise up an' I see Simon rise up out er dat grave. I see him an' he look jest as natu'al as he don 'fore dey bury him. An he look satisfy, an' he look like he taken a great interest in Bur Rabbit an' de little beasts an' birds. An' he set down on de top of he own grave and carry on a long compersation wid all dem animals. But dat ain't all. Atter dey wored dey self out wid compersation, I see Bur Rabbit take he fiddle an' put it under he chin an' start to playin. An' while I watch, I see Bur Rabbit step back on de grave an' Simon were gone.[13]

Upon closer examination of this early slave folktale, which initially may appear to the reader both childish and obscure, one can see that in the tale "the African tradition and the future flowing from it, the ground of spiritual being and the product of its flowering."[14] It is interpreted rather carefully below using Stuckey's application and my own.

Bur Rabbit. Bur Rabbit is a trickster figure (like Anansi of African folklore). In generic African style, a weak figure is used in this slave tale as protagonist. The use of the hare or rabbit as a trickster figure pervaded much of black Africa, where some trickster proverbs and tales were often told to demonstrate the shortcomings of the white man. In other words, the physically weak trickster figure was used in these tales to outsmart stronger, oppressive characters. Bur Rabbit is shown here as a "man of God" (black preacher figure). He even wipes his face with his handkerchief in black preacher style (and also like Louis Armstong, as Stuckey points out). As the "man of God" or priest figure, he can call forth the dead. This is the earliest African-American (again, rooted in Africa) definition of a religious leader: one who has the power to call forth the dead. The trickster figure is "keeper of the faith of the ancestors, mediator of their claims on the living, and supreme master of the forms of creativity."[15]

The graveyard as setting. In African tradition the burial ground or ancestral temple is the physical site of the ancestors. The slave storyteller used the cemetery as a way, precisely as in the African rite of passage of the burial of the dead, to show honor to the place of the dead. The cemetery symbolizes the wisdom of the dead or the spiritual and cultural heritage of the African ancestors. Again, the funeral, in the slave as in the African tradition, uses a circular movement to represent themes of togetherness and containment and the continuing interplay of the living and the living dead. In the emerging African-American religious tradition the living dead became the continuing memory of the wise ones of the community.

The fiddle. In African traditional culture drums were used in religious ceremonies to speak to and interpret the messages of the dead to the living and the living to the living. This was the tradition of the "talking drums." Stuckey quotes the Herskovitses: "Tradition assigns to them the...power of summoning the gods and spirits of the ancestors to appear." The drums had the power to "articulate the message of these supernatural beings when they arrive."[16] And, finally, the drums had the power to send the spirits of the gods or the ancestors back at the end of the religious ceremony.[17] In this folktale, Bur Rabbit directed this ancestral ceremony with his fiddle. He called forth the spirit of the ancestors (Simon) with his fiddle. When the ceremony was over, he fiddled Simon back into the grave. Stuckey writes that the violin was the most important instrument of slave musicians. When the whites took the drums away from the slaves (after they figured out they could send messages with this instrument), the power of the drum was transferred to the violin.

The circle dance of the community of animals. In African religious tradition one of the most important forms of worship is dancing and dance was sacred. The dancers often whirled in a counterclockwise movement. The little animals in this folktale danced in a circle (African style) with great intensity. The intensity of the dance indicates the motif of spirit possession or using bodily worship in the form of dance to come into a *unity* that transcends linear time with the supernatural presence of the past in the form of the memory of the ancestors. The animal dancers symbolize the unity of the slaves as a community linked together (the circle) in time with the living, the living dead, and the long dead, as in an African worldview.

Simon. Simon symbolizes the recently dead or the living dead. His name is still remembered, as he is himself, in the community. This is indicated by the storyteller saying that he looked as natural as he did before they buried him. It is also a way of saying that the memory of the ancestors is vital, alive, and well in the community. The storyteller says that they "wore themselves out with conversation." Simon, as the living dead, is communicating with the living community. This symbolizes the preservation and passing on of the African heritage.

In this folktale the storyteller does not relate what Simon said to the community. The storyteller may have purposely omitted the content of the knowledge that is passed on from generation to generation of the slave community (as the rites of passage were led by secret societies in Africa). This was in keeping with the need for the slave community to keep secret the wisdom of their heritage that would help them to continue life or to survive in their precarious life circumstances.

The Ring Shout

Sterling Stuckey writes, "The ring shout was the main context in which Africans recognized values common to them."[18] It can be seen as the most arcane and most widely practiced form of black religion in antebellum North America.

> In the *blacks'* quarters, the coloured people get together, and sing for hours together, short scraps of disjointed affirmations, pledges, or prayers, lengthened out with long repetitious *choruses.* These are all sung in the merry chorus-manner of the southern harvest field, or husking-frolic method, of the slave blacks; and also very greatly like the Indian dances. With every word so sung, they have a sinking of one or other leg of the body alternately; producing an audible sound of the feet at every step, and as manifest as the steps of actual negro dancing in Virginia &c. If some, in the meantime sit, they strike the sounds alternately; on each thigh...the evil is only occasionally condemned and the example has already visibly affected the religious manners of some whites. From this cause,

I have known in some camp meetings from 50 to 60 people crowd into one tent, after the public devotions had closed, and there continue the whole night, singing tune after tune...scarce one of which were in our hymn books. Some of these from their nature, (having very long repetition choruses and short scraps of matter) are actually composed as sung and are almost endless.[19]

This account by John Watson is a very accurate description of the ring shout. It is danced in worship in the present day praise house in exactly this manner by the black people of St. Helena's Island off the coast of Beaufort, South Carolina.

Albert J. Raboteau writes that Watson's account is historically important because it supports the argument that black patterns of behavior influenced white revivalists at camp meetings. However, its greater value may lie in the fact that it supports the argument of important African retentions in African-American religion. It also indicates that the black people of that time were not fully satisfied by institutional Christianity or the Methodist church, so they gathered after the integrated camp meetings and held their own worship meetings in their own way. In these meetings they used African dance and song forms.

Raboteau writes that the ring shout was the most frequently described religious dance of the enslaved on the Sea Coast Islands; there is historical evidence that it was a widespread and deeply ingrained African-influenced practice among the enslaved in other areas as well. This religious dancing was seen as a crucial part of worship for slaves and ex-slaves alike. Raboteau quotes folklorists John and Alan Lomax in their description of the ring shout:

All share basic similarities: (1) the song is "danced" with the whole body, with hands, feet, belly, and hips; (2) the worship is, basically, a dancing-singing phenomenon; (3) the dancers always move counter-clockwise around the ring; (4) the song has the leader-chorus form, with much repetition, with a focus on rhythm rather than on melody, that is, with a form that invites and ultimately enforces cooperative group activity; (5) the song continues to be repeated from sometimes more than an hour, steadily increasing in intensity and gradually accelerating, until a sort of mass hypnosis ensues...This shout pattern is demonstrably West African in origin.[20]

The above descriptions of the ring shout demonstrate a continuing memory of African values.

Stuckey writes that the ring shout was also danced annually in burial grounds in the North by the enslaved Africans from different ethnic groups:

In that field could be seen at once more than one thousand of both sexes, divided into numerous little squads, dancing, and singing, "each in their own tongue," after the customs of their several nations in Africa.[21]

Though the lyrics were not always preserved, Stuckey states that given the ring shout *context* of the songs, the overall meaning is clear:

They were songs concerning the ancestors, songs some notes of which, like those of Brer Mockingbird in Red Hill Churchyard, conveyed the pain of being on the ground of the dead in an alien land far from the ancestral home...Their annual movement to the burial ground in Philadelphia meant a continuing affirmation of their values, so they sang and danced in a circle "the whole afternoon," the ground beneath them being common ground.[22]

This ritual of dancing in a counterclockwise direction was a recognizable and vital point of cultural convergence between the Africans and the African Americans.

Interpretation of the ring shout reveals a number of significant values.

Cultural oneness. The use of the counterclockwise, circular direction of the ring shout emphasized the African concept of time moving in a unified movement in which neither time nor human continuity is seen as uni-directional or separate. Not just the mind was used in this dance, but the body as well, highlighting a non-dualistic view of mind and body and the belief that God must be worshiped with the whole self, a theology that has been retained most notably in African-American Pentecostalism. The dance permitted all to worship God together, irrespective of their many ethnic and linguistic origins, and thus fostered the social principles of unity, harmony, and cooperation in the slave community.

Participation and community. The ring shout was not spectator oriented. There was no audience or congregation (except for the white people who sometimes observed) as in Western worship practices. This, too, emphasized a worldview that is totally intertwining and interrelated. God's presence was not believed to be invoked by an individual but by the unified participation of the entire community in the closed circle in which everyone danced with the whole body with the same movements, the same song, and the same rhythms. The spirit did not possess the individual but came upon the individual in community. Spirit possession in religious song and dance is communal.

Honoring of the ancestors. The ring shout was the African American's way of respecting the memory of the ancestors by preserving African culture through worship practice directly related to African burial ceremony.

Cultural resistance. The ring shout served many purposes: (1) It was a means of retaining and honoring the African cultural heritage; (2) it served to help the enslaved interpret for themselves their new reality and to meet their physical, emotional, and spiritual needs; and (3) it helped them to resist total debasement in the New World. As such, Stuckey states, it was one of the first practices that the whites attempted to stamp out.

Though, as Raboteau maintains, the Protestant revivalist tradition in the United States was influenced by African styles of behavior, slave religious dancing was prohibited and condemned as "heathenish and sinful." Yet in the ring shout and other forms of ecstatic behavior, the African heritage of religious dance found expression in the evangelical religion of the American enslaved.

> Despite the prohibition of dancing as heathenish and sinful, the slaves were able to reinterpret and "sanctify" their African tradition of dance in the "shout." While the North American slaves danced under the impulse of the Spirit of a "new" God, they danced in ways their fathers in Africa would have recognized.[23]

Thus the African-American shout tradition originated as a reinterpretation of African traditions and served as a form to merge African patterns of response with Christian interpretations of the experience of spirit possession.

The famous AME bishop Daniel Alexander Payne, under the strong grip of European Christianity, attempted to convince black people, a little over a decade after the end of legal slavery, to stop the dance:

> About this time [1878] I attended a "bush meeting"...After the sermon they formed a ring, and with coats off sung, clapped their hands and stamped their feet in a most ridiculous and heathenish way. I requested the pastor to go and stop their dancing...I then went, and taking their leader by the arm requested him to desist and to sit down and sing in a rational manner. I told him also that it was a heathenish way to worship and disgraceful to themselves, the race, and the Christian name. In that instance they broke up their ring; but would not sit down, and walked sullenly away. After the sermon in the afternoon, having another opportunity of speaking alone to this young leader of the singing and clapping ring, he said: *"Sinners won't get converted unless there is a ring."* Said I: "You might sing till you fell down dead, and you would fail to convert a single sinner, because nothing but the Spirit of God and

the word of God can convert sinners." He replied: *"The Spirit of God works upon people in different ways.* At camp-meeting there must be a ring here, a ring there, a ring over yonder, or sinners will not get converted."...These "Bands" I have encountered in many places...To the most thoughtful...I usually succeeded in making the "Band" disgusting; but by the ignorant masses...it was regarded as *the essence of religion.*"[24]

I have placed emphasis on certain portions of this quotation because they reveal the basic conflict between African religion and culture and European religion and culture—not, as Payne claimed, between those who knew God and those who did not know God. The young band leader, with an African sensibility, was more accepting of difference and willing to allow that the Spirit of God "works upon people in different ways." Yet he firmly held on to "the essence of [black] religion"—the ring shout. He refused to be named by Europe and chose instead to be named by Africa.

The exchange between Payne and the band leader shows the early emergence of class stratification based on education and religion in the African-American community. Educated black people, like Payne, often chose the religion of Europe. Uneducated black people (those who Payne referred to as "the ignorant masses") chose more overtly the religion of Africa *and* the religion of Europe as they reinterpreted it to meet their own needs for survival in a hateful culture. Finally, it is of crucial significance that the band leader found the ring shout mandatory for conversion and for the working of the Spirit. God, for him, first and foremost, lived in Africa. Thus we see the self-definition of identity for the earliest people who were African-American being rooted not in skin color but in whether the person honored a common African-based cultural and spiritual heritage. This sensibility is identical to traditional African values.

The Praise-House Tradition

The religious dance and shouting of the slaves did not take place only at the integrated camp meetings. The enslaved also held their own regular religious meetings. In a quotation from the 1800s Raboteau cites the existence on the plantations of tiny shacks where black people worshiped that would come to be called (and are still called) praise houses:

On most of the large rice plantations which I have seen in this vicinity, there is a small chapel, which the negroes call their prayer-house. The owner of one of these told me that, having furnished the prayer-house with seats having a back-rail, his negroes petitioned him to remove it, because it did not leave them *room enough to pray.* It was explained to me that it is their custom, in social worship, to work themselves up to a great pitch of excitement, in which they yell and cry aloud, and, finally shriek and leap up, clapping their hands and dancing, as it is done at heathen festivals. The back-rail they found to seriously impede this exercise.[25]

The praise-house tradition among African Americans, which may be basically defined as an indoor ring shout, also served to allow the people to praise and worship God in their own, African-influenced way as they resisted both European worship and European definitions of God, as well as the trappings of European worship styles.

Raboteau states that the singing style of the slaves used in the ring shout and in the praise house, influenced by their African heritage, emphasized call and response, polyrhythms, syncopation, ornamentation, slides from one note to another, and repetition combined with body movements that included hand-clapping, foot-stomping, thigh-slapping, and heterophony. This complex, holistic or whole-body style could not be reduced to musical notations.[26] It was radically participatory; both song and dance depended on the participation of the entire group rather than on separate individuals or worship units (soloists, preacher, choir). Both slaves and ex-slaves sought the presence of the spirit that remained in their memory from Africa. Though the religious experience of the African Americans contained elements of the revivalist tradition of American evangelicalism, that evangelicalism was also influenced by African worship behaviors.

Drums and Shadows relates this interview with the daughter of an African who was enslaved and brought to America. Her father had "marked" her when she was a very young child.

We questioned her more closely regarding this mark which from her description seemed to have been a small scar, oval in shape and slightly raised...We returned to the subject of the mark, at the mention of which her eyes suddenly narrowed..."Yes'm, he mahk me," she admitted, "on muh ches."..."But did he tell you why he marked you?," we persisted. "No,m, he ain say wy. He jis tell me he don it wen Ise lill..." "Rosanna," we ventured, "would you let us see the scar?" She hesitated, then cautiously raised her hand to the fastening at the neck of her dress and, baring her chest, allowed us a glimpse of the scar. It appeared to be an irregular circle the size of a fifty-cent piece with faint lines which seemed to run toward the center. Time, however, had obliterated any design or pattern it might once have had.[27]

Time may have in like manner obscured the details of African religious tradition among the enslaved, but the basic outline of a unified worldview was preserved in the centrality of the circle (ring shout, praise-house tradition) as a symbol in African-American slave culture and religious traditions.

I have been to worship in a contemporary praise house on St. Helena's Island, off the coast of Beaufort, South Carolina. It calls to mind the group that asked the plantation owner to take back the furniture he donated to their worship setting. The people were polite but reticent about taking me to the praise house (I was an "outsider," even though I am an African American). After looking at me closely, they told me where it was. It is not on a well-traveled route. This praise house is a very tiny one-room shack without any furniture. Its structure is in stark contrast to the concern for elaborate edifices often present in European-influenced Christianity. It appears that the people are more concerned with the actual worship than with the building where it takes place. For them, church is the people, not the place. The people (except for myself) are elderly. They sing, pray, and dance in much the style described by Raboteau.

Black Ghost Tales

Howard University historian Al-Tony Gilmore states that whites used ghost stories as "one of the more devious—and principal—devices employed...to control African-Americans, during and following the period of slavery, a devastating system of psychological pressure based on fear of the supernatural."[28] In the same vein, black folk historian Gladys-Marie Fry points out that

> if blacks could not be sufficiently frightened with things of this earth the whites' major recourse was to play upon the belief in and deep-seated fear of ghosts and other preternatural beings that they assumed were held by most black people. The use of supernatural imagery as a powerful and compelling psychological deterrent to the nighttime movements of black slaves and freedmen was successfully employed by whites throughout the three phases of black history—during slavery, post-bellum and turn-of-the-century times.[29]

In this concerted attempt to frighten and coerce black people into submission and obedience by psychological means, systematic exploitation of black folk beliefs was practiced by slave owners and overseers who, disguised as ghosts, prevented night social visits, dances, religious meetings, and other forms of activity among the slaves. In other words, white slave owners needed only to distort and reinforce existing beliefs in ghosts and witches in the African-influenced worldview of the slaves. This factor, coupled with the slaves' world as one in which they did not always know who their enemies were and from which direction they would strike (whether white or black), led them to perpetuate originally African beliefs in the manipulation of the supernatural to either protect themselves or harm others.

It is not surprising then, that ghost tales were used in the slave community as a means of relaying "supernatural subterfuge" or as a way of protecting the community by telling stories of good ghosts (for example, Simon in *Bur Rabbit in Red Hill Churchyard*) or evil ghosts (haints, witches, a deceased wicked person) like in the following slave ghost tale.

> Nearly anyway you turn, you lived in the country, you try to go home or away from home at night, you had to go by a spooky place. It's either an old house that someone has seen ghosties there, and the reason why the ghosties be hanging around, or either it was a cemetery where some wicked person been buried, and you will see a spook around his grave.[30]

This ghost tale clearly reveals an African influence, though Western culture may have had some of the same beliefs about ghosts derived from a different tradition or worldview. The belief that the ghost is there because the person who died was wicked (and therefore, in African belief, unable to go to the abode of the ancestral spirits) is strongly present.

The following is an example given by Fry of the white planters' manipulation of black folk beliefs to control black peoples' movements after nightfall:

> Back in those days they had little log cabins built around in a circle, around for the slaves. And the log cabins, they dabbed between two logs, they dabbed it with some mortar. And of course when that fall out, you could look out and see. But every, most every night along about eight or nine o'clock, this overseer would get on his white horse and put a sheet over him, and put tin cans to a rope and drag it around. And they told all the slaves, "Now if you poke your head out doors after a certain time, monster of a ghost will get you." They peeped through and see that and never go out. They didn't have to have any guards.[31]

The above description calls to mind the Ku Klux Klan. Fry writes that there were three types of black people: those who believed the tale unequivocally, those who were uncertain, and those who simply did not believe. The numbers of those who believed must have been very large, as evidenced by the strong presence of "hidden traditions" (see below) of black religion in America.

Hidden Traditions: Black Religion, Magic, and Alternative Spiritual Beliefs

Yvonne Chireau writes that the spiritual life of black people in the United States (as demonstrated above) historically has extended beyond the church, beyond the mosque and temple, beyond all institutional expressions. Transcending institutional boundaries, it has flourished, as Chireau claims, "outside of sectarian boundaries, permeating the private sphere and the public realm, filling the spaces where everyday needs are considered and met."[32] The "hidden traditions" of black religion in America coexisted with institutionalized forms of religion, such as Christianity, but represented divergent conceptions of belief and practice based in Africa. These hidden traditions, as Chireau states, bridge African-American religion and African-American spirituality. As such they have no church, creed, or doctrine but their assumptions and codes of practice can be seen as reinterpretations and reformulations of African traditional religion combined with elements of European and Native American beliefs and practices that the enslaved encountered in America.

No illness or misfortune in the slave community, as in Africa, was seen as the result of chance or bad luck. Everything was believed to have a cause. In the testimony of every person interviewed in *Drums and Shadows* (and in many other slave narratives) there was a pronounced fear of people's enemies. Not only was the black community under the constant stress of fear from without (white racism), but it was also perpetually plagued by the fear of someone "fixing" (putting *hoodoo* on individuals through a root doctor or a witch) its members from within the community and of reprisals from the dead either because they had not been properly buried or because they had lived wickedly while on earth and, therefore, continued restlessly to roam the earth meddling in human affairs in the form of ghosts or haints.

The enslaved were constantly afraid for a plethora of reasons. They were afraid of the potential for violence and actual violence toward them by white people. Of this pervasive fear of the black community during segregation, Howard Thurman wrote: "The ever-present fear that besets the vast poor, the economically and socially insecure...is like the fog in San Francisco or London" for it is "nowhere in particular yet everywhere."[33] In addition to this fear of violence from outside their community, the slaves were afraid of each other. The slave narratives reveal how the enslaved were taught by the whites to mistrust one another. They were told that slaves from another plantation were evil and corrupt so that, sight unseen, they learned to regard each other with deep-rooted suspicion. This enhanced their belief in the need for protection from one another.

Other fears were based in the disruption of their African-based social system. In Africa the family was the basic unit for caring for the very young and the very old. Slavery disrupted social security for both very vulnerable generational groups. Sojourner Truth recounts how her elderly father, Bomefree, literally starved and froze to death in an isolated shack in the woods in the dead of a northern winter because the white people put him out there, without food, fuel, or any way to take care of himself (he was blind and partially paralyzed) when he was too old to work. She, his only child, could not care for him because she was enslaved on another farm. The circle of life had been shattered by slavery. Children could not always care for their parents nor parents for their children. Husbands could not always care for and protect their wives. All lived in fear.

In addition to the fear of other forms of existential suffering (illness, death, poverty), African Americans already held deeply rooted, African-based beliefs in the havoc that would be wrought by the dead upon the living if they were not properly honored at their burial. Oftentimes their circumstance as slaves did not permit them to do this. But when they could, the enslaved and their descendants continued to preserve remnants of the ceremony of the burial of the dead in America.

The practice among African Americans, stemming from Africa, of bringing food and the deceased person's last used personal items regularly to the grave of the dead person was sustained well into the twentieth century. *Drums and Shadows* records this and many such testimonies:

> Relative to the custom of placing food and possessions on a new grave this woman spoke earnestly. "Dis wuz a common ting wen I wuz young. Dey use tuh put duh tings a pusson use las on duh grabe. Dis wuz suppose tuh satisfy duh spirit an keep it frum followin yuh back tuh duh house. I knowd a uhmun at Burroughs wut use tuh carry food tuh uh daughtuh grabe ebry day. She would take a basket uh cooked food, cake, pies, an wine. Den she would carry dishes too an set out a regluh dinnuh fuh duh daughtuh an uhsef. She say duh daughtuh's spirit meet uh deah an dey dine tugedduh."[34]

Hidden traditions were used to bridge the gap that mainstream, institutional, or "approved" religion left in the face of all of these fears and social obligations required by an African-based culture in America. Even though denounced by European-Christianity as heathenish, pagan, anti-Christian, and "of the devil," the hidden traditions not only persisted but thrived among both black people and white people during and after slavery as a way to combat or resist all forms of evil.

Spiritual leaders

Chireau records how gifted African-American women were regarded as powerful seers and conjurers within and without slave communities. Throughout slavery both black women and men in the slave community held important and authoritative roles as spiritual leaders based on their knowledge and practice of the hidden traditions. There were at least two legitimate ways that one became a spiritual leader: (1) by being born with a caul (the embryonic sac) or double-caul covering one's face at birth; or (2) being born the seventh son of a seventh son. Both of these traditions are directly based in West African beliefs. People born in one or both of these conditions were said to possess second sight—the ability to see and hear the spirit-world just as if it were in a part of the physical realm. In order to stop the deleterius aspects of this "seeing," such as the horror of viewing evil spirits, the child's birth sac would have to be saved and a tea made from boiling it that the child must drink. If the mother or midwife failed to do this, the child would forever be plagued and frightened by the sight and sound of horrible apparitions (what, in modern language, we might call the visual and auditory hallucinations of schizophrenia) that would threaten its life and sanity. These people, gifted from birth, as in West African belief, still had to serve a period of apprenticeship in order to become proficient in interacting with the world of the spirits and the supernatural. They often used their gift of "second sight" and became respected prophets, visionaries, dreamers, and dream interpreters whose advice was sought after by the community. An illegitimate way to obtain these gifts was to sell one's soul to the devil. These people became witches (both males and females). Again, this is based in West African belief.

Healing and conjure

The folk tradition of doctoring in the African-American community emphasized healing through plants and herbs and by possessing special spiritual power. *Root work,* or the use of natural and organic substances for supernatural ends, was a prevalent method of protection against illness (mental and physical), white people, witches, ghosts ("haints") and other evil spirits, conjurers and "doctors" who may have been commissioned by one's enemies to do one harm. Root work was also used to protect or secure one's love life, to obtain financial prosperity, and to predict the future.

Conjuring included the use of objects such as charms, luck pieces, "mojos," or "hands," "tobys," amulets, and other articles used to ward off any misfortune, evil, or sickness or to draw what was desired to one's self. Chireau writes:

> The creations of "rootworkers" were particularly important to the mothers of young children, who sometimes acquired charms for their infants to wear on the body in order to thwart disease. Former slave women described homemade ornaments, small sacks with various combinations of asafetida, herbs, garlic, hog's teeth or dog's teeth, and mole's feet, which many believed, when worn around the neck of children, would prevent physical illness and encourage growth.[35]

In Africa today children are seen wearing amulets and charms for protection.

Conjuring assumed the efficacy of spiritual power and the mystical nature of cause and effect. It recognized the existence of unseen forces and the belief in the ability of humans to control these forces by using rituals, words, or objects. This tradition was used by slaves and their descendants to "regulate the inequity of power relations, including those between bondspersons and slaveowners, or among slaves themselves."[36]

The men in the community who had the gift of conjuring were called doctors. For example, the famous Dr. Buzzard of St. Helena's Island, who died in the 1990s, was descended from a long line of Dr. Buzzards extending back to slavery. His son assumed that role on the island (along with others) after his father's death. Women with the gift came to be called Mama in the black community. The most gifted and respected conjurers were able to combine physical healing (through their use of the knowledge of the healing properties of plants, herbs, and organic substances for making medicines), dentistry, midwifing, fortunetelling, predicting, and dream and vision interpretation with root working, knowledge of spiritual matters, and wisdom as general insight into the properties of nature and the behavior of human beings.

African-American novelist Gloria Naylor writes of how this tradition was used as counter-cultural resistance. Her contemporary novel *Mama Day* is set on the fictive Sea Coast Island of Willow Springs. Inhabited totally by black people, Willow Springs is based on the actual St. Helena Island, which is off the coast of Beaufort County, South Carolina. The Georgia and South Carolina Sea Coast Islands are still replete with the customs and beliefs of African-American hidden traditions. The novel's protagonist, Mama Day, is gifted with second sight and uses the hidden traditions to combat evil black conjure or root work on the island as well as evil white racism.

In one amusing section of the novel a new white deputy sheriff from the mainland, ignorant of black people's customs and Mama Day's reputation, mistakes her for a person without power. He comes to the island, without consulting the sheriff who knows better, in search of moonshiners and blithely insults the elderly black storekeeper, Parris, calling him, "nigger this and nigger that." The black people on the porch of the store become very still. Mama Day tells him he will address Parris "proper" before the night is over. The young deputy sheriff, still unaware of who and what she is, rudely calls her "Granny" and tells her nobody is talking to her.

By the time night falls, through a series of events (such as his patrol car mysteriously acquiring three flat tires and his reliance on Parris to relay the directions to where he can find the moonshiners' still), the deputy sheriff finds himself lost. He spends hours on foot in the cypress swamp in the island's worst lightning storm in ten years. For half the night he staggers up and down the road begging for shelter, but it appears no one is home. It takes him most of the rest of the night to find the bridge back to the mainland—but he dare not cross it on foot because it has metal-studded planks and he doesn't want to be electrocuted by walking over water in the midst of a furious lightning storm. At long last he sees a car and yells, "Please sir!" After the deputy has begged for a while, the driver finally rolls his window down. All the deputy sees is the driver's grin as his teeth are turned into "glowing pearls" by a flash of lightning before he speeds up, drives off, and leaves the deputy stranded. Needless to say, the driver is Parris, and the deputy never comes near the island again for any reason whatsoever.

A historical example of counter-cultural resistance is Madame Marie LaVeau, an African-American conjurer of renown. She was a devout and earnest Roman Catholic, as far as outer appearances were concerned, and reigned as the Queen of Voodoo in New Orleans from the 1830s until her death in 1881 at the approximate age of eighty-five. Her daughter, Marie II, reigned after her. The Maries were said to have control over white businessmen and city politicians. It was said they walked into politicians' offices, stated what they wanted, and it was done. People, white and black, said she was the real boss of New Orleans. Both women inspired tremendous fear in New Orleans because of their use of Voodoo, a mixture of the hidden traditions from Africa and Roman Catholic statues of saints, prayers, incense, and holy water.

Conjure beliefs were validated by the enslaved and their descendants as a source of spiritual authority. They drew upon the rich symbolism of African traditional religion and Christianity to form what Chireau calls "a subterranean core of supernatural ideas"[37] that helped people define themselves primarily by integrating mind and the soul through the rational means of the intellect and through the inner guidance of intuition.

Indeed, the intellect, they believed, worked best in service to intuition, which was regarded as the inner guidance of the soul by God. Thus the power to perceive and affect the world was not just or even primarily external but, perhaps more important, also an internal, spiritual power. Therefore *ashe*, or "the power to make things happen," was never believed to be separated or compartmentalized solely in the realm of the intellect or the material. The elders of the slave community passed on a rich spiritual legacy that included a deep respect for the integral and inseparable link between the seen and the unseen, the material and the spiritual, the natural and the unnatural, the individual and the community, and the community and God.

In summary, African Americans resisted the Western-based notion that what could be seen and established as real or true only by empirical data was all there was and all there ever would be. The needs of the community established what was real or not real—truth was not equated with fact, as defined in the Western worldview, when the community was threatened. The following narrative of an ex-slave tells how an elder painfully taught her this lesson as a little girl:

What You See, You Don't See
They always felt that the good food was not for the slaves. But in order to have a feast every now and then, some of the slaves who could trust the others, would steal a sheep and kill it...So she said she [the child] passed by the table, and childlike smoothed her hand along as she went. But due to the fact that she was raised in the house with the mistress' children, they didn't trust her. So she said this old man took her out...And he said, "I'm going to teach you how to see and not see, and hear and not hear." So she said he took her out back of the quarter house where all of these oyster shells were, and he whipped her terribly...And when he finished whipping her, he told her, he said, "Now what you see, you don't see, and what you hear, you don't hear."...She realized that they were afraid she would tell in the house that she had seen all of this lamb on the table, because they weren't given lamb, and that they had to steal it and cook it among themselves.[38]

In conclusion, the slave community established identity by defining what was real or not real as it was guided by the urgent necessity to protect the community and keep it alive. Hidden traditions were real to the enslaved and their descendants because they recognized and addressed this imperative from their African heritage in a way that institutional religion did not. African retentions were at the very heart of the community's struggle to define itself during and after slavery in the form of alternative religion as counter-cultural resistance.

THE WORLDVIEW OF THE ENSLAVED COMMUNITY

The basic principles of the way of life of the Africans in America reflected the endurance of the African legacy. In the face of the new anxieties black people experienced as generated by the Atlantic slave trade, this legacy of African retentions served as black spiritual and cultural guides for black people in developing their own self-perception and way they saw God and humanity. This black way was often in direct opposition to the perceptions of white racism. The evidence of important African retentions in African-American religion and spirituality demonstrates this cultural synthesis and black people's commitment to dignity and self-determination through defining their own identity from the very beginning of their suffering and struggle to survive with dignity the American holocaust.

The worldview of the enslaved, viewed through the lens of African retentions, was in many ways similar to an African worldview. Yet it emerged into two identifiable parts. First, the emerging African-American worldview of the enslaved was essentially guided by a unified worldview. The experience of the Africans in America added to this the second critical component of the preservation of this worldview in racial memory as a form of cultural resistance against a hostile and larger surrounding culture. Huge numbers of human beings (estimates range from Wiedner's 3.5 million to Rotberg's 25 million)[39] were forcibly imported in the Atlantic slave trade in a commercial system that removed workers from one society and transported them to another culture. This vastly different, European-based culture sought not only to exploit them physically but also spiritually and emotionally by denigrating all they were that was African. Some accepted this. This is reflected in Phyllis Wheatley's poems and letters and in Daniel Alexander Payne's description of black people who refused to acculturate to Western culture as "the ignorant masses."

Yet the great majority, as evidenced by strong African retentions in African-American religion and spirituality, did not. They embraced a unified worldview that included:

1. The belief in a sacred cosmos created and preserved by a Supreme Deity and, therefore, the belief that everyone and everything in the cosmos reflects this Supreme Deity (humankind, nature, and God are seen as a unity or distinct yet inseparable aspects of a sacred whole);
2. The assumption that the tribe (now the community of the enslaved) and the family are the principal links between the

historical world of humans and the transhistorical realm of the divinities and the ancestral spirits;

3. The belief that, in spite of the unity of Creation, human beings are capable of irreverent acts that cut them off from the sacred community and, as a direct consequence, wreak havoc on the individual, the family, and the entire community.[40]

Individuals in this last category were witches and sorcerers. One may suggest that they were also those who either consciously (by fully emulating European culture in its anti-African aspects) or unconsciously (through forgetfulness) did not share the African heritage that remained alive in slave culture.

In this unified worldview Africans in the diaspora were able to preserve "the structural dimensions of their spirituality: belief in a spirit-filled cosmos and acceptance of a moral obligation to build a community in harmony with all the various powers in the cosmos."[41] This moral obligation was evidenced in the religious expression of the black church as it sought to serve the needs and sustain the true identity of the African-American community.

THE BLACK CHURCH AND THE ENSLAVED

C. Eric Lincoln describes religion as a "change [that] mirrors the social flux" of people but, at the same time, endures in nature or "transcend[s] the flux and integrate[s] the totality of experiences by which human life is gauged and evaluated."[42] This had been the nature of black religion and spirituality in America.

Religion alone has the ability to address itself effectively to what is new and evocative while retaining the assurances of what is settled and traditional—appearing at once to change with changing institutions and to persist through change unaffected by any history but its own.[43]

Lincoln goes on to define "religiously alert" as a required characteristic for the black church. Religious alertness expresses itself in two forms: (1) as an *internal* alertness that guards the quality of the expression of faith; and (2) as an *external* alertness that serves to "stave off intrusion" and what Lincoln calls "the violation of the premises."[44] As a black church historian, Lincoln emphatically announces early in his discussion of the Negro church described in the work of E. Franklin Frazier that the Negro church is not religiously "alert":

> The Negro Church is dead because the norms and presupposi-
> tions which structured and conditioned it are not the relevant norms
> and presuppositions to which contemporary Blacks who represent
> the future of religion in the Black community can give their assev-
> eration and support. The Black Church must become the charac-
> teristic expression of institutionalized religion for contemporary
> Blackamericans because it is the perfect counterpart of the Black
> man's present self-perception and the way he sees God and man,
> particularly the white man, in a new structuring of relationships
> from which he emerges freed of the traditional proscriptions that
> compromised his humanity and limited his hope.[45]

Yet, in an African sensibility, perhaps "what's dead is never dead." The
Negro church, in this view, is simply one of the expressions in the quest
for identity on the part of African Americans, and it is to be evaluated,
as Lincoln does indeed evaluate it, in terms of how alert it was or is
(internally and externally) in helping black people to define themselves
in an authentic way in the midst of a hostile and threatening culture.

In the above statement Lincoln is making the point that the black
church in America must become subject to the internal critique of the
community. It is to be evaluated as relevant or irrelevant (and possibly
even harmful) according to the same normative principle that his ancestors employed: Does it help to promote healthy black identity? The
black church in America must listen for, in Howard Thurman's words,
"the sound of the genuine"—especially within itself and its religion.

According to Lincoln's evaluation, the church had substantially failed
in its institutional embodiment as "the Negro Church" to do what was
required to help black people establish their true identity. Lincoln demonstrates a very African worldview. He believes that if the church, with
black people in it, does not serve the needs of the black community to
thrive and survive with dignity, it is not black. It is simply a building
occupied by dark people.

> The call to full manhood, to *personhood*, and the call to Christian
> responsibility left no room for the implications of being a "Negro"
> in contemporary America. With sadness and reluctance, trepida-
> tion and confidence, the Negro Church accepted death in order to
> be reborn. Out of the ashes of the funeral pyre there sprang the
> bold, strident, self-conscious phoenix that is the contemporary
> Black church.[46]

In Egyptian mythology the phoenix is a beautiful blood-red (red is
the color of *ashe* or "the power to make things happen" in Yoruba mythology), lone bird that lives in the Arabian desert for 500 or 600 years

and then sets itself on fire, rising renewed from the ashes to start another long life. It is a symbol of immortality.[47] Thus African mythology reveals perhaps the best symbol for African-American spirituality. It is the phoenix that arises in black spirituality, which, to date, cannot be killed by American racism. Its nature is first to synthesize and then amalgamate what it encounters as "other" or alien, and then, finally, to transform the alien to its own end and purpose. For African Americans this is highlighted in their ability to detoxify the racism of American culture by combining it with the powerful African legacy.

The black church in slavery is discussed in this section over and against the measuring rod of Lincoln's criteria of religious alertness and the characteristic of the phoenix. In this regard it is helpful to analyze how black people interpreted the Bible (the Book), the black preacher, the music of the black church, and the shout or the frenzy of the black church.

The Book

Bible scholar Renita J. Weems writes, "The Bible is in many ways alien and antagonistic to modern women's identity; yet, in other ways, it inspires and compels that identity."[48] The same may be said of the relationship of the enslaved community with European Christianity through encounters with white interpretations of the Bible. This relationship was often ambivalent, because the Bible was frequently interpreted to the Africans in America as a way to set in motion a process of social change that involved the rapid disintegration of the African worldview. The European church could not separate Christian dogma or doctrine from a European scale of values or from European customs. What resulted in the white people's catechesis of the enslaved was hatred in the form of racism and cultural imperialism rather than true Christianity.

German philosopher Friedrich Nietzsche asserts that the Western worldview is based on the theory of opposites. In order to define its social norms and values, it looks at differing options in opposition to or set over and against each other. Therefore, at the heart of its influence, as a mental grid that informs the worldview of Western culture, is a "will to opposites" or "a will to power" that is essentially violent and warlike in its essential either/or nature.[49] In other words, what becomes normative, "right," and regulatory within the culture is determined by beating down or stamping out various other alternatives. Norms and values are established by way of domination. In this mental framework the possibility for both/and is destroyed. Both/and thinking is basically determined as irrational, primitive, or illogical. What results is a ravaging, hate-filled dogmatic form of establishing cultural values that leads to pseudo-spirituality or religiosity that defines itself, at its core, through a standard of antagonism toward and exploitation of difference.

African spirituality had no book, nor did it express itself through written doctrines, creeds, and tenets formulated by a religious hierarchy of councils. Instead, it was written on the tablets of the people's hearts and expressed itself throughout daily African culture to the extent that, as discussed earlier, religion was not separate from culture. These distinctive worldviews, Africa and the West, clashed intensely, yet things did not essentially fall apart among the Africans in America.

When the Africans and their descendants encountered the Bible, their spirituality allowed them the freedom to interpret it as the whites interpreted it (in some if not many instances they did) or in ways that met their own needs. In this manner, unlike the Western worldview, they were always radically free. Their worldview did not proscribe both/and thinking and this opened the way for the possibility of alternatives in their biblical interpretation. In many ways the Western worldview prohibited or circumscribed freedom, religious and cultural, because it did not allow for this possibility.

Weems writes of how African-American women read and interpret the Bible:

> How African American women read the Bible is a topic that has to do with not only uncovering whose voice they identify with in the Bible—female as opposed to male, the African as opposed to the non-African, the marginalized as opposed to the dominant. It has equally and more precisely to do with examining the *values* of those readers and the corroboration of those *values* by the text; it has to do with how the text arouses, manipulates, and harnesses African American women's deepest yearnings.[50]

This method may also be used to demonstrate how the whole enslaved community, male and female, often interpreted the Bible on the issue of the survival of the community.

Jacquelyn Grant writes that black women considered the Bible to be a major source for "religious validation in their lives" in the "interplay of scripture and experience": "The God of the Old and New Testament became real in the consciousness of oppressed black women. Though they were politically impotent, they were able to appropriate certain themes of the Bible which spoke to their reality."[51] Grant continues to write on this theme of the interplay of scripture and experience and, like many black scholars of religion (Weems, Katie Cannon, Thurman), quotes Nancy Ambrose, the grandmother of Howard Thurman:

"During the days of slavery," she said, "the master's minister would occasionally hold services for the slaves...Always the white minister used as his text something from Paul...'Slaves be obedient to them that are your masters..., as unto Christ.' Then he would go on to show how it was God's will that we were slaves and how, if we were good and happy slaves, God would bless us. I promised my Maker that if I ever learned to read and if freedom ever came, I would not read that part of the Bible."[52]

As Grant emphasizes, this reveals not simply a rejection of the white preacher's interpretation of the Bible, but, perhaps more fundamentally, an internal critique of the Bible itself. In other words, the community of the enslaved, male and female, was often able to begin from the context of experience (later James Cone will maintain that context is the true source of all theology that liberates) as the a priori for understanding a written text—even a sacred text.

Scholars of religion Hans Frei and George Lindbeck, in direct contrast, speak of theology as narrative. In narrative theology the text essentially governs the meaning of experience. Yet, one may suggest, people have not truly read in this way since the seventeenth century. The question of the enslaved, who seemingly interpreted the Bible in a profoundly modern sense, may be asked as: How can a book, any book, be large enough or true enough to alter and shape the enormity and truth of experience, unilaterally and from the outside, without seriously interacting with our experience? That would be magic—not religion. After all, even Jesus had to enter history. One may suggest that he did not impose a book upon history. Unlike the biblical Pharisees—with whom the enslaved were thoroughly unsympathetic—he chose to live with the book, day by day, intimately within his own personal history.

In slave biblical interpretation it was not always a matter of either/or in interpreting the Bible, that is, *either* the Bible *or* experience. The slaves interacted with the Bible *and* permitted it to interact with them in a serious life-and-death way that was essentially circular and back and forth in nature. The Bible, for the enslaved, was influenced by their lives and culture *and* their lives and culture were influenced by the Bible in a profoundly both/and manner.

The result was, as Howard Thurman, James Cone, and many other black scholars have stated, an exegesis of the enslaved. The Book of Exodus (and the books of the prophets) became essential for black people, as well as the Jesus of scripture, with whom they identified and understood as the God of the disinherited. They saw God, in Jesus of Nazareth, as the One who had always championed the cause of the Hebrew masses against both the Pharisees and the Roman oppressors (equivalent to the

white, privileged bourgeoisie of North America). He was crucified because of them. They believed that if Jesus had lived in America in their
time, he would have been hung as an abolitionist like John Brown, whom
many slaves and some white people considered a Christian martyr.

In summary, black people came to understand the Bible through the
lens of four essential presuppositions summarized by Latta Thomas:

1. The Bible is through and through a collective document which
   grew out of and is about God's liberation of people from human sin and human oppression, and true liberation is made
   real on earth when oppressed people and those who throw in
   their lot with them *hear* and *act* on the call of God to rebel
   against the evil in the world...
2. The Bible pictures the real God of heaven and earth and of
   Jesus Christ as *always* concentrating God's liberating efforts
   and concerns where human beings are in need, being mistreated, and held down...
3. Before the Bible can be seen in all its liberating purity and
   power, the effort must be made to identify and cut through
   those motives, myths, and interpretations whether deliberate
   or accidental, which resulted in attempts to twist the Bible in
   support of Black enslavement and white racism.
4. Black people, particularly in America but actually everywhere,
   need the liberating power and direction in the biblical faith
   as never before, and should fully embrace them...as the foundation of today's Black church in America.[53]

Perhaps equally significant is the emerging genre of contemporary
postmodern black scholars of the Bible and religion who have undertaken crucial studies demonstrating that the Bible itself may be essentially about African people. In the light of these investigations the enslaved may have had an affinity with the scriptures because they saw
much of themselves and their own culture reflected in its pages. In other
words, we can say that the enslaved often interpreted the Bible in a way
that was characterized by religious alertness.

The Preacher

Du Bois writes that the black preacher was "the most unique personality developed by the Negro on American soil."[54] The main responsibility of the black preacher was to speak a word of divine hope to the
oppressed that would inspire them in the same way as the slave spirituals. The black preacher, guided by African-American spirituality, did
not sever what Wyatt Tee Walker calls "the historical umbilical cord of

African heritage." The black preacher used it to help the people adapt to and cope with the oppressive climate of the American experience. Walker states that in the instances where the black churches became strongly imitative of white worship styles and theology, there was a parallel loss of freedom and sensitivity to the pain of the black masses. In those instances where this did not occur (notably the "invisible church" of the enslaved and the churches of the uneducated), black folk life and religion remained intact and there was a far greater potential for the churches to be engaged in social action for the people's liberation.[55]

In order for the preacher to possess the spiritual authority or *ashe* to speak an efficacious, liberating word, the preacher had to embody at least three characteristics: a strong memory and respect for black spirituality as a way to freedom, a personal rejection of Western values as evidenced by self-sacrifice over self-interest, and a deep kindness and compassion for the despised poor that evidenced itself in a "hands-on" personal touch administered to the poor. These characteristics, which also composed religious alertness, took priority over contemporary issues such as gender or ordination. In the African-American religious tradition the title preacher was accorded through considerations of whether or not the person possessed spiritual authority as evidenced by a call from God to serve the community.

The Music

In the church of the enslaved, music had an observable effect in the struggle for personal and collective liberation. Many black musicologists have traced this effect to a basic continuity with Africa and the oral tradition. This music was "rooted in African musical idioms and reflect[ed] accommodations"[56] to Christianity. But, as with every aspect of early black culture, what the people were singing religiously reflected what was happening to them sociologically—even if they were singing European hymns. Musicologist John Lovell Jr. describes seven categories by which music could function as a religious support system for the oppressed. Early black song, forged from slave spirituals, served:

1. To give the community a true, valid, and useful song
2. To keep the community invigorated
3. To inspire the uninspired individual
4. To enable the group to face its problems
5. To comment on the slave situation
6. To stir each member to personal solutions and a sense of belonging in the midst of a confusing and terrifying world
7. To provide a code language for emergency use.[57]

The sacred music of the black church was also religiously alert to the extent that this occurred within the life of the individual, congregation, and community.

The Frenzy

The striking shout tradition of the black church in slavery (and post-slavery), also described as the frenzy by W. E. B. Du Bois, was believed in as a visible manifestation of the Invisible God there could be no true communion without.[58] This belief remained firmly entrenched in the black churches of the masses in spite of the protestations of white people and acculturated black people who called it heathenish and pagan. It served to usher the people into a "spirit possession" that was a oneness or radical unity with God, family, and the black community. To the extent that a transfer of African culture and spirituality took place in the religion of the people in the frenzy, Christianity was Africanized within the black community and assisted in keeping it religiously alert.

THE VALUES OF THE ENSLAVED COMMUNITY

All the above led to a community rooted in moral and relational values that stemmed from the amalgamation of the unified African worldview expressed in African retentions and the Christianity of the black church. These values defined the identity of the African-American community and the individual in community. The values and the identity they inspired essentially may be summarized as *commitment to God, self, and others embodied in community.*

The African-American community named itself culturally through a spiritual self-understanding that evaluated everything in terms of its capability to inspire loyalty to the community. This spiritual self-understanding was based on the central conviction that they were God's children, not niggers. God was a good God who was just and extraordinarily compassionate to the disinherited and oppressed because God's self-revelation in Jesus Christ had demonstrated that God, too, had been, in the words of the spiritual, "lied on, cheated, talked about, and mistreated." God intimately knew the misery of their condition and willed their freedom. For God was understood both from their African heritage (God as head of the community and member of the family) and black Christianity (slave exegesis of the Bible through their experience) as "one of us."

The radical identification of oneness with God who was both with them and for them was lived out through the basic value of *cultural oneness* expressed in everyday life as social principles of unity, harmony, and cooperation. This value is revealed in the black ideal of family as the basic unit of black social structure. The existence of the extended family as a cooperative familial style in slave society has been well documented, but a few of its characteristics need to be highlighted to better explore the values of the enslaved community.

In slavery the definition of family actually embraced the entire black community. As in African society, children were valued by the community, and in African-American culture the definition of family came to mean that anybody's child was everybody's child. In other words, all adults were responsible for all children. All elders were required to care for and educate children by passing on the history and values of the community as derived from the ancestors or the ones who had gone before them. This African value became even more pronounced in slave culture, because children were often forcibly removed from their biological parents. Other black adults readily embraced them whenever and wherever they could.

This is not uncommon even in contemporary black culture. In my own family, my father was an only child. Yet he was raised with several other children my grandparents took in at various times as the need arose for the care of other children in the community.

It was the elders' responsibility to teach the children how to survive with dignity and grace and how to be human from an African perspective. This involved teaching them lessons and telling them stories about the collective survival wisdom of the ancestors as well as moral teachings about treating everyone justly and fairly. Lying and stealing were not permitted because the people held up honesty and a respect for the truth as absolute virtues as well as the value of education. The responsibility of educating children often led to a special relationship between grandparents and grandchildren because the grandmothers, in particular, often told the children stories about the ways of times gone by.

Children, in turn, were expected to demonstrate utter respect and obedience to elders. If the old people needed anything done for them, children were expected to do it readily and without remuneration. Old people were to live out their days at home, taken care of by their family, and they were not to be abandoned or expected to fend for themselves. Even today, African Americans are reluctant to send their elderly to nursing homes.

People were expected to be kind to the poor even though they were poor themselves. Sharing was common. For example, marriages and funerals (when permitted by slave owners) were often sponsored by the community when single families or individuals could not provide for them, and food was often shared with those in need, including strangers.

The black church was also understood as one's "church family." It operated from the same basic values and principles as the black family.

Howard Thurman wrote that his mother was concerned that Thurman's father had never joined the church, not only because of the issue of where his soul would reside after death, but also because, at that time, to be outside of the church was to be outside of the community. As church historian C. Eric Lincoln states, "To understand the power of the Black Church it must first be understood that there is no disjunction between the Black Church and the Black community."[59]

The black church was required to preserve and pass on the racial memory of the people as a legacy that would ensure the community's survival. The same values of love and equality between all people as the children of God, treating everyone fairly and justly, and respecting truth and honesty were preached as the gospel in the churches.

The black church was expected to give the people hope for freedom and liberation by helping them collectively to resist racism and anything that threatened the life of the community. It is no accident that the black church historically has been in the vanguard of the struggle for change in race relations in America. The rejection of racism as a means of protecting the community was seen as a holy and spiritual obligation. This necessity led to African-American definitions of good and evil that were integrally related to the continuing survival and welfare of the community.

The values embraced by the enslaved (through the eventual use of the form of Christian terminology combined with the content of African and African-American spirituality) informed their unique view of evil as essentially *forgetfulness* and good and salvation as *memory and forgiveness.*

Forgetfulness as evil

Slave understandings of evil can be explained in terms of a circular, counterclockwise, and unified worldview of looking to the past to inform the present and future. The African and early African-American understanding of destiny, as Paris states, "preclude[d] any radical individual autonomy in human action either in its initiation or its consequences."[60] All matters of destiny were essentially connected to and governed by the ancestors. Misfortune or sickness was attributable to ancestral punishments for "wrongdoing in general or inattentive devotion to them."[61] In the amalgamated culture of the enslaved if the community failed to live out the values prompted by an African-based or African-influenced worldview, either through conscious neglect (intentionally living out opposing values) or neglect in the form of failing to pass on the African legacy in the form of "forgetfulness" (not preserving the racial memory), evil resulted in the life, well-being, and harmony of the community and the individual was in great jeopardy. Thus the people were called to recall, remember, and remold the African legacy in each generation to guide them in "being human" and surviving in America.

Griots and storytellers focused mainly on a particular chronicle of the past out of the necessity to help the people in the present so that there would be a future. In this view, failure to survive in America resulted from the human evil of forgetting the past, thereby disrupting their oneness with all that came before (Africa and the ancestors) and destroying the possibility of all that was to become in America. Those who neglected the past were considered to be traitors to the community. Early slave storytellers used the symbol of a buzzard to speak of the traitor.

The early English-speaking Africans in America told many tales about buzzards. Stuckey writes:

> The buzzard represented something more dreadful than he [the storyteller] realized. A buzzard was not encountered; rather, the spirit of a traitor took the form of a buzzard. Tom joined in the telling of the tale and said he "hear 'bout dat ole thing 'fore 'dis," that his "pa" told him "dat way back in slavery time–'way back in Africa"–there was "a nigger, a big nigger" who as chief of his tribe tricked his people into slavery, betraying thousands.[62]

This traitor then entered "an endless journey of spiritual unrest, a punishment markedly African":

> An' when he dead, dere were no place in heaven for him an' he were not desired in hell. An' de Great Master decide dat he were lower dan all other mens or beasts; he punishment were to wander for eternal time over de face er de earth. Dat as he had kilt de sperrits of mens an' womens as well as dere bodies, he must wander on an' on. Dat his sperrit should always travel in de form of a great buzzard, an' dat carrion must be he food...An' dey say he are known to all de sperrit world as de King Buzzard, an' dat forever he must travel alone.[63]

Therefore, the greatest punishment for the traitor of the community was to be excluded from the community–"to travel alone." When black people's values are essentially communal (I am because we are), to be out of community is to be spiritually dead and therefore no longer to exist. This, for people of African descent, is the worst kind of pain and punishment.

Buzzards, or traitors to the community, were excommunicated from black societal existence. For an African-influenced society this could feel like being among the dead while yet alive. Therefore, in a very real way, being considered a part of the early African-American community of the enslaved was based not on common color or oppression but in the positive value of being loyal and committed to the healthy survival of the community.

There is a saying that has survived from slavery times into the idiom of contemporary African-American speech. When a young person is behaving outside of the communal norms and values, black people say, Where did this child come from? or to the parents, Where did you get this child from? Oftentimes older black people explain individuals acting outside of black communal norms (whether black or white) by saying, "They just don't know no better." With this, they dismiss any further conversation about the matter. The implication is, How do you expect them to act when they have not been taught by the community how to behave like human beings?

Forgiveness as Salvation

Hatred was viewed in the black community as something that would eventually destroy "the core of life of the hater"[64] for it could not be controlled once it was set in motion and it would return to the hater. Again, this is essentially a circular, African-influenced worldview: What goes around comes around. Hatred would inevitably destroy one's own soul by bringing death to the spirit through the disintegration of the ethical and moral values of the hater.

Peter Paris also notes that traditional African societies did not harbor long-term resentments against anyone. They "sought to resolve the problems as quickly as possible so as not to be exposed to the spiritual imbalance for too long a time," because it would destroy the moral balance of the community.

> African peoples have always known the great toll that hatred takes on both the personality of individuals and the life of the community. In the interest of their highest goal, community, they have shunned hatred by cultivating the virtue of forgiveness through the habitual exercise of kindness...The virtue of forgiveness is essential for the ongoing life of community.[65]

He cites the lives of Nelson Mandela and Martin Luther King Jr. as examples of the saving power of forgiveness as essential for saving the soul of the individual and the community.[66]

When United States President Bill Clinton journeyed to Africa in 1998 and visited President Nelson Mandela, President Clinton asked President Mandela why and how he advised the native South African people to forgive the descendants of the enslavers and colonizers. The South African leader said that they had to forgive the white people more for their own sakes as black South Africans than for the sake of the white people. In European-influenced Christianity forgiveness is often conceived of in terms of the restoration of a broken personal relationship in order to receive a reward from God for leading a good life. In African and Afrocentric terms it is conceived of primarily as an act required of the individual and the community for the sake of the salvation of the community.

The willingness to forgive is also encompassed in the saying, They just don't know any better. Those who offend communal values, in some cases, are seen as ignorant of what it means to be in community; therefore, in a certain sense, their behavior is all one can reasonably expect, so they should be forgiven. For example, when Eugene "Bull" Connor (Birmingham's pugnacious police commissioner) or Alabama's Governor George Wallace insulted black people in the media and ordered police dogs, police, fire hoses, and so on against the freedom fighters in the Civil Rights movement, the old people did not appear terribly upset (except for concern for the safety of the freedom fighters). Their attitude was more or less: What else can you expect? They ain't got no home trainin'. And, to a great degree, they dismissed them from further conversation, saying that they would hate to be either of them because one day they would suffer terribly (in this life and beyond the grave).

Yet when Malcolm X was quoted in the media as saying that white people were devils, they would get upset and say, "Now that child knows his mama raised him better than that!" Malcolm was expected to "act human" because it was assumed that he had been taught the traditional, African-based and Jesus-based norms and values of the black community that said *all* people are people because the same God created them. They believed that Malcolm needed to be restored to the community and returned to what they understood as the traditional values they assumed he had been taught by his elders. In a radically unified sense of community, they felt that Malcolm was "family" in a way that Connor and Wallace were not; Malcolm had been exposed to the memory and values of the community. The black community took what he said far more personally because he was believed to embody an extension of themselves and their community. They felt he had an obligation to represent the family well and to subscribe to traditional black values in public and in private, because he was one of them.

African and African-American slave ideas of good and evil were part of the whole African cosmological scheme of memory of the ancestors. When that memory was terminated through conscious or unconscious neglect, it could be said that the ancestors had died along with the possibility of community. To be saved was to be saved in community by recalling, remembering, and remolding the African past to speak to the present experience and not to allow anything—neither forgetfulness nor hate as the result of unforgiveness–to prohibit this necessity. This religious worldview antedated and interacted with European-Christianity to create the identity of the black church and the black community in America.

CONCLUSION

African retentions and spirituality continued to inform and influence the morals and values of the enslaved and their descendants and helped constitute their identity. These retentions were of inestimable importance in the cultural resistance of black people in America as they sought to name and identify themselves and seek salvation for the community. Identity and salvation could come only from a fundamentally African value system and the newborn and developing African-American spiritual tradition.

African-American spirituality empowered black religion, the black church, and the black community to become a "phoenix rising from the ashes" of the devastation caused by a larger, hateful culture that sought to eradicate black self-determination and identity. Amazingly, the strength and resilience of the black community, which allowed it to critique itself internally as well as to critique what was oppressing it externally, was not derived from numbers or violence; rather, it was a byproduct of a wise oral tradition taught by the old to the young–of folktales, ghost stories, dances, songs, art, folk cures, protective charms and amulets, and compassionate, sacrificial spiritual leaders who spoke plain, holy words of hope and deliverance through chants, incantations, visions, prophecies, fortunetelling, sermons, prayers, and their own interpretations of the Bible.

This religious emphasis, based in new-old African-American spirituality, did not paralyze action in the community or lead to resignation. Instead, it helped to foster both a vision of and the struggle for a better way for the people to name themselves and be in community. The name or identity of the black community, guided by African-American spirituality, can be found in a community that is characterized by essentially the same values described in its African heritage. The spiritual, religious, and cultural style of the name or identity of the African American in community, guided by these African-based spiritual tenets, is *relational.*

Chapter 3

The Call to Protest

Spirituality Embodied

This chapter examines black spirituality from the perspective of African Americans who lived in different periods in history in order to show both its persistence and adaptability as well as to discover its form. The conversion process of African-American spirituality is explored as it is revealed in the lives of Harriet Tubman, William Edmondson, Fannie Lou Hamer, and Ruby Bridges.

In the conversion process—viewed as God's intervention with the self in community—the convert changed from a way of being in the world characterized by radical selfishness to a way of being in the world characterized by radical compassion. In the slave and ex-slave conversion tradition, this was experienced when the former patterns of consciousness were suspended or disrupted and there was a possibility of apprehending new information that radically altered the patterns of consciousness. Once this took place, the individual experienced a change in thinking and behavior that was nurtured and acted out in community. The conversion experience touched the whole person, including both inner being and outer actions as they affected social and cultural aspects of community life.

The conversion process occurs in at least six dimensions that result in a vocation or call to protest societal values and norms that destroy the possibility for community. These dimensions include apprenticeship, the experience of alienation, rejection of the societal norm, personal sacrifice *vs.* self-interest, solidarity with the despised poor, and joy in community. These moments of conversion are not mutually exclusive or separate but are essentially related to one another. In other words, the new, truer sense of self is acquired in social roles, but the essential identity (defined as the soul or the self through which God and the individual are related) is, at the same time, not totally apprehended from the corporate existence of the individual. The primal identity is God-given, but it has to be actualized within community. Thus, in African-American spirituality, in conversion one "recovers" or "retrieves" the true, God-given self or identity that is centered and rooted in ultimate meaning expressed through and in the life and culture of the community. Pastoral counselor Edward Wimberly states the African-American conversion experience is a process inextricable from social context, the black symbolic universe, cultural modes of expression, and biblical and African eschatology.[1]

The slave community and its descendants recalled their history or racial memory in such a way that it resulted in the remolding of the past into a "remembering" that became their present experience. The converted no longer saw themselves as alien or separate in any way from God or the rest of creation—even in terms of temporality and eternity. The conversion process resulted in a vocation or call to protest societal values and norms that destroyed the possibility for community. This vocation is the foundation of the embodied soul's ability to be centered or anchored in God and then stand for God in community. When the person stands in the community, he or she simultaneously stands in the presence of the ultimate Source of meaning; the person is then able to make sense out of life and believe and act upon ultimate values that enhance the growth and well-being of the self in community. It is necessary to look at African-American spirituality as it is embodied, for it is best revealed as it is integrally interwoven in the concrete lives and experiences of actual human beings.

HARRIET TUBMAN

Harriet Tubman was born into slavery around 1820, as Araminta Ross in Dorchester County, Maryland. She knew her African grandmother, whose name was Modesty. Araminta, as Harriet was first called, or Minta or Minty, was the *basket, pet,* or *crib* name given to her by her parents to use until the time came to call her by her adult name, Harriet (also her mother's name). This would occur when the slave community recognized her as having reached the age of accountability and responsibility. The early African-American community followed the African custom of using crib names from birth to the time that children were considered to be grown-up and reliable enough to be addressed by their mature name. While children were also given their mature names at birth, they were reserved for later use. These two names were given by the parents or parent in faith that the child would survive or not suffer early death as an infant and that the child would survive life in the community or not be sold away from family and "tribe" before early adolescence. The crib name, in this regard, was used to "fix" the child's uncertain or "slippery" existence in place in the midst of temporality. If the child survived either of these forms of death, then the grown-up name would later be used by all.

Araminta survived. In later years Harriet Tubman was to say that the slave community believed that she was Ashanti because she acted like these fierce African people. A vital part of her spiritual formation lay in a solid and secure black cultural foundation, upon which she would later build her life as a hired-out slave laborer, field hand, wife, abolitionist, freedom fighter, conductor of the Underground Railroad, lecturer, Union Army spy, and nurse, caretaker, and protector of the poor, elderly and infirm. Though Tubman was a slave, there is clear evidence in her narrative[2] and biographies later written about her that her slave parents and community were able to prepare her for life in a short time in a remarkably powerful way. Indeed, the black community learned these skills first from the generation of the enslaved and transmitted their child-rearing practices to succeeding generations.

Like many other slave children, Minty was brought up during the daytime hours in the company of the plantation's other small children. All of the children who were too young to work were placed in the care of an old woman while the children's parents labored in the house, barns, outbuildings, or fields. Harriet's adult narrative does not recount the name of the old woman who cared for the children, but it does recall that all the children were afraid of her. Even though she was very elderly, she would vigorously enforce discipline among the children by using a tough switch from a black gum tree. The children were never to leave her sight or go near the creek or the woods or go into the cabins where they might get burned in the hot ashes from the fireplaces. They respected and obeyed her because high respect for elders—the rule of the community—was carefully observed.

Harriet stated that when this elderly caretaker was in a favorable mood, she told them stories of the Middle Passage. Ann Petry, Tubman's biographer, writes:

> The mumbling old voice evoked the clank of chains, the horror of thirst, the black smell of death, below deck in the hold of a slave ship. The children were too young to understand the meaning of the stories and yet they were frightened, standing motionless, listening to her, and shivering even if the sun was hot.[3]

This fierce old woman also told the children that things would change for the enslaved. She served not only as protector of the children, by keeping them out of harm's way, but she protected them as a *griot* and

storyteller by telling them their history and therein creating and preserving the racial memory out of which they could forge an identity.
She also inspired them by implanting the seed of the dream of freedom
in their young hearts and minds from the earliest days of their existence.

Ben, Minty's father, and Old Rit, her mother, were also powerful
storytellers. Ben's stories concentrated on lessons about nature; Old Rit's
stories were mostly from the Bible. She told about Moses and the children of Israel, about how the Red Sea parted so that the Hebrews were
able to walk across on dry land, and about how, on the long journey to
the Promised Land, some of the Hebrews had wanted to go back to
Egypt. Old Rit also taught Minty the words of slave songs that were
forbidden after the abortive slave uprising of Denmark Vesey in 1822
because the white people were afraid they would encourage the slaves
to revolt. The main song Old Rit taught her, under her breath so they
would not be discovered, was "Go Down, Moses." Harriet carefully
learned all the words of this song, never to be forgotten. Old Rit also
taught her daughter how to pray and believe in the power of her prayer.

In addition, as far back as Harriet could remember, stories were told
secretly in the quarters at night about Denmark Vesey. It was said that
he was a free Negro who had bought his freedom at thirty-three and
that he could read and write. He read the Bible and told and retold the
story of how the children of Israel had escaped from bondage. He told
a group of slaves who became his followers that all people were born
equal and that it was sinful and degrading for black people to bow to
white people. Finally, he planned and attempted an insurrection in
Charleston, South Carolina.

Night after night, when the enslaved slipped stealthily into one
another's cabins to talk of Denmark Vesey, some of them said he had
made life harder and worse for the rest of them because the new laws
passed after his attempted uprising took away what little freedom they
felt they had. By law, they were no longer permitted to read, to sing
certain spirituals, to gather without permission and a white person
present, to travel without a pass, or even to move about or visit one
another's cabins in the quarters at night because the white people feared
more plots. Minty's mother was of the opinion that talk about freedom
was dangerous and unproductive. She feared change and constantly
reiterated that the slave master had promised to free her, Ben, and their
children before he died. She wanted to hear nothing about escape and
insurrection.

Tubman's biographer writes that the other slaves and the plantation
master were in awe of Ben because he could accurately predict when it
would rain or frost or how many days there would be of fair weather.
He knew everything about the woods—the plants that grew there and

their properties for healing and whether they were edible–as well as the ways of the animals and birds. Ben knew all about the rivers, creeks, and swamps. He taught Minty everything he knew about nature. From a very early age she knew how to identify the North Star and how to study the sky and the flight of birds. Ben taught her the names of birds; which berries were good to eat and which were poisonous; where to look for water lilies; and how to identify hemlock, cranebill, and wild geranium as plants with medicinal value. The slaves used these plants to cure all kinds of ailments, fevers, and intestinal disorders. He also taught her the valuable skill of picking a path through the woods and the underbrush without making a sound.

Though they never spoke of it, she says that she knew deep inside that Ben was training her for the day when she would become a runaway. A successful flight to freedom depended heavily upon what he taught her about nature. By the time she was six years old, she had consciously and unconsciously absorbed much of the knowledge she needed to run for her freedom. She ran away from slavery for the first time when seven.

Harriet recounted that at night inside the cabin with her family she felt safe. The slave community provided her with this warm sense of security. She spoke of the joy she felt there when they sang; when there was warmth from the fireplace, and her family and friends from the quarters were gathered around it together; and the happiness they all felt in the time between Christmas and New Year's when, by tradition, they had little work to do. They were always happy when they were together, and she deeply loved and was loved by her family.

Yet as an enslaved person she also had the growing awareness that she was a slave and that white people were hateful to and mistreated slaves. As Howard Thurman wrote:

> The doom of the children is the greatest tragedy of the disinherited. They are robbed of much of the careless rapture and spontaneous joy of merely being alive. Through their environment they are plunged into the midst of overwhelming pressures for which there can be no possible preparation.[4]

The slave community struggled to prepare the children, as best it could and in very powerful ways, for that for which there could be "no possible preparation." While the adults could teach the children how to survive, they could not protect them from the pain of cruel and inhumane treatment. The children lived with as much concentrated insecurity, terror, and stress as the adults.

Early in life Minty learned how to recognize the sound of the overseer's horn, which called her parents and siblings to work. She did not know exactly how or when she learned that she was a slave, yet she knew that she, her brothers and sisters, her father and mother, and all the other people who lived in the quarters were slaves. She had been taught early how to address white people as "Missus" and "Massa." At night and during the day she heard the frightening sound of the rapid hoof beats of patrollers going past in pursuit of runaways. She also heard the screams when runaways were caught, whipped, and often sent to certain death on a chain gang. By the age of six she already knew a great deal about fear and terror.

In the summer of 1826, when Minty was six years old, she was considered by plantation standards to be old enough to work. Edward Brodas, the plantation owner, "hired her out" for a small amount of money to work for Mrs. James Cook, a white woman whom she had never seen. She became more and more frightened as she was taken away in Mrs. Cook's wagon, farther and farther away from her family and the quarter where she had grown up. She slept in the kitchen in a corner near the fireplace and placed her feet in the fireplace ashes at night to keep warm. Harriet spoke of how the people fed her scraps of food, "as much as they might have fed a dog." She also remembered and told of how the children on her mother's plantation were fed from a common trough on the ground in the yard "like pigs." They ran with oyster shells and pieces of roof shingle to scoop up cornmeal mush. She said that whoever ate the fastest got the most food and that the children were always hungry. There was never enough.

Initially, Minty was supposed to help Mrs. Cook, who was a weaver, inside the house. She hated being confined indoors because she had grown to love the outdoors from the time spent in apprenticeship with her father. When Mrs. Cook complained that she was useless in the house, Mr. Cook assigned her the task of taking care of his muskrat traps on the bank of the river. One morning she woke up weak, coughing, and feverish, but Mrs. Cook forced her to go out into the freezing-cold river to inspect the trap lines. As a result, she became even more seriously ill. When her mother heard about it (Harriet stated that the enslaved had a highly sophisticated, covert, and rapid communication system), she asked her owner if she could bring the child home and look after her. He agreed because he did not want to lose a slave.

Minty had a serious case of the measles and looked like a skeleton from being almost starved to death. Her mother nursed her back to health for six weeks. But for the rest of her life she had a huskiness to her voice as a result of being so ill. Her biographer wrote that it gave her voice "an undertone that made her singing voice memorable. It lent an added timbre to her speaking voice."[5]

As soon as she recovered, she was sent back to the Cooks. She said she felt like the muskrats that were caught in the traps. She refused to learn to weave, and the Cooks sent her back to the plantation for good. But she was soon sent away in a wagon, once again, to be hired out at a different location. At the age of seven she became the full-time care-taker of a white infant. Whenever the baby cried, she was severely beaten.

> She was whipped so often that the back of her neck was covered with scars, crisscrossed with scars, so deep that they would be vis-ible for the rest of her life. Finally she learned to sleep without really going to sleep, learned to listen while still asleep, head nod-ding, eyes closed, but all her senses alerted to the slightest move-ment from the cradle.[6]

After many weeks of this torture, she began to think about running away.

One day she was caught sneaking a lump of sugar from the sugar bowl. The mistress took out a rawhide whip to beat her. She ran away and kept going until she was completely exhausted. From Friday to Tuesday she hid in "a great big pigpen." She states she was

> fighting with those little pigs for the potato peelings and the other scraps that came down in the trough. The old sow would push me away when I tried to get her children's food, and I was awfully afraid of her. By Tuesday I was so starved I knew I had to go back to my mistress. I didn't have anywhere else to go, even though I knew what was coming. So I went back.[7]

This was the height of her experience of alienation. The message com-municated to her was that the white infant was important and she was not only unimportant but less than human and of worth only as it re lated to the care of white people.

At seven years of age she was broken in heart as well as body. She must have felt totally alone, a stranger on the face of the earth. Yet through the memory of the love and training of her parents and com-munity, her spirit held fast and did not break. After she returned to the mistress, she was sent back to the slave quarter literally skin and bones and covered with filth and new wounds from a fresh beating.

The horror of this early alienation from the human community through severe mental, emotional, and physical abuse heightened the extreme contrast between being in community and being out of com-munity in young Minty's heart and mind. For the rest of her life it caused her to treasure and long for family and community as the greatest and highest good. The experience of slavery, for Harriet Tubman and many others, was hell in its most evil and virulent manifestation because it withheld from them the love in community that was the supreme joy of their existence. Slavery destroyed families and the "tribe"; this, in turn, destroyed the individual. Harriet Tubman would commit her body and soul to the struggle for community for the rest of her life with astonishing faith, courage, wisdom, and success.

Minta performed the back-breaking, spirit-killing labor of a field hand from the time she was returned to the plantation until she ran away for good. The plantation owner soon hired her out to a man who worked her as hard as a full-grown man, even though she was only a child. By the age of eleven she began wearing the bandanna or head covering that was worn by young slave women as a sign of maturity.

It was in this year, 1831, that she first began to hear stories about an Underground Railroad that slaves could journey upon and become free. In her mind she imagined a steam train running in an underground tunnel. That same year she also heard of Nat Turner's insurrection. The slave owners became more frightened, and therefore more cruel, than ever before, while the enslaved spoke more and more of freedom.

One night, while the slaves were in a barn shucking corn, she saw a slave run away. The overseer went after him. He caught him and ordered Minta to help hold him. The man ran away and Minta, in an instant, made a decision from which there could be no turning back. She cast her lot with the runaway. Not only did she not help to hold him, but when the overseer tried to get out of the doorway to catch the man who was escaping again, she blocked the overseer from leaving. He picked up a 200-pound weight and tried to throw it at the escaping slave. The weight missed the runaway but hit Minta directly, with full force, on the forehead. She was knocked unconscious and left with a great, gaping wound in her head that bled profusely. Everyone was sure that she could not survive. If she *did* survive, they believed sure death awaited her in the form of being sold to a chain gang as punishment for aiding a runaway.

She would suffer from headaches for the rest of her life and fall suddenly into a trancelike sleep over which she had absolutely no control. She said that after these strange periods of sleep, she would wake up knowing what to do about whatever had been worrying her before she fell asleep. She knew that if this happened while she was on the chain gang, she would be beaten to death. And she also knew the same thing might happen if she tried to run away and fell asleep exposed on an open road.

She remained in a stupor from before Christmas until March. During that time the plantation owner foolishly tried to sell her, even while she was still inert. When she regained consciousness, she began to pray for the slave master. At first she prayed, "Change his heart, Lord, convert him."[8] Then the word came to her from the slave community that she had been sold as part of the next chain gang.

In desperation she changed her prayer to *"Kill him,* Lord!"[9] One morning, a few days later, the master suddenly died. In utter despair and filled with guilt, she agonized because she believed that her prayers had killed him. Yet it strengthened and reinforced her belief that God would always hear and help her in her struggle to survive in freedom.

The other slaves began to admire her because of her courage and audacity in defying the overseer. They stopped using her pet name and everyone in the slave community began to call her Harriet. Even the old ones listened to her ideas and deferred to her. The severe wound to her head that she had sustained while protecting and standing in solidarity with the oppressed was her rite of passage in the slave community from childhood to adulthood. The community granted her adult status and respected her participation in the struggle for the freedom of another person in the community. This initial act of rejecting the norm of slavery in order to save someone else, set in motion her capacity to defy the system of slavery.

As Harriet's beloved husband, John Tubman, was a freed man, they were permitted to live together in their own cabin. Even though she still performed back-breaking labor as a hired-out field hand, the time she spent at home with him was the happiest of her life. Yet when she spoke of the urgent necessity to run for her freedom because slaves were being sold regularly to pay the plantation owner's overwhelming debts, he refused to run away to the North with her, and he told her he would betray her to her master if she tried to escape. This wounded her to the depths of her spirit; she deeply loved this handsome man who was her family and fondest hope for the future (children). Family was to be treasured, protected and held together. Finally, in tremendous grief, she sacrificed her love for him and the possibility of having children. She made the decision to leave him and run for her freedom, even though this left an emotional void, a hole in her heart, for the rest of her life. In spite of her fears about going alone with a trance-inflicting illness, she decided to trust God for her life, safety, and security, and she fled to the North alone.

Later she would sacrifice her own safety over and over again to return to Maryland and to help over three hundred other slaves make their way to freedom on the Underground Railroad. She said that she did not enjoy freedom without her community. These trips included the rescue from slavery of all of her family members who had not been sold away on the chain gang as well as total strangers. After the John Brown insurrection, the reward offered for her capture went up to twelve thousand dollars. For a top-rated, strong, male field hand, the reward was usually two thousand dollars.

Harriet developed skills as a black preacher. She was always able to speak a word of divine hope to the runaways she helped by using the memory of the tradition (songs, prayers, stories, the Bible, knowledge of healing powers of plants and herbs, belief in the intuitive and mystical, and so on). Runaways would become discouraged from extreme exhaustion, starvation, cold, heat, and the unspeakable stress of the sheer fear and terror of being captured and punished. Some talked about going back. In spite of her painful headaches and sleeping condition, Harriet drew upon her own strength and emotional resources by using her beautiful voice to pray, constantly singing spirituals to them and telling them stories of what awaited them in a life of freedom in the North. She also used Bible stories to keep them motivated and inspired to go on in the face of overwhelming emotional pressure and external obstacles. Sometimes, when the pressure became unbearable, they stopped believing in her stories and insisted that they were going back because slavery could not be as bad as what they were presently suffering. So, when all else failed, she pulled out a gun and told them that she would shoot whoever tried to go back. Following an African sensibility, she believed that the safety of the entire group and all of those whose homes were used as stops on the way could not be jeopardized by a single individual. In later life she said, "I never lost a passenger."

Amazingly, none of them ever tried to leave when she was overtaken by sleep. They sat patiently and waited for her to wake up; when she woke up, she knew what to do next. It did not matter if the question was how to feed them, which road to take, or how to inspire them to go on. She said that God always told her exactly what direction to go so that they would not be captured by patrols. She simply prayed and asked God, and when she woke up from her trance, she knew.

Harriet did not look to the community of the oppressed or her vocation as a servant of God to support herself financially. In between trips as a "conductor" on the Underground Railroad, she worked as a common laborer, among other things, to support herself and many other people. She never accepted money as payment from anyone for her sacrificial acts of service. Later, when she worked as a nurse for the Union Army and heard that others complained about her getting free food rations, she refused them and sold pies at night to earn money to buy food. During this time she also made medicine from roots and herbs and healed many people. She also began giving lectures on the Underground Railroad to earn money to support herself and her growing household.

During this time Harriet not only helped many slaves out of bondage, but she also supported her elderly parents and her new husband, Nelson Davis, who had tuberculosis. They had been married nineteen years when he died in 1888. She took in elderly and sick slaves, former slaves, and basically anyone who came to her door who had nowhere to go and no resources or help whatsoever. She created her own welfare system for the stranger and the poor by inviting them to live in her home and going out to work in order to feed them.

Eventually, she gave her home in Auburn, New York, and twenty-five acres of land to the African Methodist Episcopal Zion Church as a free home for the elderly. She criticized the church when it began to charge the people to stay there. Near the end of her life she said:

> When I give the Home over to Zion Church, what do you suppose they did? Why, they made a rule that nobody should come in without a hundred dollars. Now I wanted to make a rule that nobody could come in unless they had no money. *What's the good of a home if a person who wants to get in has to have money?*[10]

Her African-American spiritual temperament led her to expect the institutional black church to be as kind and compassionate toward the poor as she had been. And she criticized it when it was not living up to a black spiritual standard. Her solidarity was ultimately with the community of the despised poor—not institutional religion.

Harriet continued to live in her home with the poor after she donated it to the church for free housing of the indigent elderly. Eventually her parents and her husband died. In advanced old age she continued to care for her "created family" or community of the poorest of the poor. Ironically, the Union Army gave her a pension when her husband died because he had been in the army, but it never gave her one for her own work as a Union spy and a nurse. She spent her last days peddling vegetables as an excuse for visiting with her neighbors up and down the road and telling them spellbinding stories of the Underground Railroad.

> Finally, she became a tiny little old woman, peddling vegetables from door to door in Auburn. She didn't make many stops in the course of a day. There wasn't time. At each house, she was invited inside, told to sit down, and urged to tell a story about some phase of her life…It was as the storyteller, the bard, that Harriet's active years came to a close. She had never learned to read and write. She compensated for this handicap by developing *a memory* on which was indelibly stamped everything she had ever heard or seen or experienced…She had memorized verses from the Bible, word for word…[She was] *a superb storyteller.*[11]

In the end, as Wole Soyinka writes about an African cosmology, neither child, nor mother, nor grandmother was a closed chronological concept. The child Minty became the "mother" of the elderly grandmother-*griot* Harriet as Harriet recalled the stories of her life. The remembering of her youth helped remold the world as it continued in its eternal circle of life. Harriet Tubman died of advanced old age (approximately ninety-three years old) on March 10, 1913.

WILLIAM EDMONDSON

I first encountered the limestone sculptures of William Edmondson, the son of former slaves, several years ago on one of my visits to the Cheekwood Fine Arts Center in Nashville, Tennessee. As usual, I visited the gallery early on a weekday afternoon because I knew I would have the luxury of being in the exhibition rooms alone. After looking at the oil paintings that I always enjoyed viewing, I aimlessly wandered into a small room dedicated completely to William Edmondson's work. I didn't know who he was or at which medium I was looking. I hadn't even known that his work was there. But, as I looked in awe at the simple art, there was one thing of which I was certain. I knew immediately that I stood on holy ground, that I was in the presence of the holy. It felt like being in church. An immediate calm came over my spirit and, when I left, after sitting on a little bench and gazing at the sculptures for a while, I felt that I had gained more strength to carry on with day-by-day life. That peace stayed with me.

I went back to "church" in the tiny, solitary, Edmondson "cathedral" many times. Eventually I sought out the curators to ask for more detailed information about the artist. The placards on the walls were not enough. It turned out that Edmondson, a native of Nashville, Tennessee, was the first black person to be honored with a one-man show at New York's Museum of Modern Art in 1937. The works I had been looking at were decorations taken from tombstones he had carved.

William Edmondson was born to ex-slaves from the Edmondson and Compton Plantation in segregated Nashville, Tennessee, around 1883. The family Bible in which his birth was recorded was destroyed in a fire. He worked for the Nashville, Chattanooga, and St. Louis Railway shops until about 1907, when an accident left him disabled. He subsequently worked as a servant, fireman, janitor, and orderly at the Women's Hospital (later to become Baptist Hospital) in Nashville until it closed in 1931. He then began to work in his large vegetable garden, do odd jobs around the neighborhood, and finally he retired from his life of hard labor and started to "cut away on some stones." In his book *Visions in Stone* Edmund Fuller quotes Edmondson:

> I was out in the driveway with some old pieces of stone when I heard a voice telling me to pick up my tools and start to work on a

tombstone. I looked up in the sky and right there in the noon daylight He hung a tombstone out for me to make. I knowed it was God telling me what to do. God was telling me to cut figures.[12]

A deeply religious man, he believed that God had called him to carve gravestones.

Edmondson said of his work, "I didn't know I was no artist till them folks come told me I was. Every piece of work I got carved...is a message...a sermon, you might say. A preacher don't hardly get up in the pulpit but he don't preach some picture I got carved."[13] In the beginning, before he became recognized as a great artist by white people, Edmondson saw the stones he carved as a personal odyssey of self-discovery between himself and God, tightly interwoven into the everyday existence and needs of the black community. He designed and created the gravestones because God told him to and because black people needed them to carry out the spiritual tradition of respect for the dead.

For African Americans, the cemetery has long had tremendous significance; the graveyard was originally the most important place where an overt black identity could be asserted and maintained. Sometimes the gathering of black people at the cemetery for funerals provided the occasion for discussing and planning political direction that led to plans for escape and rebellion. Eugene D. Genovese writes:

> The slaveholder's regime tried to supervise slave funerals and feared their providing the occasion for insurrectionary plots. In 1687 authorities in the Northern Neck of Virginia banned public funerals for slaves because they had become convinced of their role in hatching a dangerous conspiracy. In 1772 the corporation of New York City required that slave funerals be held during daylight hours and that maximum attendance be held to twelve.[14]

Art historian John Michael Vlach states that when Edmondson's creations are understood within the complex system of belief and identity located in black graveyards, it can be seen that Edmondson's work as a maker of tombstones was not that simple.

> The complexity of Afro-American funerary customs lends a level of complexity to his stone markers. While the stones themselves were often only modest tablets with just the name of the deceased and his or her dates of birth and death inscribed upon it, the purposes for which they were intended and the motivations of those who requested that the stones be carved were quite elaborate.[15]

Even though African-American funerary customs had assimilated much of Western culture by the 1930s, when Edmondson began to carve, the tombstone was still used by the African-American family as "a grave offering conveying care and concern equivalent to a personal item even though it did not possess the same degree of intimacy."[16]

Edmondson's work was the means by which many black people in Nashville continued to observe traditional black customs. His gravestones functioned within a complex social system. Vlach states:

> While the request for a tombstone could be construed solely as a monetary negotiation, the significance of death and funerals in Afro-American culture converted that request into a religious matter. Edmondson's gravestones cannot then be considered apart from the shared beliefs of Nashville's black community. They are not just his expression, but an ethnic statement created out of the context of well-known Afro-American rites that insure the necessary respect for the dead.[17]

The gravestones, then, were rooted in a traditional belief system that resulted not only from the individual's skill but also from collectively maintained attitudes within the black community. According to Vlach, the gravestone "represents communal attitudes; that is, it is a physical statement of the interactions among community members and between the carver and his clients."[18] Edmondson's vocation involved a call by God to be of service to the community. The ordering of grave markers allowed the community to fulfill its obligation to the dead, but it also allowed Edmondson to fulfill his obligation to God through the community and fulfill his own personal destiny as an artist.

Graveyards were a vital source for the maintenance of African-American identity. The graveyard continued to reestablish black identity as well as to satisfy the need of families to communicate with their deceased family members and placate the needs or potential fury of hostile spirits. Vlach writes, "In the black cemetery it was finally their order that was followed."[19] Edmondson's place, therefore, as a gravestone carver expressed his connection to black communal life and the black spiritual tradition.

He said of his work of almost twenty years:

> "Dis here stone 'n' all those out there in de yard—come from God. It's de word in Jesus speakin' his mind in my mind. I mus' be one of his 'ciples. Dese here is mirkels I can do. Cain't help carvin' I jes' does it. It's like when you're leavin' you're goin' home. Well, I know I'm goin' to carve. Jesus has planted the seed of carvin' in me."[20]

He never considered himself an artist in the sense of creating an object simply to be observed. His tools for carving were the tools of a handyman rather than those of a stonemason or sculptor.

Edmondson's carvings were secured after his death at little or no cost from demolished city buildings, curbs, and rebuilt city streets to be placed in museums and galleries because white people believed them to be objects of beauty. They were that, but black people knew that they were so much more. They represented the miracle of the link between the spirits of the living and the dead. I felt the connection the first time I happened upon his gravestone decorations in the Cheekwood Fine Arts Center. Though he was later commissioned to make other things, he never abandoned carving gravestones. Even today he continues to strengthen the black community through the work that was the result of his conversations with God. Increasingly arthritic, he died on February 7, 1951.

FANNIE LOU HAMER

Fannie Lou Hamer was born to Jim and Ella Townsend on October 6, 1917, in Montgomery County, Mississippi, the youngest of twenty children. Two years later her family moved to the E. W. Brandon Plantation to sharecrop in the Delta flatlands of Sunflower County. The family's diet was poor, with equally poor medical care. Her biographer records that Fannie Lou "limped badly throughout her life either from polio or from a childhood accident—a fact never clearly established."[21] In the cold winter the plantation owner would tell them that they could gather cotton scraps left in the fields. She remembered:

> We would walk for miles and miles and miles in the run of a week. We wouldn't have on shoes or anything…The ground would be froze real hard. We would walk from field to field until we had scrapped a bale of cotton. Then [my mother would] take that bale of cotton and sell it, and that would give us some of the food that we would need. Then she would go from house to house and she would help kill hogs. They would give her the intestines and sometimes the feet and the head and things like that and that would help to keep us going. So many times for dinner we would have greens with no seasoning and flour gravy.[22]

They were often near starvation, even though the large family picked tremendous amounts of cotton, fifty-five to sixty bales of cotton (at five hundred to six hundred pounds per bale). The toil was endless, but there was never enough food, clothing, housing, heat, electricity, in-door toilets, water, medical care, or education.

In the midst of this quasi-slavery, the people lived with severe vio-lence. The Mississippi Department of Archives and History preserved the newspaper accounts of the murder in February 1904 of African-American John Holbert and his wife, who were accused of killing a prominent Sunflower County planter, James Eastland. They were never taken to trial; instead, a lynch mob chased them for three days across two counties through the dense swamps and marshes of Sunflower County. Under the headline "John Holbert and Wife Are Burned at the Stake" the newspaper account read:

> Bruised and Battered Almost Beyond Recognition; Bleeding From an Hundred Tortures; With Ears Shorn From Their Heads; Pal-sied Limbs and Fingerless Hands–More Dead Than Alive–They are Led to Their Horrible Doom.[23]

On a Sunday evening, after the white people had been to church, they burned them alive at the stake.[24] The planter's nephew, James O. Eastland, a powerful plantation owner from Sunflower County, later became a United States senator and controlled appointments to the fed-eral bench in his role as Judiciary Committee chairman.

Olaudah Equiano (Gustavus Vassa), one of the earliest slave narra-tors, who vividly remembered his African heritage, asked a white slave owner who treated black people with barbarity and cruelty, "Do you not fear God?" The white man replied that God and heaven were later, slavery was now.[25] European-Christianity permitted him to compart-mentalize his religion into the sacred and the secular in such a way that he saw God as separate from the business of his everyday affairs, espe-cially making money. This worldview permitted slothful and greedy white people to exploit black people to death and still go to church.

The white people did no work that young Fannie Lou could see. It was her parents, her brothers and sisters, and her black neighbors who did all the work.

> "Being a very small child I thought it was because of our color that made something wrong. I remember telling my mother one day. I said, 'Mother, how come we are not white? Because white people have clothes, they can have food to eat, and we work all the time, and we don't have anything.' She said, 'I don't ever want to hear you say that again, honey.' She said, 'Don't you say that, because you're black!'…'You respect yourself as a little black child. And as you grow older, respect yourself as a black woman. Then one day, other people will respect you.'"[26]

Later she watched helplessly as her mother became blind after an eye injury because of lack of medical care. She said, "I began to get sicker and sicker of the system there."[27] She vowed that she would improve life for her mother and black people in the South "if it would cost my life; I was determined to see that things were changed."[28]

Fannie Lou Hamer painfully recalls an incident that happened when she was six years old:

> "I will never forget, one day—I was six years old and I was playing beside the road and this plantation owner drove up to me and stopped and asked me, could I pick cotton?...I told him I didn't know and he said, 'Yes, you can. I will give you things that you want from the commissary store,' and he named off things like Crackerjacks and sardines," a Daddy Wide Legs gingerbread cookie, and other treats for which the child would never have money for herself. "So I picked the 30 pounds of cotton that week, but I found out what actually happened was he was trapping me into beginning the work I was to keep doing, and I never did get out of his debt again." It was clear Fannie Lou knew how to work. The next week she had to pick 60 pounds. "By the time I was 13, I was picking two and three hundred pounds."[29]

Black people were locked into the sharecropper system because they were never able to get out of debt. Each spring the landowner advanced the seed for the crop and "furnish" money to pay for food and clothing and other goods until the crop was harvested. They had no choice but to use the plantation commissary, where the plantation owner set the prices and kept the books on their line of credit. When "settling day" arrived, the plantation owner, no matter how hard the people had worked and how much money they had actually made, cheated them and said they were in debt. The black people knew they were being cheated but had no recourse because they would be murdered if they protested, and there was no one to appeal to in white-supremacist controlled Mississippi. But they could, and did, appeal to God.

Fannie Lou's mother had sung children's songs and spirituals to her when she was very young. The family sang regularly in the fields and in their local black church. The church also taught her spirituals and hymns and gave communal validation to her unusual gift. She sang in the tradition of her ancestors. James Weldon Johnson described this tradition as "fashioned out of the raw materials of hard and cruel experience, softened and mitigated by the resilient sense of community that was palpable among slave worshipers.[30] " Folksinger Pete Seeger described her extraordinary singing voice as "African." Harry Belafonte said her singing was not for amusement:

It's another thing to sing where there is a passion behind what you
do, because the singing in and of itself is created for the purpose of
touching something and someone. And Fannie Lou sang that way.
I don't think there was ever a wasted hum when she sang.[31]

Belafonte recalled that for Fannie Lou Hamer every song had a purpose, and he said that one could hear "the struggle of all black America...I
thought that when she sang, there was indeed a voice raised that was
without compromise the voice of all of us."[32]

She recognized the power of song in her early life and in later life as
the unofficial song leader of the Civil Rights movement as "one of the
main things that can keep us going."[33] Her favorite song was the spiritual "This Little Light of Mine." She related it to the Beatitudes in
Matthew's gospel and felt it brought out the soul of the human being.
All through the dangerous days of the movement she used her powerful
singing voice and knowledge of black sacred music just as her mother
had used her singing—to comfort, motivate, and inspire the people to
struggle against pain and evil and hold on for just another day. The
same songs she had learned from her mother along the rivers and bay-
ous and in the fields and in the black church she sang on marches and in
jail. The people came to depend on her songs to conquer fear and inspire action. Then, finally, she taught and passed on this legacy of black
sacred song to college student Bernice Johnson Reagon, the movement's
next great song leader and the future director of Black American Studies at the Smithsonian Institute.

Fannie Lou attributed her own greatness to the greatness of her
mother, whom she deeply trusted, loved, and revered. Though she joined
the Stranger's Home Baptist Church at twelve and had much of the
Bible memorized, she said that many of her religious principles were
learned at home from her mother. One of the most important lessons
she was taught was that hating made one weak. Her mother said that
she must forgive. She was able to embody this spiritual teaching in the
face of incredible racism.

In addition to having to forgive white people for working, cheating,
undereducating, and miseducating (she asked white people why they
had withheld black history from black children in the schools and learned
it thoroughly on her own), as well as starving herself, her family, and
her community almost literally to death, without her knowledge or
permission she was sterilized by a white doctor in 1961. She had gone
to the doctor about what she called "a knot on my stomach." Later,
Vera Alice Marlow, cousin of the doctor and wife of the plantation
owner, told the cook and Fannie Lou eventually learned that she had
been given a hysterectomy. The involuntary sterilization of poor black
women was later to become a national issue. But at this time, poor,

rural black women had no legal recourse. When she went to the doctor and asked him, face to face, why he did this to her, he simply refused to answer.

For Fannie Lou and her husband, Perry or "Pap," this was the greatest of tragedies. They loved children and wanted to have a family. They were raising two girls—the poorest of the poor—one of whom had been born to an unwed mother, and the other was a girl from a large, impoverished family who had been badly burned when a tub of hot water was spilled.

In 1962 Mrs. Mary Tucker, who could be called Fannie Lou's "play Mama,"[34] went out to the country to get Fannie Lou and take her to a voter registration meeting that was to be held at her home. Fannie Lou refused to go. She said, "Tuck, they taught us that mess in school and that's turned me off like that."[35] Mrs. Tucker said, "I felt real bad but I wouldn't let on."[36]

Fannie Lou, who had been thoroughly brought up in the black tradition of high respect for elders, also felt bad about it. She went back later to Mrs. Tucker and said: "Tuck, I come to beg your pardon. I never sassed you before in my life and it hurt me so bad when I thought about what I had said to you. I come to beg your pardon."[37] So Fannie Lou went to the next meeting, not because she believed in the cause, but because she had been taught, in the African-American spiritual tradition, to love and respect her elders. The result was that when she went to a second meeting at Williams Chapel Church led by James Bevel, she was the only one who raised her hand when he asked who would register to vote. In doing so, she was defying decades of racist, restrictive laws. Later, because of this decision, she became a fugitive. Her biographer wrote, "Once Fannie Lou Hamer tried to register to vote, there was no turning back to life on the plantation. Her course, and that of her husband, was irrevocably altered."[38]

On June 9, 1963, a Sunday morning, Fannie Lou and other freedom fighters were arrested and jailed in Winona, Mississippi. She was severely beaten by another black inmate who was told he would be beaten if he did not carry out the white officer's order.

One of the officers called her "Fatso," and they took her to the bullpen. The highway patrolman gave one of the inmates a black-jack, and Mrs. Hamer remembered that he said, "I want you to make that bitch wish she was dead." The inmate told her to lie down on the bed. "You mean you would do this to your own race?" she asked him. "You heard what I said," the highway patrolman ordered. "So, then I had to get over there on the bed flat on my stomach, and that man beat me—that man beat me until he give out." No one else was ever beaten.[39]

She was not allowed medical treatment or phone calls. Another black prisoner, Euvester Simpson, said, "The only way we could manage to get through that ordeal was to sing any song that came to mind."[40]

Locked in her cell, Fannie Lou wondered how Christian people could do that to her. She even talked with the jailer's wife, who claimed to live a Christian life. The beatings continued. Andrew Young came to get her out of jail.

> "She was instinctively an extremely nonviolent person who really was so polite and was so generous to her jailers, for instance—the people who had been beating her," Young said, "that we could not conceive of the way they were chatting—that these were the same people who had been beating her for a week. But that was deliberate on her part."[41]

"Instinct" had nothing to do with it. Fannie Lou had been *taught* how to be human by her parents, her church, and the black sharecropper community through the legacy of the ancestors. She forgave those people.

Unita Blackwell tells of Fannie Lou's own recounting of the story of the brutal treatment she had received. Blackwell said, "She could just keep you spellbound. I was so angry that day...She said, 'Baby, you have to love 'em.'"[42] When Unita Blackwell thought she was crazy, Fannie Lou went on to explain to her that she had to love white people because they were sick and America was sick and it needed a doctor and that black people were the hope of America. Martin Luther King Jr. and Malcolm X expressed the same sentiment.

Though she knew the Bible well and attended church regularly, Fannie Lou Hamer criticized the church. She said Christianity should be "being concerned about your fellow man, not building a million-dollar church while people are starving right around the corner." She said that "Christ was a revolutionary person, out there where it was happening. That's what God is all about, and that's where I get my strength."[43]

Finally, incorporating an African worldview, she often quoted Galatians 6:7: "Do not be deceived; God is not mocked, for whatever a person sows, that they will also reap." She said that one day, she didn't know how white people "are going to get it, but they're going to get some of it back."[44]

In conclusion, she firmly believed in a Source much greater than herself to whom she had accountability. Of struggling for the freedom of the community, she said, "Whether I want to do it or not, I got to. This is my calling. This is my mission."[45] Later, she would speak powerfully as the vice chairperson for the newly formed Mississippi Freedom Democratic Party at the 1964 Democratic National Convention (and the tumultuous Chicago convention of 1968) to protest the state of Mississippi denying African Americans their basic right to human freedom. Though from the humblest of beginnings, black, poor, female, and unlettered, and from the most repressive state of the South, she rejected the compromise of President Lyndon Johnson when he offered the MFDP two token seats at the convention and roared at him, "We didn't come all this way for no two seats cause all of us is tired." After a revelatory trip to Africa, she went home to found the National Women's Political Caucus and the Freedom Farm Cooperative. On March 14, 1977, Fannie Lou Hamer died of heart failure brought on by complications from cancer, diabetes, and hypertension.

RUBY BRIDGES

Ruby Bridges (now Mrs. Ruby Bridges Hall) was born in 1954. She desegregated the Louisiana school system in 1960 when she was six years old. I quote Pulitzer prize winner Robert Coles's children's story below extensively, because storytelling is crucially important in African-American spirituality. Theological truth was and is communicated primarily in story and only secondarily by theories, axioms, and abstractions.

Perhaps if this story had been told in the community of the enslaved they—practical and realistic people—would not have left out some of the more frightening details. One such detail is that little Ruby Bridges would eat only packaged or bottled food. When other food was presented to her, she said she wasn't hungry. Finally, after many days and much questioning, she reluctantly told her mother that she was afraid to eat because white women (many of them the mothers of her classmates) in the mob gathered outside her school yelled that they were going to poison her. These same white women held up little coffins and dolls hanging by the neck and signs with death threats and racial epitaphs as the marshals hurried her through the crowd. Or the community of the enslaved may have included the detail that Ruby ended up going through this all alone because the other black parents, at the last moment, became so afraid that they would not allow their children to go to the school. They probably would have included the fact that her father was fired from his job and could not obtain another job because of white retaliation because his daughter went to the formerly all-white elementary school. Finally, they may have added that a Northern white woman, the only teacher who would teach Ruby when the other white teachers refused, was also a courageous heroine who was ostracized by the white community.

The Story of Ruby Bridges

Every Sunday, the family went to church. "We wanted our children to be near God's spirit," Ruby's mother said. "We wanted them to start feeling close to Him from the very start."

At that time, black children and white children went to separate schools in New Orleans. The black children were not able to receive the same education as the white children. It wasn't fair. And it was against the nation's law.

In 1960, a judge ordered four black girls to go to two white elementary schools. Three of the girls were sent to McDonogh. Six-year-old Ruby Bridges was sent to first grade in the William Frantz Elementary School.

Ruby's parents were proud that their daughter had been chosen to take part in an important event in American history. They went to church.

"We sat there and prayed to God," Ruby's mother said, "that we'd all be strong and we'd have courage and we'd get through any trouble; and Ruby would be a good girl and she'd hold her head up high and be a credit to her own people and a credit to all American people. We prayed long and we prayed hard."

On Ruby's first day, a large crowd of angry white people gathered outside the Frantz Elementary School. The people carried signs that said they didn't want black children in a white school. People called Ruby names; some wanted to hurt her. The city and state police did not help Ruby.

The President of the United States ordered federal marshals to walk with Ruby into the school building. The marshals carried guns.

Every day, for weeks that turned into months, Ruby experienced that kind of school day. She walked to the Frantz School surrounded by marshals. Wearing a clean dress and a bow in her hair and carrying her lunch pail, Ruby walked slowly for the first few blocks. As Ruby approached the school, she saw a crowd of people marching up and down the street. Men and women and children shouted at her. They pushed toward her. The marshals kept them from Ruby by threatening to arrest them.

Ruby would hurry through the crowd and not say a word.

The white people in the neighborhood would not send their children to school. When Ruby got inside the building, she was all alone except for her teacher, Miss Hurley. There were no other children to keep Ruby company, to play with and learn with, to eat lunch with.

But every day, Ruby went into the classroom with a big smile on her face, ready to get down to the business of learning.

Then one morning, something happened. Miss Hurley stood by a window in her classroom as she usually did, watching Ruby walk toward the school. Suddenly, Ruby stopped—right in front of the mob of howling and screaming people. She stood there facing all those men and women. She seemed to be talking to them.

Miss Hurley saw Ruby's lips moving and wondered what Ruby could be saying.

The crowd seemed ready to kill her.

The marshals were frightened. They tried to persuade Ruby to move along. They tried to hurry her into the school, but Ruby wouldn't budge.

Then Ruby stopped talking and walked into the school.

When she went into the classroom, Miss Hurley asked her what happened. Miss Hurley told Ruby that she'd been watching and that she was surprised when Ruby stopped and talked with the people in the mob.

Ruby became irritated.

"I didn't stop and talk with them," she said.

"Ruby, I saw you talking," Miss Hurley said. "I saw your lips moving."

"I wasn't talking," said Ruby. "I was praying. I was praying for them."

Please, God, try to forgive those people.
Because even if they say those bad things,
They don't know what they're doing.
So You could forgive them,
Just like You did those folks a long time ago
When they said terrible things about You.[46]

Robert Coles, the author of the book quoted above, was a child psychiatrist who happened to be passing by the Frantz Elementary School when little Ruby Bridges, under the protection of federal marshals, was hurried through a raging, white mob. He watched, stupefied and amazed by the courage and utter dignity of such a small child in the face of such bitter and virulent hatred. Later he secured permission from her parents to become her therapist, because he was afraid that the stress, terror, and extreme alienation of her experience would cause her emotional damage. For most of that terrible semester he was continually puzzled by her ability to withstand the storm. He could not understand the source of what he called her "resilience" and her mature ability to forgive.

The primary source of Ruby's strength was the African-American spirituality that was born, nurtured, and sustained within her family, the church, and the black community. It not only helped little Ruby to survive incredible hatred and danger, but to forgive and thrive. At the end of the semester, her grades were extremely high and her scores on standardized tests were well above grade level.

CONCLUSION

In the conversion experience of African-American spirituality, personal and communal liberation are a whole process and a unity of experience. Reality is essentially a whole in that people, society, institutions, the spiritual realm, and nature are interpenetrating and interacting entities vitally related to one another in a circular and unified worldview. God is active, in the midst of this interrelatedness, to deliver people from bondage to freedom—freedom to be in community.

This spiritual worldview led directly to conversion that was not simply an inner event. It was a total transformation of the individual that led to an inextricable outward concern for the social environment. The urgency of this concern, characterized by radical compassion for the poor, was ultimately God's concern. God called the individual toward an active vocation of social liberation. It was embodied in the individual's struggle for the freedom of the community. The spiritual journeys of the four individuals discussed above reveal this conversion as the vocation or call to protest societal norms and values that destroy the possibility for community. In the conversion process the convert changed his or her life to one wholly engaged in active struggle for the community to be liberated.

Chapter 4

The Community

The values inspired by the African legacy of a unified worldview that helped the Africans and their descendants to create an individual identity also created a *group identity* expressed in black communities in the New World. George Ofori-atta-Thomas, scholar of religion, states that the African spiritual heritage prevailed for one hundred and fifty years before European-Christianity significantly influenced the folk practices of Africans in this country. This African heritage, as the preceding chapters suggest, should be the organizing principle for understanding the cultural and spiritual identity of black people in America. In addition, cultural historian Lawrence Levine points out that at the heart of this cultural transformation was a shared emphasis on certain virtues and ideals, certain manners of independence and hospitality, general ways of looking upon the world, which gave black people a similar lifestyle. This lifestyle, derived from this "fundamental outlook," became the black community in America. This outlook led African Americans to seek to change human attitudes toward the loving acceptance of a society that is sufficiently spiritually motivated to create the possibility for social togetherness in a way that would allow society to embody, as Martin Luther King Jr. said, "a constructive equality of oneness" in which all people would be treated justly as the children of God.[1]

Though the Africans did not bring with them a unified or uniform African culture, they did share a fundamental outlook toward the past, present, future, and common means of cultural expression that helped to constitute the basis of a sense of common identity. The black enslaved engaged in widespread exchanges and cross-culturation with the whites among whom they lived, yet throughout the centuries of enslavement and long after the emancipation, their fundamental outlook remained. Over the centuries black scholars and black religionists have called it by various names—*Négritude* (Senghor); the "souls of black folks" (Du Bois); the "black aesthetic" (Swann), and "soul" (singer James Brown and the general black populace)—but, at its core, is the constant of the peculiar spirituality that has fueled its nature. This nonmaterial aspect of black culture, which began in the African past, is of the deepest significance even today because it defines the values that have shaped African-American life, church, and society. Almost unconsciously drawn upon, it determines and measures the validity of the community's self-definition and practice.

Building Community

John Mbiti emphasizes that at the base of African cosmology is the understanding that the individual exists or has being in relation to the community; this is expressed in the saying, I am because we are; and because we are, I am. The basic orientation for existence in an African worldview is that life cannot exist in isolated individualism but must be experienced as part of a whole. For the enslaved, who were much closer in outlook to this African traditional worldview than to a European-American worldview, the loss of community meant the loss of self. The spirituality of the Africans—as revealed in the earlier discussions of slave tales, narratives, spirituals, folk religion, slave or invisible church, and black church—was drawn upon as a crucial source of strength and release in the face of the crisis caused by chattel slavery. This spirituality helped them preserve and create their own definition of self and of community (essentially perceived as the same) by influencing their systems of establishing meaning in the face of new experiences in a new world. This meaning-making then led them to create their own communities on North American soil, for in order for the self to exist, there had to be a community. The African legacy helped to "instruct" the enslaved in the building of a new world as community in at least two ways. First, it encouraged them to remember their African past as a source for defining community rather than accepting solely European-American standards. Second, it urged them to leave bondage, at any and all costs, so that freedom to build community might be possible. Thus community was created from the spiritual interaction of at least two essential sources: the memory of the African past, and the emerging African-American identity with its bent toward freedom.

The African-American community is not of any singular opinion or consensus about the ideal of community. Yet, as guided by African-American spirituality, these ideals of community do commonly denote "some determinate object, a particular type of social life and experience, e.g., a sense of belonging, a sense of place, a sense of identity, or shared values."[2] The ideal of community in the life of the community is "well balanced" enough, in terms of African-American life and identity, to reveal *continuities* in a way that echoes the collective spirituality of a people.

This chapter draws upon the values demonstrated in community practice in Bainbridge, Georgia, that persisted from the African legacy of a unified worldview. These values are the "Africanity" or ancestral patterns of social and cultural conduct based in African retentions at the core of the transplanted African family; the patterns act as the central organizing force that has sustained Africans in America throughout the centuries. In Bainbridge, as they did in African societies, these values governed both personal and social conduct in the community as family morals and community morals.

Bainbridge is selected for two reasons. First, the African-American community of Bainbridge, historically self-contained, exists not as a mere vestige of aspects of African traditional culture but as a black community that is rich with African retentions that are still a dynamic, living, creative part of its group life in America. Second, I was born in this community, as were all the generations of my family on my mother's side of the family since chattel slavery. This affords me an intimate knowledge of this community that spans several generations from slavery to the present. My family history, for the most part, is very similar to that of many other black families who originated in Africa and were forcibly taken to labor as slaves in the American South and then later migrated to the urban North. It is this very "ordinariness" that is helpful in examining family history to understand African-American spirituality.

The Setting

Bainbridge, Georgia, was incorporated in 1829. It is forty-two miles north of Tallahassee, Florida, and just north of Attapulgus, which is south of Camilla. Self-described as Georgia's "first inland port," Bainbridge's economy was originally based on cotton and other crops grown and harvested with slave labor. It is now an industrial town and the county seat of Decatur County, where cotton fields, pecan, peanut, and pine tree plantations and a large Amoco plant dominate the picture-postcard beautiful, Southern rural landscape just outside of town. The Amoco plant was featured in a "60 Minutes" documentary in the early 1990s. The documentary investigated the plant's exploitation of the town's poor people by paying salaries just above minimum wage and blocking other industries from coming into town.

Much of the vast acreage of pine-tree-studded property immediately surrounding downtown Bainbridge and going further south toward Tallahassee has been owned for several generations by wealthy, Northern, industrialist families who use it seasonally for deer hunting. People are always cautious about driving in the fall of the year because of the abundance of deer. The mighty Flint River, which has overflowed twice in living memory, runs close to the downtown business district. Present-day Bainbridge is a curious mixture of a very old, large black community—still poor, but with an old and established middle class—whites who are wealthy, and a number of mostly white farmers and small business owners.

Bainbridge and the adjoining counties were historically supported by the close but outlying cotton plantations that imported large numbers of slaves from Africa in the Atlantic slave trade to plant and harvest the cotton, pecan, and peanut crops as well as perform other forms of labor in the plantation economy. As a direct result, large numbers of Africans were gathered together on the plantations, with black people far outnumbering the whites in the county. This allowed the black community to retain much of its African heritage. This large, self-contained community enables my mother's family to trace its heritage back to slavery and the settling in Camilla and Decatur County from as far back as the 1800s. Many black people from Camilla (the farm community just outside of Bainbridge) look entirely African. By this, I mean that they (including my mother's people) look like Harriet Tubman and Sojourner Truth.

After the general Emancipation, the plight of the black community of Bainbridge continued to be plagued by low wages, disenfranchisement, segregation, poor housing, inadequate school and medical facilities, unfair courts, lynching, and other types of violence. It is generally held that as many as 350,000 black people left the Southern states during 1916 and 1917 (my father's generation). About 50,000 of that number fled Georgia. The area of the state that was most affected by the black migration was the southwest corner—Georgia's Black Belt and a portion of its wiregrass area. State history shows that in 1916 twenty counties in this section were heavily damaged by the boll weevil, an insect that breeds on cotton and feeds on the cotton boll. The damage to cotton in these areas ruined many farmers and forced many farm laborers to seek better wages in the North.

Decatur County was heavily damaged by the boll weevil. In 1917 the local newspaper, *The Bainbridge Post Search Light*, accused Germans of encouraging black people to leave the South and its fields in order to cripple the nation's economy. The newspaper attempted to discourage black people from leaving Bainbridge by printing articles that pictured terrifying portrayals of suffering black people who had gone North. Articles often had headlines such as "Negroes Suffering in Philadelphia," "Hardships in Cincinnati," and articles referring to black people's subsequent return to the South under titles such as "Another Negro Is Now Cured."[3]

Like many other Georgia towns during this period, Bainbridge passed laws to ensure a steady, cheap, black labor supply. For example, one of the "work or fight laws" provided that all black women who did not work outside of their homes would have to find work. The motivation behind this law was to secure cheap domestic laborers for white homes. Non-working black housewives were arrested and fined fifteen dollars each. Other extremely oppressive conditions also existed in Bainbridge. For example, black people were not allowed to be treated in the privately owned Bainbridge Hospital, which advertised itself as "for Whites exclusively."[4] And in 1920, 28.7 percent of black citizens ten years old or older in Decatur County were illiterate. Ten years later, in 1930 the illiteracy rate among black people remained alarmingly high. In 1930, 20.2 percent of black people were illiterate as compared to only 3.8 percent of whites. In 1930, the county was spending only $4.08 a year to educate each black child, while it spent $23.57 for each white child.[5] My mother's teachers[6] said that when they were teaching my mother (born in 1926), these conditions were prevalent.

During the World War II years, the social and economic conditions for black people continued to degenerate. After the war, black soldiers returned to the United States to find that throughout the South black people would face another half century of cruel discrimination, race hatred and violence.

The Preservation of Black Birth Customs and Rituals

My grandmother "dreamed" I was going to be born even before my mother knew she was expecting. My mother, never assuming her mother could be wrong about such a thing, immediately began telling the family and the community that I was expected before she went to a doctor for confirmation. When she did make a doctor's appointment, the examination revealed that she was not pregnant. However, my mother still believed my grandmother and kept announcing my coming birth and the community began celebrating my future arrival. My grandmother also dreamed that I was a girl and proceeded to name me Flora, the name of her own mother and her mother's first cousin who was a preacher, whom it was believed that I would resemble. Though they would not have labeled this "knowing" as African retentions, it is clear that this practice resembles both the African beliefs in the close linkage between the past and the future (the grandparent and the child) and in the African naming practices. In this way my grandmother played a key and crucial role in my birth and identity in the community.

At the time of my birth, black doctors still could not practice nor could black children be born in Bainbridge Hospital because of the Jim Crow laws of segregation. I was delivered in the black infirmary built by Dr. Joseph H. Griffin, a relative by marriage. In Bainbridge, everybody in the black community claims to be family and knows everybody's history—again, an African worldview.

The community, to say the least, tends to be close-knit. For example, a few years ago I came to Bainbridge from Atlanta to preach on the occasion of an anniversary of the First African Baptist Church of Bainbridge. On the way out of town, I ordered food through the speaker at the local Wendy's. Before I drove around to the window where she could see me, the black teenager who was working at the window asked through the speaker, "Didn't you preach this morning at First African?" Whenever I drive through the black community, I have to keep one arm continually raised in greeting—without putting it down until after leaving the boundaries of the community—because everybody calls out to greet me from porches and the roadside. I do not want to risk missing anyone because, in black tradition, it would be considered extremely rude and a reflection on my grandparents' (even though they are now deceased) and my parents' abilities in the "raising" of children. I was also compelled by longstanding custom about what constitutes respect to visit all the old people who knew my grandparents, parents, and other relatives of that generation, even though I was only in town overnight.

When other black people were fleeing to the North by the thousands looking for less oppressive life circumstances, Dr. Griffin, the son of prosperous rural Georgia farmers, returned to the Deep South after interning at Meharry's Hubbard Hospital and completing postgraduate work in surgery at the Medical School of the University of Pennsylvania and at Cook County Hospital in Chicago. Historian Barbara Cotton documents his life story in her book *Non Verba Opera*. Dr. Griffin would have to fight relentlessly against white Bainbridge's determination to maintain white supremacy in the South from 1917 until his retirement in 1977. He had conquered enormous odds against racism by successfully completing his medical studies. Like many black families of that time, his parents taught him to respect and value hard work and education. He became one of the first black doctors in southwest Georgia.

Dr. Griffin was barred from treating his patients in the white hospital, though he did treat whites after earning a reputation as a good doctor during the nationwide influenza epidemic of 1918, when both black and white people were dying rapidly and in large numbers. In the beginning he practiced out of a small office on Ward Street. When patients needed surgery, he had to travel forty-one miles to use the hospital facilities at the Florida Agricultural and Mechanical College for Negroes in Tallahassee.

White doctors, who would not treat black people, forced him to tolerate the racial slurs of malevolent plantation owners. His brother, Dr.

David Griffin, recalls accompanying him to a plantation and being met by a white man who shouted, "Doc, I got a nigger sow down here trying to birth a young 'un and the granny lady (black midwife) there but she can't handle it. I thought I better call you. You go down there and see what you can do with her. Cause I want her back in the fields as quick as possible."[7]

Dr. Griffin, who had worked so hard to become a physician, was frequently the target of racial abuse. In the late 1930s a black man in Bainbridge was accused of a sex crime against a white woman. The Bainbridge newspaper said he was killed under "mysterious circumstances" while awaiting trial. What actually happened was that white people forcibly took his body from the mortician's parlor and set it on fire and dragged him around town. The men also made threats against the lives of Dr. Griffin, the black mortician, and other black leaders in the community who were accused of "not knowing their place." The black people of Bainbridge said that Dr. Griffin sat on his front porch with his shotgun across his knee and vowed that he would shoot anyone who crossed his property and that they "would both go to hell." Shots were fired into his driveway, but he wasn't harmed.

Dr. Griffin's colleague, whose work partially overlapped his own, Dr. Edward Adolphus Rufus Lord Sr.—a black doctor, originally from Guyana, who delivered me—was also killed under "mysterious circumstances" in Bainbridge on October 30, 1960. Dr. Lord's granddaughter, Itabari Njeri, writes about his death in her autobiographical novel, *Every Good-Bye Ain't Gone,* winner of the 1990 American Book Award.[8] As a journalist for a Miami newspaper, she journeyed to Bainbridge to find out exactly how Dr. Lord had died after being hit by a car driven by a white man. Allegedly, Dr. Lord, still clad in his robe and pajamas as a result of hurriedly leaving his home in response to an urgent medical crisis, was returning from a late-night house call. Njeri interviewed the then-oldest living white person in Bainbridge, Dr. Mortimer Alfred Ehrlich. Dr. Ehrlich and others she interviewed said that Dr. Lord was a "bad man," primarily because Dr. Lord had attempted to start a branch of the NAACP in Bainbridge. The white southerners of Bainbridge, by and large, believed that the NAACP was subversive, and they condemned Dr. Lord for being political and belonging to it. Dr. Ehrlich said, "If he hadn't been killed in an accident, he would have been shot. Better he was killed that way so we didn't have the bother of a trial for whoever shot him."[9]

As a result of this hostile racial climate, Dr. Griffin used his own capital to open his first hospital, the Johnson Memorial Hospital, in Bainbridge in 1930. It was an eighteen-bed facility named in honor of his wife's parents.

"In 1950, only 23.7 percent of African-American infants in Bainbridge were delivered in hospitals, compared with 94.4 percent of white infants.[10] The infant mortality rate among black people was 50.3 percent, compared to 30.6 percent among white people."[11] Dr. Griffin was particularly concerned to reduce infant mortality by providing prenatal care in a modern medical facility where black women would be able to deliver their babies under appropriate sterile conditions. On August 3, 1950, he opened the fifty-bed Griffin Hospital and Clinic in downtown Bainbridge. It cost $250,000 to construct and was financed entirely by Dr. Griffin. *The Bainbridge Post Search Light,* notorious for racist stories about black people, wrote favorably in the special "Colored Corner" of the newspaper about Dr. Griffin's hospital, because it was in sympathy with keeping black people out of white facilities.

African-American novelist Tina McElroy Ansa quite accurately describes the climate of these early black infirmaries in her contemporary novels *Baby of the Family* and *The Hand I Fan With.* Though fictional accounts, they reveal her experience of being born and brought up in Macon, Georgia. In a 1997 lecture at Spelman College, Ansa described her use of black birth rituals and customs in her novels as a way of responding to the ridicule of white people who misunderstood and disparaged African-based traditional beliefs. Ansa's work reflects the concern of the contemporary African-American artist to "free" the beliefs and spirituality of the African ancestors from the cloud of ignorance and suspicion surrounding them created by the dominant American culture.

Though Dr. Griffin and Dr. Lord had to suffer terribly and undergo tremendous personal sacrifice to provide adequate medical care to the black community, the isolation of black mothers and their babies in the small black infirmaries of the Deep South allowed the continuance of African-based birth customs and rituals. One particular concern was for children born with a caul or the embryonic sac covering their faces at birth. These children were considered, as were all children, to be valuable to the community. It was believed that they were extraordinarily connected to the spirit world with the intuitive gift of second sight. As in Africa, procedures were followed at birth to ensure that these children would be helped rather than harmed by this gift.

I was born with this veil or sac, and because I was in a black infirmary, the nurses followed the traditional custom. The sac was carefully removed, boiled, and the juice from it was made into a tea that was put in a bottle and fed to me as a newborn. The sac was then dried in tissue paper and kept in a safe place. The old people believed this custom would protect me from evil spirits in the universe.

Belief in a Circular, Just, and Moral Universe

My maternal grandmother was a servant (as were all of the women of her family prior to her) for a wealthy white Bainbridge family surnamed Rich. She worked very hard and was severely underpaid. In addition, because of segregation, she could not sit at the table she was compelled to serve. Yet, for reasons I could not understand as a child (even then I knew about the exploitation of black people), she was never bitter about it and performed her strenuous job thoroughly and cheerfully without complaint. She often sang the Negro spiritual "I'm Going to Sit at the Welcome Table One of These Days." This spiritual proclaims that "one of these days" black people will be treated as well and as fairly as whites. My grandmother was able to carry on in the face of extreme oppression because she believed that "what goes around comes around" and that eventually God would even up the score in terms of racial relations in America. On the other hand, I was bitter and angry and could appreciate neither the spiritual she sang nor the faith that caused her continually to draw dignity, strength, and courage from it.

I did not come to understand her faith and her song until long after her death. When my younger sister graduated from West Point Military Academy, my family was seated at a banquet table prepared by the United States Army to celebrate the cadets' graduation. Our family was seated at the table with the Rich family of Bainbridge, Georgia. The Army must have seated families by state or region of the country. I did not really notice them until the father of their family looked at my mother in shocked amazement and said, "Agnes! Is that you?" Then they all embraced my mother like she was a long-lost family member. The great-granddaughter of slaves and the great-grandson of slave owners were sitting at the same table. My grandmother was right all along; in the end, God "evened it all out," even though we had been emancipated only a few short decades before.

Communal Child-Rearing Practices

Children in the black community of Bainbridge were often brought up, like in slavery times, in a complex relational system that extended throughout the community. In many ways the entire community was the family. This system required all adults to be responsible for all children, and children were required to respect and obey all adults. This was necessary because parents often worked long hours away from their children and because black people never truly felt safe under the constant threat of racism. My mother's neighborhood of tiny two-room houses was in the poorest section of the black community. It is still called, for reasons no one seems to be able to explain since there are no pear trees, the Pear Orchard.

Fathers in the community labored at various jobs. Mothers often worked as domestic servants. Some were employed to wash and iron articles of fine clothing by hand in the laundry owned by a Chinese proprietor. The older people tell stories of the women of my grandmother's generation leaving home for work before dawn and returning at dusk. These women skillfully balanced large baskets of laundry on their heads as they walked great distances to and from their jobs. Miss Mamie, my grandmother's next-door neighbor, had six children. Miss Mamie left for the Chinese laundry before daybreak at a pace so rapid she almost ran. She ate her breakfast from a plate as she hurried down the dark road.

They were very sad and downhearted when they left their children and their community early in the morning, but they were jubilant when they returned. My mother told me that her parents' generation would sing when they came home from work at dusk. She said they could hear them singing, field holler style, on the road "way, way before they got to the Pear Orchard and all the way to the door!" The night air would be filled with their joy and their songs about the goodness of God.

The children were watched by the elderly. My mother still speaks of how she always loved old people when she was a child. She was taught to bring them meals and clean their houses, at no cost to them, from an early age. When she reached middle age, my mother became vice president of the missionaries at First Church of Deliverance on Chicago's Southside. This black church had a missionary society of several hundred. Among other things, they cleaned elderly people's homes and did volunteer work such as feeding and bathing the elderly in the Senior Citizens Home that the church built and owned. My mother felt sorry for them. When her own mother suffered a stroke, my parents brought her to our home to live with us in the North. My mother believed the elderly should be taken care of by their children, not institutions.

My sister and I sometimes laugh about how, when we were young in the South, we were sent by our parents to look after the elderly. My sister was sent to take food to elderly people who were bedridden. She recalls being terrified because sometimes their homes would be surrounded by barking dogs, but she would march valiantly through the dogs with the hot food to be delivered because she was more afraid of going home without having fed the old people than she was of the dogs.

One summer, when I was older, an operator called my grandmother's house and asked if she would send someone to check on an elderly neighbor. The operator believed the neighbor was in distress because her phone was off the hook. My father asked me to run down the road and "see about her." We all suspected something was seriously amiss because she was diabetic. Sure enough, when I entered the house, I saw her lying on the floor. She was dead. I was uncomfortable because it was the first time I had been alone with a dead person. I called my father and told him. He told me to stay in the house with her until he got help. Though I was somewhat afraid, I stayed because it would have been considered disrespectful to leave her body alone.

Children in the community were also routinely expected to run errands and perform tasks for adults, especially the elderly. The old people invariably offered to reward the child, but if the child's parents found out later that these small rewards were accepted, sure and swift punishment followed. The children were beaten, as the black community says, "like they stole somethin'." As far as their parents and grandparents were concerned, they had. The gift was then returned and the child was whipped for being disrespectful. Mothers, fathers, grandparents, and great-grandparents felt a sense of personal injury and embarrassment if this breach of courtesy occurred. More than one generation of the family would be informed of the child's actions, whether they were good or bad. This, in many ways, was far worse than any physical punishment.

Much to my own discomfort and embarrassment, my parents continued this practice well into my teenage years, after we had moved to the urban North. In my fifteenth year I replied too abruptly to a question my mother asked. She, in horror, accused me of "talking back." My mother then proceeded to call my father at his job—an extreme measure usually resorted to only in the event of death or near mortal illness—all of our relatives in that city, and the relatives in the South, as well as the minister of the church. I believe the only reason she didn't call my teachers was because, by then, I was in a predominantly white school. My father came home from work early with the minister in tow and they lectured, preached, and strongly advised me that I had better "return unto [my] right mind" for the sake of my salvation in this world and the next.

Later that year I was to read a scene in Ralph Ellison's classic novel *Invisible Man* that reminded me of their method of discipline and correction. In Ellison's novel an African-American man named Trueblood impregnated his young daughter. The pastor of the black church and other respected elders in the black community came to confront Trueblood about his unspeakable act. Their collective presence served as a warning to him that the community, not just his victimized daughter, was violated by his reprehensible, ungodly behavior. Unfortunately, the white sheriff and his officers had been rewarding Trueblood with alcohol and cigarettes to come to the police station and describe to them, over and over again, what happened. Trueblood told the black community elders that because he was in favor with the whites, they couldn't do anything to him. He refused to respect the moral, ethical, and spiritual values of the black community.

My parent's methods also reminded me of conflict management among the Kalahari, an African people. The Kalahari people use a system of communal conflict management that is similar to the discipline prescribed for offenders in the New Testament. If someone in the Kalahari tribe believes he or she has been wronged, the person is advised to go to the offender, one-on-one, and ask that individual to make right what is wrong. If this is ineffective, the person is then advised to go back to the offender with two or three elders. If he or she still refuses to change, the whole tribe goes to the offender's home and asks him or her to straighten up their evil ways! When the tribal leader was asked what they did if the offender still refused to do right, he smiled and said, "We have not experienced that yet." In other words, the idea of being ostracized by the whole community served as a serious and important deterrent to destructive individual behavior.

An act of good behavior was as widely and rapidly broadcast as a bad one. When I was a young child, my siblings and I loved to visit my grandfather in the summer at his restaurant. While my older brothers delivered lunches to the offices of white customers, my grandfather always sat me up on the lunch counter and asked me to show black customers eating their lunches how well I could read from the newspaper. After I read a paragraph or two, they all applauded enthusiastically and told me how smart I was. For reasons I was too young to understand, my grandfather and the other black adults took endless delight in this performance time after time. Before long, my reputation was established in the community as a "smart child who is going to be somebody" in life. The older people did not tell me until I was an adult that my grandfather, a prosperous business man who owned the first black restaurant and taxicab company in Bainbridge, could not read or write.

When I was licensed and being trained for ministry in my home church, our minister of Christian education, also a native Georgian, taught us, "Never call on anyone unexpectedly and ask that person to read the Bible in church." We asked him, "Why not?" He said, "The person might not be able to read." In his seasoned wisdom he was teaching us to be gentle with people, especially older people, by never humiliating them in public.

In the days of segregated schools, teachers in the black schools of Bainbridge were expected by parents to spank and discipline children if they misbehaved. By some mysterious means, parents and neighbors always knew of the child's transgression before he or she arrived home. The child received another spanking from the parents upon arriving home and sometimes a spanking or two from neighbors along the route home if the child's parents were at work.

Teachers and ministers were frequent and welcome guests in homes, never disconnected or isolated from the children's total environment. The nuclear family, grandparents, great-grandparents, aunts and uncles (these people were not solely restricted to blood relationship), godparents, neighbors, play mama, play daddy, doctor, pastor, teachers—the entire adult community—locked hands in a unified, intertwining, unbroken circle to protect and support its children and bring them up with the spiritual values of the community.

The Moral of Hospitality as Giving

Many of the elderly in Bainbridge had refused to leave with children who had moved away to the North in search of a better standard of living. They still lived in small homes on tiny incomes. Yet whenever I entered these homes, food was offered. I ate it irrespective of how many homes I had already visited or had left to visit in a single afternoon. The issue was never one of hunger but of respect. It was considered disrespectful to refuse hospitality, especially when it was extended from the poor, who had so very little for themselves. They would have felt less than gracious if they made no offers.

At the end of these visits, when I announced it was time for me to leave for Atlanta before the hour grew late, they always rose from their chairs and looked around the room. At first I was puzzled by this behavior. After they quietly slipped a little gift in my hand, I understood they had been looking for something to give me because I was departing. I left these homes feeling that they were rich, not poor. It was only when I returned to my own large home and prosperous neighborhood in the Buckhead section of Atlanta that I felt bereft with loneliness and a strong sense of spiritual poverty.

One afternoon I visited Mrs. Ruth Brown, now deceased, who had lived across the street from my grandfather's home for as long as I can remember. Upon my leaving, Mrs. Brown said, "Wait just a minute!" She looked around her house and then smiled as she shyly gave me a tiny packet of Bible verses printed on little cards. Mrs. Brown knew that at that time I was an ordained minister, a doctoral candidate in religion, and a lecturer of religion at Spelman College. I treasure that little packet of Bible verses to this day.

My mother told me that the black community of Bainbridge survived in former times by sharing. People did not lock their doors. Those who needed sugar or some other food item when the neighbor was away from home felt free to go to the neighbor's house and borrow it. They replaced it when they were able.

Howard Thurman, the grandson of slaves, spoke of this same kind of sharing in the black community in which he grew up at the turn of the century. Everyone assisted in paying for the cost of burying the dead because the expense was often beyond the means of a single family. His father died when Thurman was seven years old. Young Howard was sent to ask neighbors to help with the funeral costs by giving whatever they could. He said that he was not self-conscious and there was no embarrassment. In Bainbridge, too, this was a way of life in the community. People helped and shared with each other. This was the way black people lived. They helped one another and survived.

Conclusion

Several values and the modes of their expression have been outlined as emerging from within the beliefs and practices of traditional West African societies. These same values are inherent in African-American culture as a spiritual legacy that functions as a sort of mental "grid" through which African Americans see the world and standard by which they judge human behavior.

In the African-American community of Bainbridge, Georgia, these same values are expressed in the racial memory and cultural context. They are revealed in many ways, including a "high" view of the importance of family as derived from African retentions; birth customs and rituals that reveal an essential memory of and respect for black alternative religion as derived from African traditional religion; the valuing of both the very old and the very young as revealed in the vital link between these generations as respect and care for the elderly and community-wide responsibility for the care and upbringing of children; respect for education (both formal and as racial memory in the form of black history) and hard work as paths toward freedom; hospitality in the form of sharing resources; and finally, defining the essence of black religion as belief in a circular, just, and moral universe where God can help one transcend earthly woes.

Chapter 5

Scaling the Mountain Peaks of Spirituality

Thurman, King, and Malcolm X (El-Hajj Malik Shabazz)

The values of the African-American community shine clearly in the lives and prophetic visions of the ideal of community of three great giants of the African-American spiritual tradition—Howard Thurman, Martin Luther King Jr., and Malcolm X—who made spiritual contributions of national and international magnitude. Their values, based on African retentions, helped to shape their mature ideals and prophetic visions.

HOWARD THURMAN

Howard Thurman was born in 1899 as the grandson of ex-slaves in a small, two-room house in Daytona Beach, Florida. He transcended the segregated South to become one of the greatest religionists and theologians in this country and the world. People tended to describe Thurman's appearance in opposites. Some of his friends said he was ugly, others said he was handsome, but all said he was a deeply spiritual prophet. His worldview and theology were under the powerful sway of African-American spirituality in a life that bridged the generations between slavery and desegregation. As a pioneer, mystic, scholar, poet, preacher, and theologian, Thurman's ideal of community, identical to that of his African ancestors, erased all barriers between God and humankind and among human beings. It embraced the idea of unity—the unity of life including men, women, plants, animals, and all living and growing things.

After serving in various pastorates and as dean of chapel for Morehouse and Spelman colleges, he was given another appointment of national significance as the first African-American dean of chapel at Boston University. He subsequently helped to found and pastored the nation's only interracial congregation of its kind, The Church for the Fellowship of All Peoples in San Francisco. As a champion of the disinherited and an advocate for justice in an unjust society, Thurman's life and theology shaped and guided the generations of great African-American freedom fighters and theologians (notably Martin Luther King Jr. and James Cone) who came after him.

The Influence of Nature on Thurman's Ideal of Community

In his autobiography, *With Head and Heart*, Howard Thurman includes among family pictures a photograph of his "special oak tree." Thurman's early predilection for nature can be explained, "in part, by the hardships of his family environment and his inner need for security and affirmation."[1] Yet one may also suggest that young Thurman, like his slave ancestors who toiled in the fields from "dark to dark," spent most of his waking hours outside in solitary enjoyment of nature. He learned to love and listen to nature. Like Harriet Tubman, he spent hours of his young life in the woods. He writes:

> When I was young, I found more companionship in nature than I did among people. The woods befriended me. In the long summer days, most of my time was divided between fishing in the Halifax River and exploring the woods, where I picked huckleberries and gathered orange blossoms from abandoned orange groves. The quiet, even the danger, of the woods provided my rather lonely spirit with a sense of belonging that did not depend on human relationships. I was usually with a group of boys as we explored the woods, but I tended to wander away to be alone for a time, for in that way I could sense the strength of the quiet and the aliveness of the woods.[2]

In a similar way, in traditional African society most of life is lived outdoors. In the villages small dwellings are built primarily for sleeping. The planning and architecture of the entire community is designed to nestle the community in the immensity of nature. Traditional worship sites are located beside certain species of trees that are considered to be spiritual and holy places.

In Kenya I sat outside in an immense outdoor "cathedral." The people had built row upon row of numerous mud "pews" to sit on under huge, mature trees. The branches of the trees were the "ceiling," and the site of the "cathedral" had been determined by the presence of certain trees rendered as holy because of the people's long history of worshiping under their shade. The trees were not worshiped nor were they viewed as holy objects. Instead, they symbolized the memory or history of the people's traditional worship site. As a result of their direct participation in nature, African people are deeply connected to, intimately knowledgeable of, and respectful toward nature. In African society of precolonial time "no freeborn person who required land needed to go outside his own area. Even if he went into another community, his freedom in obtaining land was not affected. Redeemed slaves were hardly in a different position."[3]

The majority of the people were engaged in agriculture. In Yoruba society the males in the community tilled the fields, planted the crop, and did the reaping. Women were expected to harvest the crops. "The more important part of women's work on the farm, however, consist[ed] of changing the form of the various crops harvested so as to bring it nearer to the point of ultimate consumption."[4] The entire family and community worked collectively on farms, and this was seen as an expression of kinship solidarity or, as N. A. Fadipe emphasizes, a form of public spiritedness.[5] In African traditional worship an offering always was set aside to ritually and ceremonially pay respect to nature.

Howard Thurman, born at the turn of the century, was nurtured within a black community that worked in, lived in, loved, and understood nature in an intimate way. In *Deep River and the Negro Spiritual Speaks of Life and Death* Thurman writes of the world of nature as material for the spirituals:

> The world of nature furnished the spirituals much material that was readily transformed into religious truth...For instance, in the South there is a small worm that crawls along in a most extraordinary manner...He is familiarly known as an "inch worm."...Observing this creature in the early morning on the cotton leaf, the slave felt that here was characterized much of his own life; hence the song:
> Keep a inchin' along,
> Massa Jesus comin' by an' by,
> Keep a inchin' along like a po' inch worm,
> Massa Jesus comin' by an' by.[6]

In another example he writes that the spiritual "Deep River" is the slaves' reflection upon the fascination of the flowing stream as "a constant source of wonder and beauty to the sensitive mind."[7]

Thurman's own ideas of religious truth were first drawn from his deep, mystical communion with nature.

> Eventually, I discovered that the oak tree and I had a unique relationship. I could sit, my back against its trunk, and feel the same peace that would come to me in my bed at night. I could reach down in the quiet places of my spirit, take out my bruises and my

joys, unfold them, and talk about them. It, too, was a part of my reality, like the woods, the night, and the pounding surf, my earliest companions, giving me space.[8]

That "space" was spiritual space that allowed him to commune with God through nature. It was also "free space" to sort out the loneliness and the racism of his day.

Thurman also befriended the night. The nights in Daytona Beach, Florida, were particularly black—as black as the nights he experienced in visiting Africa.

> Nightfall was meaningful to my childhood, for the night was more than a companion. It was a presence, an articulate climate. There was something about the night that seemed to cover my spirit like a gentle blanket. The nights in Florida, as I grew up, seemed to have certain dominant characteristics. They were not dark, they were black...The night had its own language...This comforted me and I found myself wishing that the night would hurry and come...I felt embraced, enveloped, held secure.[9]

He compares the Florida nights of his childhood to nights spent at the University of Ibadan in Nigeria. He wrote, "Here, too, the night was alive!"[10] In this regard, Thurman also writes of his deep communion with the Halifax River and the mighty Atlantic Ocean. His childhood was immersed in nature.

In summary, nature, for Thurman, was a spiritual space within which he experienced a deep sense of belonging and a vital connectedness with all of life. In *The Search for Common Ground* he writes of the origin of life as "never separate from the origin of the world":

> When we examine the various accounts of how the world began, the origin of life in general, and man's work in particular, we are face to face with what has been aptly called "the memory of a lost harmony."...The origin of life is never separated from the origin of the world...It is as if the sense of common origin is inescapable. Brooding over the bill of particulars of creation there is the notion of an active continuum, or spirit, or vital complex that is being demonstrated.[11]

As Thurman scholar Walter Fluker emphasizes, "All these early childhood experiences with nature provided Thurman with clues to the inner unity of all living things that would constitute the central concern of his life."[12]

The Influence of Family on Thurman's Ideal of Community

Family and extended family were also dominant influences on Thurman's view of community. He wrote that his father, Saul Solomon Thurman, a big man, was "quiet, soft-spoken and gentle" and did not attend church, but that his mother, Alice, was a "devout, dedicated, praying Christian" who attended church regularly. After his father's untimely death when Howard was only seven years old (and, later, the death of his stepfather), his immediate family consisted of his mother, Alice, his grandmother Nancy, and his sisters, Henrietta and Madaline. His mother and her mother took care of the family by themselves. He writes of their relationship:

> A communion existed between Grandma and Mamma so deep that there was never a discernible vibration of tension, or anger, between them. There must have been disagreements, but no discord affected the climate of our home.[13]

This deep communion or unity between his mother and grandmother formed his earliest impression of and model for community, a *harmony* that he would long for the rest of his life. It seems as if the profound harmony of the outdoors carried over and permeated indoors, into his family life of the connected and harmonious relationships among his elders.

Nancy Ambrose, his grandmother and day-to-day caretaker, taught him a sense of dignity and worth by telling stories about how she and others in the slave community survived with dignity in slavery. In *griot* style she told about strong slave preachers who told them they were all God's children. In this manner she began to implant in him, as other mothers and elders did in slavery, the idea that he was of equal worth. She also taught him how to interpret the Bible and to trust in a relationship with God, who would sustain him in the midst of any suffering or hatred based on race.

Like many of the generation of the enslaved, Nancy Ambrose had a high respect—which Thurman described as bordering on the "magical"—for the power of education. She was illiterate because of the restrictions placed upon her generation in slavery. But, as a famous black poet was to later capture in poem, she was of the generation that tried to give its children the books that they themselves could not read. For Nancy Ambrose's generation, education was a way to liberation.

The racial memory and wisdom of Thurman's grandmother comforted him and gave him a clear sense of direction in the face of a lonely childhood painfully influenced by the death of his father and the feeling of not quite fitting in with other children, due, in part, to his introspective, solitary nature. They also helped him to withstand the spirit-crushing forces of racial segregation in the American South. Substantially because of his family's strong and nurturing support, he would be the first child in his community to graduate from high school and eventually matriculate at Morehouse College and later Rochester Theological Seminary.

Thurman also spoke of the entire black community, called Waycross, as an extended family:

> In our tiny neighborhood within Waycross, were what today is called an extended family. The children were under the general watch and care of all adults. If we were asked to do an errand by any of the older members, it was not necessary for us to get permission from our parent. Reprimands were also freely given to the children by all the adults...My father's death was only one of the many experiences that I recall that bore the aura of caring of all...In every aspect of the common life, there was the sense of shared responsibility.[14]

In this African-influenced view of community, Thurman was taught to respect elders. In turn, all children in the community were everyone's children. They cared for each other in everyday concerns as well as in times of crisis. Thurman's ideal of community, shaped by his early experiences of family, was one of shared responsibility.

The Influence of the Black Church on Thurman's Ideal of Community

Thurman's mother and grandmother were faithful churchgoers and saw that he attended church regularly as well. He speaks of these early experiences of church as community:

> In the fellowship of the church, particularly in the experience of worship, there was a feeling of sharing in primary community. Not only did church membership seem to bear heavily upon one's ultimate destiny beyond death and the grave; more than all the communal ties, it also undergirded one's sense of personal identity. It was summed up in the familiar phrase, "If God is for you, who can prevail against you?"[15]

The black church as primary community served to shape his ideal of community as one of understanding God in radical solidarity with the oppressed community. With this black God's help, the church, in Thurman's mature ideal, was to become a model for inclusive religious fellowship that would inspire and empower the individual within the ritual worship community to struggle toward the realization of the ideal of community in the society as a whole.

Other influences on Thurman's ideal of community include Morehouse College (1919-23) as perhaps the most "crucial period of his intellectual development."[16] Thurman studied under Benjamin Mays, Gary Moore, and Lorimer Milton, who shaped and guided his intellectual and spiritual journey in ways that would significantly influence his view of community. Their teachings reinforced those he received earlier in his family life and taught him both to banish any feelings of inferiority based on race and to struggle against the evil influence of segregation.

Thurman next attended Rochester Theological Seminary, where he encountered George Cross, a professor of systematic theology. He credited Cross, along with Rufus Jones, with being the most influential intellectual source of his life. Cross emphasized "the infinite worth of the individual and her/his relationship to the creation of human community"[17] as most definitively demonstrated in the person and work of Jesus Christ as ideal. The ground for community then lay in the idealization of this perfect personality.

Olive Schreiner, a white, South African woman, was also an important intellectual influence. She emphasized the universality of truth, the oneness of all life, and the redemptive role of the solitary individual—concepts for which Thurman had established an earlier affinity through the teachings of Cross. Schreiner openly denounced racism and sexism.

Finally, Thurman came under the tutelage of the Quaker mystic Rufus Jones. Fluker states, "While Thurman acknowledges Cross as the most important influence upon him intellectually, it was Jones who provided him with a methodology that did not violate the validity of spirituality and its relationship to social transformation."[18] Jones's mysticism was rooted in theological personalism:

> He refers to religious experience as the "conjunct life," which is the divine-human fellowship between persons and a Person. Personality cannot exist without other persons, and a society of finite selves cannot exist without a Consciousness which transcends the entire group of selves.[19]

In the tradition of mystics and Quakers, Jones was also suspicious of formal creeds as being divisive; he held the conviction that truth was not defined by contexts of belief. Thurman was predisposed to this point of view from childhood, when the church initially refused to hold his father's funeral because his father was not a member. Also, later, his grandmother had confronted the deacons of the church when they were not initially inclined to accept him for church membership. From this early experience of alienation, he would come to mistrust anything that divided the human community—not only segregation but also religious creeds and doctrines.

Jones, as Fluker emphasizes, helped Thurman to develop his understanding of the relationship between the inner life and social transformation. Thurman's spiritual temperament, one may suggest, was ideally suited for the solitude and inwardness of mysticism. Yet, as an African American born in the Deep South at the turn of the century, his connection to his identity-in-community was so strong and the threat of racism so virulent that Thurman had intellectually to reconcile the relationship between the spiritual and the existential. In addition, he may have had an affinity for Jones's ideas because, in many ways, they corresponded to and resonated with the views of God and religion he had developed within the black community.

In summary, all of the above influences, along with his travels around the world, particularly trips to Africa and India, and his ministerial work as dean of chapel at Morehouse and Spelman colleges, lecturer of religion, and pastor of Mt. Zion Baptist Church and The Church for the Fellowship of All Peoples, led Thurman to identify his lifelong quest for community as "the search for common ground." This ideal is one of radical inclusion of all of human society and nature.

The Impact of Racism on Thurman's Ideal of Community

For Thurman, segregation in the American South represented a devastatingly evil means for destroying community; it was the antithesis of community. Segregation, with its Jim Crow laws that restricted social interaction between blacks and whites, was a "wall" that precluded the possibility for community. In Thurman's thought and experience community was the goal of all of life, the ultimate expression of the purpose, or good, to which God called human beings, consciously and on the level of being, to seek and restore.

Thurman's Ideal of Community

Thurman's ideal of community was the wholeness, integration, and harmony of creation. This, he wrote, was the teleological end toward which all life moved. Sin was the "lost harmony" or the loss of innocence with the disintegration of harmony[20] in creation. Community was to be restored by individuals made ready through two spiritual disciplines of prayer as meditation and suffering. These two disciplines had the possibility to lead the individual into a "creative encounter" with

God that would result in the individual's *consciousness* of the integral relationship between the inner and outer dimensions of life and the individual's *commitment* to the possibility of the actualization of community.

Individuals would then seek to restore the ideal of community—whether or not they believed it could ever be realized in their experience—in a hope that they would also restore harmony in creation. The restoration of the harmony of community would be achieved when the individual freely and voluntarily chose to make a conscious, deliberate choice to strive for wholeness, harmony, and integration within self and in relations with others and the world.[21]

There is an order or pattern given to existence by God that is realizing itself in time. Within this order, living structures reveal a "consciousness" of interrelatedness and dependability as they strive toward community. The nature of community is utopian as an instinctual dream of the human race to realize harmony and order. It is also a common consciousness in the form of the kinship of all living things. Life is one, and there is a fundamental unity at all levels of existence. Identity is the ground of community as self-awareness that seeks wholeness and integration in a dynamic urge toward order and harmony. The individual finds identity in the communal contexts of family and society.

The nature of the actualization of community is threefold. It involves the individual, God, and the world, with the individual as a point of departure. The task of the individual is to cultivate an inner life in order to develop an inner consciousness that corresponds to the individual's original connectedness to Reality, which is the ground of all awareness. This cultivation of the inner life is the basis for the development of a genuine sense of self and authentic existence in the world.[22] The genuineness of this identity is to be validated outwardly, as a guard against self-deception, by the rule of orderliness. "Whatever seems to deny a fundamental structure of orderliness upon which rationality seems to depend cannot be countenanced."[23]

The individual's outer mode of existence is characterized by human freedom and responsibility. Freedom is twofold. It is the individual's God-given birthright, and it is a sense of options or alternatives in the locus of the will. Freedom entails the responsibility for the individual's actions and reactions at both personal and social levels of existence. In *The Search for Common Ground* Thurman explains this in terms of the "potential for disharmony" and the potential for harmony in individuals. This potential is triggered or actualized by the free exercise of human choice or volition. Good (harmony as humankind's experience of community) and evil (disharmony or "against community") exist as potentials in human beings.

God is the second actor in the actualization of community. God, as omnipotent and sovereign, is the Lord of history. Existence itself is divine activity. Yet God is also personal and immanent. The life and ministry of Jesus is the highest example of the immanent God. When the individual encounters the love of God in the experience of the human struggle, "what is disclosed in his religious experience he must define in community."[24] Thus on the ground of the creative encounter, the individual is enabled, by the love of God, consciously and voluntarily to seek to actualize community. The individual is to seek to actualize restored community in the world as harmonious relationships in human society and with animals and all that is living.

Thurman's ideal of community is rooted in African-American spirituality as he experienced it growing up in the segregated South. It caused him to believe that the "highest act of celebration of the human spirit is the worship of God."[25] In this act of worship, all barriers of division between God and the human and human to human are eliminated. But, he stated, this experience of universality was only "derivative from the ground" of one's own cultural context. In other words, "a man cannot be at home everywhere unless he is at home somewhere."[26] Home, for Thurman, was in the spiritual legacy of an African worldview. Thurman's spirituality influenced contemporary understandings of black theology today.

MARTIN LUTHER KING JR.

In his collection of King's work, *A Testament of Hope,* James Washington cites the citation of the Presidential Medal of Freedom presented to the Reverend Dr. Martin Luther King Jr. on July 4, 1977.

Martin Luther King, Jr., was the conscience of his generation. A southerner, a black man, he gazed on the great wall of segregation and saw that the power of love could bring it down. From the pain and exhaustion of his fight to free all people from the bondage of separation and injustice, he wrung his eloquent statement of his dream of what America could be. He helped us overcome our ignorance of one another. He spoke out against a war he felt was unjust, as he had spoken out against laws that were unfair. He made our nation stronger because he made it better. Honored by kings, he continued to his last days to strive for a world where the poorest and humblest among us could enjoy the fulfillment of the promises of our founding fathers. His life informed us, his dreams sustain us yet.[27]

This citation accurately presents the life and struggle to build community of Martin Luther King Jr. King was born in segregated Atlanta, Georgia, in 1926. He became a world figure and one who significantly influenced liberation movements throughout the world in his role as theologian, preacher, freedom fighter, and martyr in the American Civil Rights movement, which sought to eradicate segregation in America. King articulated a vision of a "new South" wherein the ideal of the "beloved community" could be realized. His prophetic vision expanded to include a vision of "the world house"—a global vision of liberation for the poor in the entire world order.

Martin Luther King Jr. in many ways continues in the theological tradition of Howard Thurman; they converge at the "meeting place" of African retentions in African-American spirituality that urged them to seek to build community. But King, as is the task for each successive black generation, gave this spirituality unique expression according to his gifts and the needs of the community of his particular age.

The Influence of Family on King's Ideal of Community

Lewis Baldwin writes that the close, loving, comfortably middle-class family setting of Martin Luther King Jr. is "enormously important" in seeking to understand his personal and intellectual formation. He quotes King's view of the relationship between his mother and father: "I was born in a very congenial home situation...Our parents themselves were very intimate, and they always maintained an intimate relationship with us."[28]

The intimacy between Martin Luther King Sr. and Alberta Williams King later became "a metaphor for King's relationship with his own wife and children"[29] as well as for his relationship with his siblings. The family regularly ate dinner together, and these family gatherings were the setting for the reading of the Bible, prayers, and conversation that allowed them to share ideas and instill cultural and family values. Baldwin writes, "This closely knit family, in which a concern for family unity, loyalty, and interfamily cooperation was consistently expressed, was a chief source of King's early understanding of community."[30]

King's maternal grandmother, Jennie C. Parks Williams, lived in their home and was of crucial significance in his spiritual development. "The prestige and importance of Jennie C. Parks Williams in the King home were essentially as great as that of the black grandmother during slavery. She was a strong spiritual force, a bearer of culture, and a pillar of strength."[31] Much of King's early life pivoted around his grandmother, "who helped instill in him a strong sense of identity, self-esteem, and mission."[32] Their profound "connectedness" is illustrated in an incident when young Martin actually tried to kill himself by jumping out of a window because he thought his brother had accidentally killed their grandmother. He blamed himself for not being present when she died. After her death, when he was twelve years old, Martin assumed a new maturity. His childhood ended with the death of his beloved grandmother.

It is very important to note that both at home and in the church Martin was taught an African view of death. The living include the living and the living dead. This view allowed him to believe that when his grandmother actually died, her presence was still with him. This was deeply reassuring to his spirit and emotions and led him to believe firmly in the black church's teachings on personal immortality.

The King family taught its children to value education as the path to success and to work toward excellence. The two were believed to be synonymous. Daddy King, a powerful and domineering father, had graduated from Morehouse College and Alberta from Spelman Seminary, both bastions of the aspiring black middle class. Daddy King wanted the boys to become ministers like himself and daughter Christine to become a teacher like her mother. He also wanted to continue the family legacy with the boys succeeding him in the leadership of the prominent Ebenezer Baptist Church where his father-in-law and then he himself served as pastor.

The King children received excellent schooling in Atlanta's segregated schools. A good student, Martin Jr. read a number of books about black history and black culture. His mother had explained the history of slavery, the Civil War, and the roots of segregation in America. She, along with his father and his grandmother, continually reassured the children that they were equal to other human beings, as good as anyone else, and destined to be special. All of the above served to ground Martin in a strong, traditional sense of black identity. Martin was also embraced by the extended family of the black community, an environment that prepared him for a life of strong social involvement.

The Influence of the Black Church on King's Ideal of Community

Ebenezer Baptist Church was founded in 1886 by the descendants of slaves. The values and spirituality of the church were deeply and directly linked to slave religion and spirituality. Martin's maternal great-grandfather, the Reverend Williams, was its minister. His maternal grandfather, the Reverend Alfred D. Williams, "was one of the most active and popular black Baptist preachers in the South"[33] in the twentieth century. Martin's father was also a prominent Baptist minister, and both of Martin's grandmothers and his mother were active and respected in women's groups in the black Baptist church associations. As a result, his church family, the Ebenezer Baptist Church, was as key to his early development as his biological family. In many ways Martin became the "crown prince" of the family's intergenerational leadership legacy of Ebenezer. When older brother A. D. wanted no part of "assuming the mantle," Daddy King's hopes began to center around Martin. Baldwin writes:

> He drank from the wellsprings of that curious mixture of African and European spirituality concocted in the southern black Baptist Church, and that institution became an important part of his religious self-understanding.[34]

Martin joined Ebenezer at the age of five, under his father's pastorate, and remained a member until his death. Later, he would speak of his conversion as "a kind of inherited religion" that was a "gradual intaking of the noble ideals set forth in my family and my environment,"[35] most of which he absorbed unconsciously.

During his church experience he continued to learn to recite the Bible and sing the sacred music that had been created by his slave ancestors. He said that the Christian teachings of the church taught him how to love and get along with people from an early age. Exposed from an early age to the genius of the black church and the black community in its task of socializing human beings, these teachings helped to ameliorate his growing bitterness toward white people and became the root of his later conviction that American society must become socially integrated.

In "An Autobiography of Religious Development"[36] King cites his religious experience. At an early age he felt some resistance to religious fundamentalism and began to question the European-based method of interpretation of the Bible taught in the church's Sunday school. In later life (in *The Strength to Love*) he would critique two extremes of the religious expression of the black church: the excessively emotional, anti-intellectual black church, and the classism of the middle-class, "frozen" Negro church. These concerns reflected an early awareness of the problems of a European-based, privatized Christianity that could threaten the formation of authentic community, and the divisiveness of money or class as a barrier to the realization of community. He believed the black church should be more involved in a relevant social gospel and objected to the apparent apathy of the black preachers of his day in their subordination of social and economic concerns to other worldly concerns.

The Influence of Black Education on King's Ideal of Community

Martin entered a program for exceptional high school students at Morehouse College. The Morehouse culture and environment, with its long and respected tradition of preparing young black men for lives of leadership and excellence, continued to ground him even more deeply in the values of his culture and provide him with a sense of destiny and "specialness"—as a "Morehouse Man"—that was recognized by his family, church, and the broader community. In this historically black college environment, like young Howard Thurman, he encountered many of the great black men of his day, including distinguished professors Benjamin Mays, George Kelsey, Walter Chivers, Gladstone L. Chandler, and Samuel Williams. In addition, he was exposed to black business leaders, physicians, morticians, lawyers, and other professionals who, in addition to his father, served as successful and strong black male role models of moral excellence.

The Morehouse experience prepared King to understand the necessity for wholesome relationships between black people and white people. By his college years he had decided to hate all white people; however, his professors at Morehouse and his participation on the Atlanta Intercollegiate Council, combined with his early home and church teachings on the love and forgiveness ethic of Jesus, encouraged him to seek positive solutions to the race problem. It was at Morehouse that he acknowledged his call to the ministry, and he was ordained at Ebenezer Baptist Church at the age of nineteen. This call to responsibility to community, and to his family legacy proved to be stronger than his concern about the irrelevancy of the Negro church. This conflict was somewhat reconciled by his professors at Morehouse. King credits the teachings of Morehouse College professors, who taught biblical hermeneutics from the African-American tradition, with freeing him from the shackles of fundamentalism[37] and preparing him for the liberal theological tradition of Crozer Theological Seminary.

Other Influences on King's Ideal of Community

King began his studies at Crozer Theological Seminary, located in Chester, Pennsylvania, in 1948 and graduated as valedictorian of his class. He credited George W. Davis, a professor of Christian theology, with being most significant to his development while at Crozer. King began his formal study of personalism with Davis. Later King would acknowledge a great debt in shaping his theological perspective to the influence of evangelical liberalism through the Social Gospel Movement. He would later continue his study of personalism in the doctoral program at Boston University. King, like Thurman, recognized in personalism ideas that were congenial to the spiritual and social value system of the black community. He found personalism's idea of God as a personal God consistent with the black church teachings concerning the personality of God. Personalism is the belief that conscious personality is both the highest value and the highest reality in the universe.

At Crozer he also encountered the works of Walter Rauschenbusch, Karl Marx, Mahatma Gandhi, and Reinhold Niebuhr. The ideas of these greater thinkers provided a theoretical base and, in the case of Gandhi, a method to live out the social ethic of love as expressed by Jesus in the Sermon on the Mount and as he had experienced it in the black community. He graduated in 1951 and entered Boston University.

At Boston he continued his studies of personalism and began to study Hegel's analysis of the dialectical process. "Drawing on Hegel, King argued that an adequate understanding of religion is found neither in the thesis of this-worldliness nor in the antithesis of otherworldliness, but in a synthesis that reconciles the limited truths of both."[38] He stated:

> Religion deals with both earth and heaven, both time and eternity. Religion operates not only on the vertical plane but also on the horizontal. It seeks not only to integrate men with God but to integrate men with men and each man with himself. This means, at bottom, that the Christian gospel is a two-way road. On the one hand it seeks to change the souls of men, and thereby unite them with God; on the other hand it seeks to change the environmental conditions of men so that the soul will have a chance after it is changed. Any religion that professes to be concerned with the souls of men and is not concerned with the slums that damn them, the economic conditions that strangle them, and the social conditions that cripple them is a dry-as-dust-religion.[39]

This philosophy of religion was congenial to black religious experience, which had traditionally understood the nature of religion in this way before it became increasingly assimilated to the Christianity of the dominant culture.

King acknowledged Edgar S. Brightman and L. Harold DeWolf, directors of his philosophical and theological studies, and Walter Muelder and Allen Knight Chalmers with making the most significant contributions to his intellectual journey at Boston University. All of these men were renowned pacifists.

King encountered Howard Thurman, who was dean of Marsh Chapel, on at least one occasion in his last year at Boston University. Thurman was impressed with King's moral and spiritual thought in his preaching and would later recommend him to The Church for the Fellowship of All Peoples in San Francisco, although King would be unable to assume this pastorate. After graduating from Boston University, he became the pastor of the Dexter Avenue Baptist Church in Montgomery, Alabama.

The Impact of Racism on King's Ideal of Community

King's early experiences with racism as the cause of non-community caused him to search for a method to overcome the barrier of segregation.

> I had grown up abhorring not only segregation but also the oppressive barbarous acts that grew out of it. I had passed spots where Negroes had been savagely lynched, and had watched the Ku Klux Klan on its rides at night. I had seen police brutality with my own eyes, and watched Negroes receive the most tragic injustice in the courts. All of these things had done something to my growing personality. I had come perilously close to resenting all white people.[40]

These experiences, coupled with his own vital experience of love expressed as profound community in his home, church, and black community life, led him to dedicate his life to the quest for community in all of human society.

Though he grew up in a secure and comfortable black middle-class environment, Martin was aware of the poverty of his neighbors in the black community. From an early age he felt compassion for the despised poor—black and white—and he realized that they were being exploited by the wealthy. Baldwin credits his later openness to the philosophies of Karl Marx and Walter Rauschenbush to this early childhood exposure of living in close proximity to people who were forced to reside in desperate and brutal poverty. Martin had seen the police and the Ku Klux Klan brutalizing and beating black children and adults, yet he said his own black community was characterized by both "a minimum of crime" and "deeply religious families." From a very young age, this stark contrast caused him to feel a sense of responsibility toward the poor in the community. He increasingly came to understand his personal identity and the meaning of his life journey as discovering a way to eliminate the evil of non-community caused by segregation in order to usher in the "Beloved Community."

In Montgomery, as pastor of Dexter Avenue Baptist Church and an emerging community leader, King came to embrace fully the power of nonviolent resistance as a means to secure his vision of community. He stated:

> From the beginning a basic philosophy guided the movement...It was the Sermon on the Mount rather than a doctrine of passive resistance, that initially inspired the Negroes of Montgomery to dignified social action. It was Jesus of Nazareth that stirred the Negroes to protest with the creative weapon of love.[41]

Nonviolent resistance was seen by the black community of Montgomery as a way of embodying Christian love, and its theory and concepts were disseminated in mass meetings held in the black churches throughout the city and eventually throughout the South and other parts of the nation.

King's theology becomes implicit and explicit in the use of nonviolent resistance to overcome segregation in the Civil Rights movement. It can be seen as a trifold understanding of conversion as embracing God, the individual, and the world as interconnected and interrelated actors participating in the struggle to realize the ideal of the Beloved Community.

King stated that "God is on the side of truth and justice."[42] Explicit in this statement is the African-based belief in a circular, moral, and just universe. King believed that when the individual encounters God in "the limit experiences" of life, one's life becomes converted and transformed to have the hope and courage to suffer and to sacrifice without violently striking back at one's enemies (the Sermon on the Mount) and to have the endurance to persevere in the struggle for justice for all people in spite of all obstacles because God is on the side of justice.[43]

King wrote in *Stride toward Freedom* of his initial emotional understanding of this. During the period of his emerging leadership of the movement in Montgomery, although he had attended church all of his life, he had not personally *felt* the presence of God. He tells of reaching the point of complete hopelessness and despair after his home was bombed, fearing for the safety of himself and his family. Beset by worry and sleeplessness, he sat alone at his kitchen table in the wee hours of the morning. When he reached the absolute limit of despair for the first time in his life, he felt the overwhelming presence of God comforting and reassuring him that God was with him in the struggle against segregation. It was at this point that he decided to go on in self-sacrificial solidarity with the despised poor, and from this point on he never turned back. He begged his father, Daddy King, who would weep heart-rending tears because he feared for his beloved son's life, never again to ask him to relinquish his leadership of the movement and, in so doing, King gave up a comfortable, private, quietly middle-class family life forever.

King believed that a religion that focused exclusively upon the individual was a truncated form of religion.[44] In his theology the individual selves were seen as converted when they recognized their interdependency. Individuals must be nurtured toward this recognition for the sake of the emergence of the whole as the collective Beloved Community. Drawing on an African-based sensibility he saw the community rather than the individual as the starting point, and he sought to make the base of the emerging movement as broad as possible to engage people collectively. The individual was brought into wholeness and true identity as the individual lived sacrificially for the sake of protecting the harmony, reconciliation, and well-being of the Beloved Community.

King's Ideal of Community as the World

King scholars Kenneth L. Smith and Ira G. Zepp Jr. write that "King's conception of the Beloved Community is best described as a transformed and regenerated human society,"[45] transformed by means of the integration of the poor into the total human community, principally through the alleviation of racial and economic inequity. King believed, like Fannie Lou Hamer, that Christianity was a radical and revolutionary faith that could help to bring this vision into existence in history.

King thus described the goals of the Southern Christian Leadership Conference: "The ultimate aim of SCLC is to foster and create the 'beloved community' in America where brotherhood is a reality...SCLC works for integration. Our ultimate goal is genuine intergroup and interpersonal living—*integration*."[46] Therefore, his ideal of the Beloved Community was of an integrated society, both in America and also in the broader global context, where segregation would be vanquished and all people would be equal in every aspect of social life and, he would maintain later, economic life. In the "Letter from Birmingham Jail," written in 1963, he emphasized an economic withdrawal program as a means of nonviolent direct action.

King's version of this inclusive human society of the Beloved Community was not characterized simply by inclusiveness as racial justice. It also included an egalitarian, socialistic approach toward wealth and property. Long concerned about the inequities brought about by capitalism—and drawing upon the teachings of the black church of hospitality to the stranger and the theories of Karl Marx—he began to advocate for the United States to bridge the gap between abject poverty and inordinate wealth[47] as a barrier to community.

King saw the Civil Rights movement—where black and white people were joined together in love in a common struggle for justice and equality for all—as a microcosm of the Beloved Community. His concern eventually broadened internationally to embrace public disapproval of the United States' policies toward Vietnam and apartheid in South Africa.

Until his final sermons and speeches (notably "Remaining Awake through a Great Revolution," delivered on March 31, 1968, and "I See the Promised Land," delivered on April 3, 1968), he continued to call for the boycotting of racist companies and enterprises by advising African Americans to withhold their thirty billion dollars of collective wealth. In the sermon "A Time to Break Silence," delivered at Riverside Church on April 4, 1967, a year before his assassination, he began to speak of the "importance of Vietnam" as an example of "war as an enemy of the poor." King revealed his mature understanding of the economic roots of war as the greed on the part of America—as old as the impulse that fueled chattel slavery—for misbegotten power and wealth. He called the Vietnamese war "madness." He demanded that America see "the enemy's point of view," meaning those whom this nation labeled as communists, as a way to explode the political myths that masked the "basic weaknesses of our own condition." In this way, he maintained, the "true meaning and value of compassion and nonviolence" would become apparent as America was able to learn, grow, mature and "profit from the wisdom of the brothers who are called the opposition." King, to the consternation of many Americans, began to expand his vision of non-community caused by white racism to include culpability for the victimization of the earth's entire population of people of color and, in so doing, he completely and irrevocably identified himself and the collective African-American community with the world's despised poor.

The Beloved Community was to be realized, in an extended family model, through personal and social relationships of love that would overcome both racism and classism all over the world. He expressed this ideal first in the theme "Black and White Together," the title of one of the chapters in *Why We Can't Wait,* published in 1963, as well as a line from the hymn "We Shall Overcome." Drawing upon his own cultural beliefs, King also envisioned the solidarity of the human family.[48] As early as 1963, in his "Letter from Birmingham Jail," he spoke of the interrelatedness of all communities and states. This theme was repeated in the now famous words of his last Sunday morning sermon:

> We are tied together in the single garment of destiny, caught in an inescapable network of mutuality. And whatever affects one directly affects all indirectly. For some strange reason I can never be what I ought to be until you are what you ought to be. And you can never be what you ought to be until I am...This is the way God's universe is made; this is the way it is structured.[49]

In this statement King expresses a unified worldview. In this radically inclusive worldview the Beloved Community is seen to comprise the social condition of all human beings living together in an interdependent and interrelated whole created by the presence of love in human society. King's vision included all of the poor of whatever racial or ethnic group. In his last book, *The Trumpet of Conscience,* he contended that our loyalties must transcend our race, our tribe, our class, and our nation so that we may become "citizens of the world" in a concern for the condition of the poor globally.[50]

In his final sermon, delivered on April 3, 1968, at the Mason Temple headquarters of the Church of God in Christ in Memphis, Tennessee,

King exhibited a clear concern in his vision of the ideal of community for personal sacrifice *vs.* self-interest. He called for the African-American community to embody a "dangerous unselfishness" as displayed by the Samaritan, a racial outcast in the parable of the Good Samaritan. He also spoke of his own near-murder by a crazed woman while he was autographing his first book in Harlem. Though he does not say directly that this was the measure of his own great personal sacrifice, he does imply in this sermon that one must be willing to give up even one's own life, property, and most cherished religious ideas if they interfere with or disrupt community. To this end he felt that the African-American community represented the "hope" in the world for all people of color. In this vein Lewis Baldwin's book *Toward the Beloved Community: Martin Luther King, Jr. and South Africa* is an important contribution emphasizing King's understanding of the South African context in the 1950s as sharing a common destiny with challenging Jim Crow and apartheid in America in the 1960s.

Theologian Noel Erskine affirms that King was the model theologian for the twentieth century and that his unique theological contribution, which arose from the context of black culture and the black church, consisted of the following:

1. The theologian must work from within the struggle to relate Christian faith to the concrete conditions that affect both body and soul.
2. The mark of a theologian is a commitment to the struggle to change the world coupled with a willingness to lay down one's life in the quest for justice. The concrete problems of the community must provide the content of theological reflection and issues of justice, poverty, and powerlessness must be brought from the edges to the center of theological awareness.
3. Reconciliation should be the main key upon which theology is posited.
4. Faith and praxis should be joined as the gospel of Jesus is related to the condition of those who suffer and who are oppressed.[51]

King felt that it is "absolutely necessary for the Negro to have an appreciation of his heritage."[52] The spiritual strength and values of the slaves were used in his life as resources that helped him lead his people in their drive toward freedom. He wrote, "Something of the inner spirit of our slave forebears must be pursued today."[53] In many ways, the same strong, black cultural and spiritual foundation present in the life of Howard Thurman helped King to develop a life committed to action.

Thurman and King differ in their individual responses to overcoming the barrier to community expressed in the evil of segregation. Thurman's basic concern was this evil where it touched the individual. Though he does thoroughly comprehend and address the complex social dimensions of evil, his emphasis is on the creative and constructive transformation of the will of the individual at the ground of the individual's creative encounter with God as it challenges the individual's personal center to commit to the realization of the ideal of community. King's life as a black person in the segregated South allowed him to witness and experience many of the same atrocities and violations of human personhood and identity that affected Thurman. Yet the same spirituality empowered King to lead a mass movement to overcome the barriers to community through group protest.

The spiritual formation of both Howard Thurman and Martin Luther King Jr. included living contact with the generation of the enslaved; respect for elders maintained through strong and powerfully loving grandmothers and parents who preserved racial memory by teaching their children black history and promoting black values; black spirituality and religion; empowering the children with the ability to understand the Bible from an African-American hermeneutic; teaching a personal morality defined by an identity of dignity and responsibility to the community; and finally, calling for the child to aspire to excellence through hard work and education.

MALCOLM X

Many contradictions of belief and ambiguities of emotion characterize the spiritual life of Malcolm X. Malcolm's Black Muslim worldview was marginal, as theologian James Cone emphasizes in his book *Martin and Malcolm and America: A Dream or a Nightmare*[54] not only in America as a whole but in the African-American community as well. Yet Malcolm, like Thurman and King, shared some of the same cultural, racial, and spiritual roots and identity that would also shape the content of his social vision and the nature of his mature reflections on American society and the urgent necessity to realize community within both an American and a global context.

Distinct regional, religious, and class differences influenced the meanings and styles of the leadership of Thurman, King, and Malcolm. King, particularly, and to a much lesser degree Thurman, emerged from within an upwardly mobile, ever-expanding Southern, black middle class, while Malcolm was born among the more rigidly oppressed black poor of the urban North. Thurman and King's spiritual genius arose from the context of "folk, black, and southern"[55] influences that, in almost all ways, were directly in touch with the slave generation. Malcolm's spiritual genius, on the other hand, may be seen to be "twice removed"—by his life in the Northern urban ghettos and his early life of crime—from the direct influence of this traditional black socio-historical context.

Millions of African Americans, like Malcolm's father, had left the fields and farms of the Deep South and headed for the big cities, where they hoped to find the economic comfort and legal rights that were denied to them in the Jim Crow South. This great migration, which occurred in more than one wave, changed the United States from a country where race was a regional issue and where black culture existed mainly in rural isolation or in Southern, inner-city neighborhoods with healthy black enclaves. By the mid-twentieth century, race relations affected the texture of life in nearly every city in America. While the North was viewed by these early black migrants from the South as a "Promised Land," what they found when they moved to the North, full of hope, were broken promises, disillusionment, disease, crime, poverty, and racism "Northern style."

It is crucial to understand that this Northern urban and suburban setting filled with disappointment, desperation, and despair characterized the landscape of Malcolm's life. His experience was that of millions of African Americans in the North, and his rhetorically aggressive posture toward white racism captured the imagination of young and urban African Americans and young white Americans in a way that King could not.[56]

Yet, at the same time, his revolt against non-community was rooted in the traditions of African-American spirituality, as were Thurman's and King's. For Malcolm, one generation removed from rural Georgia on his father's side of the family, profoundly reflected black spirituality in drawing upon racial memory to embody his great love for his people. His was a self-sacrificial life devoted to actualizing an inclusive human community within history. His actions, too, came from the store of his own unique gifts as he attempted to translate the ethical ideals of black culture and black religion in America into the practical reality of community.

It is important to note that Malcolm also actively sought to include not only black people who were experiencing American apartheid through white segregation, but also to address apartheid within the black community itself. Black poor had been largely forgotten or neglected by the black middle class. Malcolm's ideal of community sought to bring those people from the margins of black and American life—the black, urban, underclass of the working and nonworking poor, and black convicts, ex-convicts, prostitutes, and substance abusers—into the circle of life of the "mainstream" African-American community (people who valued honest labor, feared God, and did not commit crimes against self and society). Precisely because of being among the poorest of the black despised poor, Malcolm's spiritual journey shows, with startling clarity, this more wide-angled view. His was markedly a vision of unifying the African-American class groups as well as larger American society. And eventually, in the reflections and actions of his last years of life, he reached out to all of human society in his vital concern for unifying beleaguered and oppressed Africa, the people of the African diaspora, and all people of goodwill who seek to recognize God through harmonious, reconciled community.

The Influence of Family on Malcolm's Ideal of Community

Malcolm Little was born on May 19, 1925. In his autobiography[57] he narrates that when his mother, Louise Little, originally from Grenada, was pregnant with him, the Ku Klux Klan surrounded their home, shooting guns and demanding that his father, the Reverend Earl Little, come outside. His earliest memory was of a terrible night in 1929 when he woke up as his father shot at two white men who had set their house on fire. Thus, even before his birth he was affected by the violence of white racism, which would continue throughout his life. He also remembered continual friction between his mother and father.

Scholar of religion Michael Dyson asserts in *Making Malcolm* that Alex Haley, who assisted in the writing of the autobiography, may have manipulated Malcolm's autobiography so that the actual details of his father's death are not clear. He writes that Haley may have dramatized Malcolm's life story, or Malcolm may have embellished it in the telling. In spite of Dyson's claim, it is clear that Malcolm, like Harriet Tubman and many of the children of the generation of the enslaved and their descendants, lived through very early experiences of extreme and arbitrary white violence that threatened the security of his family. Another important factor to consider is that these stories may have survived in the family's memory and continued to function as a life-defining family mythology that caused him to develop, much like King and many others, an early fundamental mistrust of white people.

Malcolm's parents taught their children the need for self-improvement through education and racial dignity. Indeed, Malcolm excelled in school and was elected as president of his all-white class in the seventh grade. He had early aspirations to become a lawyer, but when he was competing with two other students (both white) for the top academic position in his class in the eighth grade, his white teacher told him that that was not a proper aspiration for a "nigger." Young Malcolm was devastated and sought no more formal education. Later, in prison, he became extremely well-read. The love for education instilled in him by the teachings of his parents never left him.

Malcolm's father, originally from Reynolds, Georgia, was a Baptist minister and a dedicated organizer for Marcus Garvey's Universal Negro Improvement Association. Garvey (1887-1940), an immigrant to America from the Caribbean, was a controversial and influential black leader who advocated that the black masses return to their African ancestral homelands. Garvey taught that "nationhood" was the highest ideal of all peoples:

> Education is the medium by which a people are prepared for the creation of their own particular civilization, and the advancement and glory of their race. Be as proud of your race today as our fathers were in the days of yore. We have a beautiful history, we shall create another in the future that will astonish the world.[58]

These teachings were identical to those of the enslaved Africans to succeeding generations of their children. Malcolm's parents taught him the ways of the black Baptist Church, but they also taught him the philosophy and opinions of Marcus Garvey. He would choose Garvey's teachings over those of the church.

The Early Influence of Black Nationalism

Garvey was by no means the first pan-African prophet. He was connected to a long line of slave predecessors, primarily from the United States and the Caribbean, dating back to the early nineteenth century. Many of the ablest leaders of the black community from the time of slavery, such as Paul Cuffee, who became a wealthy Quaker, Daniel Coker, a leader of emigrant black people, AME Bishop Henry McNeil Turner, and Lott Cary, an influential Baptist preacher from Virginia, were dedicated to the pan-African ideal.

Historian Hollin Lynch contends that the primary motive for pan-Africanism was the conviction that African peoples everywhere faced common problems and should seek a common solution. The goal was dignity and respect for black people everywhere through making a distinctive cultural contribution to world civilization. From the inception of the pan-African idea there was widespread agreement that its major political base should be Africa, where a progressive society was envisioned that would combine the best in traditional African and Western cultures. These proud racial views were instilled in Malcolm from early childhood, when he attended the Garvey meetings with his father and listened to his father discuss black history and the ideal of Garveyism as a vision for the realization of the actualization of community.

The Influence of the Black Church

Malcolm had a different experience in the black Baptist churches where his father Earl Little served as a visiting preacher. Malcolm could neither understand nor approve of what he saw as the anti-intellectualism and emotionalism of the black church. Unlike Martin Luther King Jr., he never found relevance in the black church experience.

> My brother Philbert, the one just older than me, loved church, but it *confused and amazed me.* I would sit goggle-eyed at my father jumping and shouting as he preached, with the congregation jumping and shouting behind him, their souls and bodies devoted to singing and praying. Even at that young age, I just couldn't believe in the Christian concept of Jesus as someone divine. And no religious person until I was a man in my twenties—and then in prison—could tell me anything. I had very little respect for most people who represented religion.[59]

Even though he would disavow belief in the black church as an adult, Malcolm's pronounced skills as a public orator were definitely grounded in the black Baptist oratorical tradition in terms of form if not content. Malcolm's adult spirituality is also powerfully rooted in these experiences of his earliest childhood. His father was brutally killed by whites when Malcolm was six. As a direct result the family had to seek help from the welfare system in order to survive.

The Influence of the Welfare System as Non-Community

Malcolm tells of his mother's inability to cope with the degrading and inhumane treatment and conditions of the American welfare system. He said that being on welfare caused his family a kind of "psychological deterioration" that began to eat away at their pride. They were deeply humiliated because they had always felt proud that their family had never "gone on relief." Constantly plagued by desperate poverty and what she saw as enslavement to a racist system of public welfare, Louise Little was forced to go against the bedrock black value of dignity through self-determination and self-support. By the time Malcolm was ten, his mother could no longer bear up under the strain of having to choose between feeding her children and human dignity. She descended into a depression from which she never recovered. Louise Little eventually died in an asylum, and years before she died, the children were split up and sent to different homes as wards of the state. They were never to live together again. Malcolm blamed white people, both personally and systemically, for destroying his family—the first principle of black identity. His subsequent actions, I believe, were a reaction to this belief.

Prison as Community

Malcolm left Michigan at fifteen and went to Boston to live with his older stepsister, Ella. There he succumbed to the lure of street life. During these years and afterward in Harlem he learned to become a hustler, pimp, drug pusher, and thief. Eventually and inevitably (for surely it was divine providence) in February of 1946, when he was barely twenty-one years old, Malcolm was sentenced to prison. He served a total of seven years, a period of time that would prove to be crucial to his conversion and spiritual growth.

A great deal of his early time in prison was spent in vicious, antisocial behavior caused by the pain, rage, hostility, and despair over the loss of his family, and also, one may suggest, by the frustration of a brilliant and spiritual human being trapped by personal and systemic racism in channels far too narrow for genuine self-expression. He lashed out against everyone and everything—but most, significantly, against God. He was nicknamed "Satan" by the other inmates because of his antireligious attitude.

Malcolm's conversion came about in prison. Prison provided the occasion for the period of stillness that he needed and the spiritual space to turn his life in another direction. After his tantrums or rages against God ebbed, he began to return to the value of education through the influence of a well-read inmate named Bimbi. Bimbi ended Malcolm's vicious diatribes against religion in what Malcolm called a "framework." The superiority of Bimbi's approach embarrassed Malcolm to the extent that he took Bimbi's advice to take a correspondence course in English. For Malcolm, Bimbi was the beginning of a renewed experience of community. Bimbi inspired him to return to the value of his family and his ancestors—education—that had been ruptured when he was in the eighth grade. His incredible drive to acquire education was additionally fueled by an overwhelming hunger for truth—the truth of his own identity and that of his community. During this time he turned away from his false identity as Satan and began to turn toward his identity as Malcolm X.

The Influence of Black Alternative Religion

Malcolm began to turn toward the teachings of the Honorable Elijah Muhammad in 1948, when his brother Reginald wrote him a letter that started him on his long journey with the Nation of Islam. Reginald "lured" him into studying the teachings of Elijah Muhammad by telling him that if he stopped eating pork, he would become free. Above all, Malcolm wanted to be free. So, without knowing why or how it would happen, he followed Reginald's advice as a first step toward the spiritual discipline of becoming a Black Muslim.

In the teachings of the Nation of Islam, Elijah Muhammad constructed an alternative cosmology that placed black people at the center with Yacub, the black scientist who created evil white people, and used race as its central category. Malcolm likened his conversion to Islam to that of Paul on the Damascus road. This new black vision of God and creation captured Malcolm's heart and imagination and transformed his life into a spiritual odyssey. It led him to turn to God in prayer as the second step of spiritual discipline. His life as an antireligious person ended as he embraced the idea of a God who cared for the oppressed.

Black Muslim doctrine is summarized by James Fowler as follows:

> Allah is a deterministic divinity outside of history, who as an all-knowing and all powerful ruler, will impose his judgment on white devils by future intervention in history. "Allah" expresses a fatalism about the present and the future. Whoever goes against Allah's truth will be cursed in this life, and "everything that is written" according to the future is set...Human effort to bring about change (is) very secondary.[60]

After many years as a loyal zealot in the Nation of Islam, this deterministic theology would eventually prove to be constraining to Malcolm's vision of the inclusiveness of community and his emerging belief in the necessity to work for social change in history.

It is important to note that during this period Malcolm became a religious ascetic in an attempt to gain the trust and approval of Elijah Muhammad. He willingly sacrificed personal gain and materialism for the sake of the community. Malcolm tells of that period and the sacrificial behavior that would characterize the rest of his life:

> I went without a lot of sleep trying to merit his increasing evidences of trust and confidence in my efforts to help build our Nation of Islam...I had nothing that was mine but my clothes, wrist watch, and suitcase. As in the case of all the Nation's ministers, my living expenses were paid and I had some pocket money. Where once you couldn't have named anything I wouldn't have done for money, now money was the last thing to cross my mind. [61]

Malcolm adored Elijah Muhammad and, deeply grateful to Muhammad for literally saving his soul, he had faithfully and scrupulously adhered to all of the Nation's teachings. When he discovered that the Prophet lied and did not himself live up to the standards by which he held others accountable in the Nation, Malcolm was devastated. Malcolm had changed and dedicated his whole wayward life to truth, as he then understood it in the Nation. As an all-or-nothing believer, he could not bear the lies embodied in the immoral lifestyles of the Black Muslim leadership. He eventually left the Nation of Islam.

For several years before his break with the Nation, Malcolm had increasingly attracted national and international attention as a Black Muslim leader, eventually rising to become the Nation of Islam's official national spokesperson. This incited jealousy in the Muslim ranks, and in November of 1963 he was suspended by Elijah Muhammad from any public speaking for ninety days. He felt betrayed and excluded–alienated from the very movement that he had worked so hard and so sacrificially to build. This new form of being an outcast, *within* the community of the oppressed as well as *without*, precipitated the completion of his conversion process as he made an irrevocable decision in 1964 to leave the Nation of Islam.

Malcolm's Ideal of Community

In the last year of his life, in his continuing quest for truth, Malcolm made pilgrimages to Mecca and Africa and embraced orthodox Islam. The teachings of orthodoxy challenged the Yacub myth that he had, for the most part, already ceased to believe. Though there is still much controversy over precisely to what degree he rejected the Black Muslim movement, Malcolm clearly stated:

> My thinking had been opened up wide in Mecca. In the long letters I wrote to friends, I tried to convey to them my new insights into the American black man's struggle and problems, as well as the depths of my search for truth and justice. "I've had enough of someone else's propaganda," I had written to these friends. "I'm for truth, no matter who is for or against it. I'm a human being first and foremost, and as such I'm for whoever and whatever benefits humanity as a whole."[62]

He then took on the new name, El-Hajj Malik Shabazz, and worked for the rest of his short life for the ideal of community as God's truth of justice for black people in the United States, including the ignored black American under class, Africa, all people of the African diaspora, and the poor (white and black) all over the world.

Malcolm felt that there was a movement of hope among young white people for a reversal of racism.

> But as racism leads America up the suicide path, I do believe, from the experiences that I have had with them, that the whites of the younger generation, in the colleges and universities, will see the handwriting on the wall and many of them will turn to the *spiritual* path of *truth*–the *only* way left to America to ward off the disaster that racism inevitably must lead to.[63]

This new, more inclusive ideal of community and his new openness to white people and to the established Civil Rights movement caused his more militant black followers in the United States to become suspicious of him. Even months before his break with the Nation of Islam, Malcolm's speeches dealt primarily with the social problem of human rights facing the nation and the world.[64] He stated that he spoke "less and less of religion" and taught social doctrine as well as current events and politics to the Muslims.

Malcolm believed that the movement away from oppression for black people in America was to be found, first of all, in reeducation based in black history so that black people could come to understand their true identity. This, he believed, was a necessary precondition for any meaningful social action. Second, he appealed to orthodox Islam for truth, and specifically the Islamic principle of kinship, which he believed was capable of producing a society of love, humility, and kinship while affirming a broad measure of diversity in its tenets. Malcolm stated:

> America needs to understand Islam, because this is the one religion that erases from its society the race problem...I have never before seen *sincere* and *true* brotherhood practiced by all colors together, irrespective of their color.[65]

In the practical realization of his ideal of community, Islam was needed by white people even more than black people as a channel to create kinship among the races of humankind. He also believed that the major shortsightedness of black leaders in America was their lack of connection with the broader international community. Thus, the establishment of a kindred spirit in order to motivate people to build a just and harmonious global human community was a religious task. Nearing the end of his life, Malcolm proclaimed, "The *brotherhood*! The people of all races, colors, from all over the world coming together as *one*! It has proved to me the power of the One God."[66]

The bitter fight with the old Muslims persisted. Yet he never turned back. His home was bombed, and after weeks of death threats El-Hajj Malik Shabazz was murdered at the age of forty. Peter Paris writes, "Phoenix-like, he was destined to rise from ignominy to great fame."[67]

CONCLUSION

It is clear that the ideals of community in the lives of these great spiritual leaders of the African-American community and tradition were guided by an African-based African-American spirituality with a unifying concept of God, human being, and community. To a great extent the energy that sustained these individuals' ideal of community as a just and inclusive world order and the urge that drove them to seek its realization was drawn from African-American spirituality in a life-and-death conflict with the non-community of white racism. As they struggled to clarify their own identity, this spirituality led them to assume personal responsibility for the realization of community the world over.

The spiritual formation of each leader was critically informed by an African-based worldview of *relationality*, based in a unified worldview. As a result, the unified and relational basis of their spirituality, as it emerged from the teachings of the black family and the black community, continued to expand their awareness until they embraced all the earth, including all of humanity and nature (Thurman), all people of goodwill, all people of color and the poor all over the world (King), and the poor of the world community as well as the despised within the communities of the poor (Malcolm X) in a unified, relational vision of the ideal of community.

The visions of the ideal of community in the lives and practices of Thurman, King, and Malcolm X demonstrate that African-American spirituality caused the spirit of compassion of these leaders to expand rather than to constrict, and thereby it reduced their selfishness by enabling them to see commonality more than difference. In the final analysis, the "other" is no longer perceived as an alien or as an enemy to be feared, but as a sister or brother in the human family. In addition, this spirituality encouraged them to measure the value of the ideal of community from the standard of the bottom of the society rather than the top. That is, community could only be realized when the poorest of the poor were empowered to stand in equal relationship with the dominant sector of the world community. God, in this spirituality, is to be seen in the condition of suffering humanity, and therefore all effort must be expended to honor God by standing in solidarity with the poor.

Chapter 6

Black Film as Theology

In a poignant article written for *Ebony Magazine* in 1977, black historian and *Ebony* senior editor Lerone Bennett prophetically outlined "the crisis of the Black spirit" in a way that clearly reflects his understanding of good and evil as it is governed by a thorough grounding in African-American spirituality.[1] For Bennett, the problem of explaining evil does not find its locus in any of the classical notions of sin as rebellion against God in the primordial realm. Nor does he view evil as a necessary aspect of any finite order in which there are free beings. And evil is not an illusion of finite or temporal experience that does not exist from the standpoint of eternity. Bennett's short article also reveals, in a classically African-American spiritual temperament, that he does not believe there is no theoretical answer to the so-called mystery of evil and that humankind, therefore, must passively hope that all will be well.

Rather, Bennett locates the origin of evil in the greed-inspired cultural values and hostile cultural chauvinism of the Western world. This belief makes no appeal to mystery, nor does it require the explicit qualification of the omnipotence of God. Instead, it presupposes the utter freedom and responsibility of human creatures in the midst of the intrinsically evil power of a decadent culture that worships the god of materialism rather than the true God of love, justice, and compassion.

In a similar vein, Theophus H. Smith suggests that "the theme of captivity" for contemporary African Americans no longer rests around the issues of the abolition of slavery or the abolition of desegregation, as it did in the past; rather, it is bondage to "physical gratification as the purpose of life."[2] I suggest that it also includes the conscious avoidance or turning away from a spiritual heritage that identifies salvation with a just and equal social order rooted in harmony and love among all that is—heaven and earth—in history. Smith writes:

> The identification of black liberation with the material success of a
> few, physically and mentally severed from the black masses, makes

151

mockery of the unity essential for all. Accordingly, "captivity" rather than "promised land" may best represent the historical present for the two major groupings in black society: the poor and the more successful. The black poverty class is barred from a fulfilled promised land configuration...At best it has also become a partial socioeconomic reality in black experience. But the cocaptivity of the poor and of the successful to social structures that maintain their respective economic and spiritual impoverishment indicates the ambiguous, if not entirely vitiated, status of that reality.[3]

He then appeals to the rhetoric of the Black Muslims and the Black Panthers, two militant groups of the 1960s. Smith suggests that the Panthers, sophisticated in Marxist analysis, translated the Black Muslim's "white devil America" to mean "a decadent society."

African-American spirituality can in this present age address the contemporary spiritual crisis of black people in America who have become "white black people" to the extent that they are ignorant of black cultural values. This may occur through the evil of *forgetfulness,* a failure to pass on the black spiritual legacy, or through *willful neglect,* having no concern for and personal sacrificial solidarity with the "tribe" of marginalized black Americans, the poor in Africa, and the poor in the entire world order. In either instance the human community is ultimately responsible for the eroding moral and spiritual foundations of black culture. Human beings can voluntarily decline to commit themselves to its continued vitality, or they can take responsibility for its regeneration by committing themselves to its continued vitality. Bennett writes of this with great urgency:

We have come to a great fork in the road of Black destiny. We have come, by a strange and circuitous route, to a place of danger and decision which requires a mobilization of all the resources and energies of the Black community. The danger is real and pressing. For the first time in our history, the inner fortresses of the Black Spirit are giving away. For the first time in our history, we are threatened on the level of the spirit, on the level of our most precious possession, on the level of the soul. And what that means is that we are threatened today in this country as we have never been threatened before. A Great Black Depression and policies of malign neglect are eroding the material foundations of our communities, and the fallout from this is eroding the moral and spiritual foundations of Black culture. The signs of crisis are everywhere...To come right out with it, *we are losing a whole generation of people.* And this fact, which is cultural, political and economic at the same time, constitutes the gravest challenge we have faced in this country since the end of slavery.[4]

One may be certain that the African ancestors felt a similar sense of urgency and fear for the survival of the Beloved Community as they were transported in the holds of slave ships across the Middle Passage to provide slave labor for a slovenly and greedy culture.

Lerone Bennett *does not see black people as victims.* He understands the destiny of black people as essentially a matter in the hands of God and black people. Black people must be willing to heed God's summons to true community by making the decision to turn away from the values of a decadent society and toward compassion for and solidarity with the despised poor. They must maintain allegiance to a spiritual and cultural heritage that is, itself, the legacy of the poorest of the poor—those African people carried off from their homes to slavery in a foreign land. It is to this extent the people will be saved.

This notion of salvation proposes that white racism does not predetermine the ultimate condition of one's black soul or the soul of the black community. What determines it is one's own personal decision to either live out or to reject personal sacrifice for the sake of the despised poor. This "shape" of the contemporary African spirit of resistance within African-American spirituality is inspired by the continual struggle of an oppressed people to be free from the domination and control of captivity. This theme of turning away from the decadence of Western cultural values and returning toward the communal values of the African spiritual heritage in order to be "saved" is to be found, with astonishing regularity, in the work of many leading and prophetic contemporary black filmmakers.

EVIL AND SALVATION IN CONTEMPORARY BLACK FILM

Three contemporary black films reveal contemporary black understandings of evil and salvation that are governed by African-American spirituality: *Sankofa,* by Haile Gerima; *Daughters of the Dust,* by Julie Dash; and *The Piano Lesson,* by Pulitzer prize-winning playwright August Wilson. All of these films were written and/or produced by black artists in the 1990s and contain the spirit of "truth" or the voice of God as it is currently revealed with remarkable spiritual acumen and continuity. They also highlight the African worldview of a community of contemporary black artists both nationally and internationally.

These were all, at some point, underground films. The artists were not able to get them mass-produced or distributed in theaters in America and had to struggle to find the resources to finance these projects themselves. Yet a huge number of black people managed to find out about them through word of mouth, because there were no budgets for advertising, and sought out the handful of theaters where they were shown for very short runs. Julie Dash's film was finally shown on some public television stations.

Sankofa

The film *Sankofa,* written, produced, and directed by an Ethiopian filmmaker, is set in the eighteenth-century antebellum American South during the beginning period of the enslavement. It clearly reveals the contemporary African artist's crucial concern with the plight and history of African Americans and black people who were enslaved by the Western world during the African diaspora.

Gerima views history in a counterclockwise, circular worldview. The film begins in present-day Africa at the now famous tourist site of the former British governor's castle in Sierra Leone on the shore of the Atlantic Ocean. This was where slaves were held in massive, underground dungeons, sometimes for over a year, before being taken out at night and transported to be sold in the slave ports of the New World. An African-American woman, Mona, who is a high-fashion model, is being photographed in front of the castle by a white male photographer. As she postures for the camera, the photographer encourages her by saying, "That's it, Mona! More sex! That's it, baby!" She is wearing a red-blonde wig, a heavy gold necklace, a revealing tiger print bathing suit, six-inch long plastic fingernails, and very heavy make-up. She laughs and cavorts before the camera in sexually provocative poses.

An elderly African man, Sankofa, who is a priest, *griot,* and the self-appointed guardian of the castle, confronts Mona as she dances around for the photographer's camera. As he silently stares at her, she hides behind the photographer. Sankofa speaks commandingly to her in the African language of Akan (subtitles translate what he is saying) and rebukes and admonishes her: "Back to your past! Return to your source!...This is holy ground. It is special ground...Blood was spilled here!" The word *sankofa* is Akan for "one must return to the past in order to move forward." Sankofa carries a staff with the Ashanti bird symbol (head facing backward, feet facing forward) carved on the top. Sternly he rebukes Mona's embodiment of Western decadence and materialistic values as he continues to stare unblinkingly into her eyes. His look compels and "conjures" her to look into the dark heart of America's false materialistic promises.

The film's narrator chants a powerful, seductive prose poem in the voice-over: "Spirit of the dead, rise up! Lingering spirit of the dead, rise up and possess your bird of passage...Step out and tell your story! Step out and tell your story! Spirit of the dead, rise up and possess your bird of passage! Spirit of the dead, rise up!" Sankofa begins rapidly to beat a ceremonial drum, which symbolically possesses the power to call up the ancestors, and stares out over the ocean toward the West. A huge buzzard (the symbol of the traitor or the African slave trade) flies over the ocean to the Western world.

The scene shifts, and Mona is suddenly transported underground (the symbol of the unconscious racial memory) to the eighteenth-century and the slave dungeons. In the dark recesses of the dungeons are hundreds of slaves chained around the neck to each other. White slavers approach her and hold her down. She screams, "I am not an African! I am an American! I'm not an African!" She has forgotten who she is. Sankofa has sent her back to the memory of the past and the ancestors, the living dead, so that she can recall, remember, and remold her identity. The white slavers tear off her modern clothing and brand her as a slave. She is chained in a coffle with the others. The buzzard flies over the ocean to America. In the next scene Mona is Shola, a house slave on an American plantation. In the background is the haunting sound of Negro spirituals and the lash.

Shola's story is the story of the horror of American slavery and her struggle to redefine her identity and values in the light of her people's history of cruel bondage and oppression. She begins as a house slave, baptized into Christianity and believing that everything African is "heathen" and evil. But through her love for the man Shango (the name of the high African God), who was sent to the plantation from Jamaica, and the pain and anger caused by her repeated brutal rape by the slave owner, she becomes a rebel insurrectionist. She embraces an African-based identity and becomes an initiate in the slaves' secret society.

Haile Gerima combines African-American and Jamaican slave history in the telling of his story. Shola participates in a slave uprising that is fomented by a secret society reminiscent of the famous Jamaican Maroons. Maroons were slaves who escaped from the lowland plantations of the Jamaican cane fields and lived in freedom in the hills. Periodically they would raid the plantations and bring more slaves to hide out in the freedom of the hills, where the white people could not find them.

Crucial to the story's development is Nunu, a pure African woman who is Akan. Nunu is the wise and gentle mother-figure and spiritual leader of the plantation's slave community. Filled with a recent African memory that gives her a healthy and genuine sense of identity, she is the community's midwife, healer, priestess, and rebel leader. As a result of being raped on the slave ship from Africa by an overseer, fourteen-year-old Nunu gives birth to her mulatto son, Joe.

Joe is Gerima's visually striking symbol of the Africans of the diaspora, the mulattos who are of mixed racial, religious and cultural heritage. He is utterly confused. To Nunu's horror, Joe becomes a cruel headman on the plantation, one who carries out the biddings of the slave owner. A traitor to the slave community, he is feared and despised. Joe is baptized and taught by the plantation's Catholic priest, Father Raphael, to regard Africa and African beliefs as evil and "of the devil." He encourages Joe to denounce his own black mother and the values of his ancestors and worship at the altar of the plantation chapel that is dominated by a huge Italian Renaissance painting of a white madonna and child. Father Raphael tells blue-eyed, red-haired, yellow-skinned Joe, "She is your mother! She is pure!" He also tells Joe that his own dark black African mother Nunu is the devil and that Joe is "different" from "these other heathens." Joe, in his confusion and fear of all things African, murders gentle and loving Nunu because she rips a Catholic medal of one of the saints from around his neck and because he believes she has fed him some food that poisoned him. Nunu, who loves her mixed-up child, believes that he will be saved and protected only by the God of Africa—not the god of European-Christianity.

When Joe realizes that he has murdered his own mother, in a rage of fear, grief, and confusion with profound sorrow and repentance he carries her lifeless body to the altar of the chapel and lays her there on the communion table, under the picture of the white madonna and child. Father Raphael confronts him, saying, "What in Christ's name is going on here? Take that heathen woman out of this sanctuary!" Instead, Joe falls to his knees and begins to pray before the table and Nunu's lifeless body. Father Raphel shouts angrily, "You are just like the rest of these niggers. You have no soul!"

Joe shouts back at him, "You are going to have to stop disrespecting this woman! She is my mother. Her name is Afriya (Nunu's African name). She has been dragged through the mud and she has suffered for everybody! Now *ain't* she a saint!" In this declaration Joe acknowledges that salvation comes from the story of the suffering, oppressed, abused, and lied-about black woman, and that Africa is the collective "saint" of the world. He is no longer confused. He turns away from the white god of European-Christianity (the symbol of the Catholic church) and toward Africa.

When the priest tries forcibly to remove Nunu from the altar, Joe strangles the priest to death and burns down the chapel with the priest, Nunu, and himself inside. The secret society slaves revolt and burn down the plantation. Shola kills the slave master when he tries to rape her again.

Finally, the scene shifts once more as the buzzard flies over the ocean away from the American plantation and toward Africa and the slave castle. Shola again becomes the contemporary Mona. But her face is clean and without make-up. Without her long, plastic fingernails, wig, and gold jewelry, she is dressed in modest African clothing. Sankofa furiously beats the ceremonial drum. In the final scene Mona and black people of all colors ranging from yellow to brown to black, dressed in African clothing, and the smiling Nunu (alive and risen from the fire as a symbol of memory and the phoenix-like nature of African-American spirituality) sit in a circle around the drummer as they stare out over the water to the West. The narrator chants the same prose poem as at the film's beginning, "Spirit of the dead, rise up! Lingering spirit of the dead, rise up and possess your bird of passage! Step out and tell your story! Step out and tell your story!...Spirit of the dead, rise up!"

In this film Gerima clearly uses art to communicate the truth that evil is forgetting the African past and adopting the decadent Western values of greed and materialism. Mona is "saved" by going back in black history to the story of her ancestors and rejecting white religion and cultural values. In going backward, she goes forward into the present of a healthy African-based identity. She is able to join in the eternal "circle of the saints" as they recall, remember, and remold the story of the enslaved Africans and call forth to others the spiritual challenge to remember. In many ways Gerima's vision of community is the most radical contemporary call for people of African descent to reject and renounce completely European-Christianity and embrace African traditional values. His vision transcends black nationalism. In *Sankofa* he is not asking for a "back to Africa" movement, as did Marcus Garvey and others. Instead, he is advocating a return to the spirit of African cultural values rooted in community rather than materialism.

Daughters of the Dust

Julie Dash is African American, originally of the Gullah people of St. Helena Island. Her film is set in the Middle Period of African-American history, 1902, when the Peazant family, Gullah people from the imaginary Ibo Island patterned after the Georgia and South Carolina seacoast islands, are on the eve of their family's migration North to look for the Promised Land. They are participants in America's extraordinary internal black diaspora, which led black people into both urban disintegration and rural poverty.

Dash's film, like Gerima's, revolves around the central concern of retaining black memory. Nana Peazant, an "old soul" and the great-grandmother and oldest living elder of the family, is against her family's migration away from Ibo Island. She is afraid that in the North they will forget their history and thereby lose their true identity. Dash places the majority of Nana Peazant's scenes in the graveyard as she tends the graves of deceased family members. Nana Peazant says, "It's up to the livin' to keep up with the dead...respect your elders, respect your family, respect your ancestors...Let 'em guide you. You need their strength."

She always carries with her a small tin container filled with "scraps of memories." Inside is a lock of her mother's hair, which her mother gave her before she was sold away in slavery. It also contains other precious personal objects that remind her of family members who have passed on. Nana Peazant's hands are permanently stained blue from having worked as a slave dying cloth from the indigo plants on the plantation. All of the women in the film wear white except Nana Peazant. An elder from slavery times, she wears an indigo-colored dress that symbolizes the brutal labor of her generation. Nana Peazant cautions her descendants, "Those eighteenth-century Africans, the old souls, they watch us, they keep us...There must be a *connection*, a bond between those what are going North and those what are here and those across the sea."

In order to stave off the threat she perceives to her family, Nana Peazant begins to call forth her great-great-grandchild to be born. In traditional black belief the grandmother and grandfather are close to the grandchild. Dash uses the character of the unborn child to symbolize this circular worldview. The film's narrator is this unborn child, who is able to bridge time and generations. In one scene she enters the past and sees the people in slavery dyeing cloth in huge vats of indigo. Then she enters her future and sees her father agonizing over her mother's rape as he wonders if she belongs to him. She enters her mother's body when she is visiting the family graveyard. One of the film's characters, Viola, steeped in black belief, says that the children and the old souls are the most important members of the family.

Dash employs three characters in her film to symbolize the three major strands of black forgetfulness that threaten the life and vigor of the black community. Hagar, an educated woman who has married into the family, and Viola, a Peazant from birth who left for the mainland and became educated, are both Christian and oppose Nana Peazant's "old, heathen ways." Hagar says of the old ways of the "freshwater Africans": "Hoodoo mess! Who do it dis' way don't have *nothin'*today! I'm an educated person and I'm tired of those old stories! They ain't got no religion in them...I don't want my daughters even to hear all that mess!"

Ignorant of traditional black culture and spirituality, she mistakenly believes Nana Peazant worships the things in the tin container. She believes the old ways have kept them poor and the new way of life in the North, the way of the people of the white mainland, will give them material prosperity. Hagar represents the strand of forgetfulness that leads people to worship at the altar of the god of materialism. At bottom, she is angry with black culture and spirituality. She believes it is ineffectual pagan superstition and inferior to the culture of a people who appear to own everything. Haughty, arrogant, and extremely bitter, Hagar is outwardly disrespectful toward Nana Peazant.

Viola, on the other hand, has gone to the mainland and sincerely been converted to European-Christianity. She starts to believe in European-Christian notions of heaven and hell as somewhere else and sometime else. Nana Peazant does not believe in otherworldly notions of heaven and hell. She believes in the teachings of the old souls who survived and then passed on a legacy to their children as a heritage of survival. When Viola mentions heaven to her, she dismisses her theology and says, "No I ain't gon' be watchin' from no heaven as long as soil be here for me planting." At one point Viola bursts into tears and exclaims in utter frustration to the great-grandmother whom she dearly loves but whom she cannot convince, "Old folks supposed to die and go to heaven! It ain't right!" Viola believes that traditional black spirituality cannot get her into heaven.

Eli, Nana Peazant's great-grandson, is also against the old ways and believes they are ineffectual "foolishness." His beloved wife, Eula, was raped by a white man, and he is hurt and angry because he believes the old ways cannot protect them from the white man. In a fairly typical African-American male point of view, he judges the value of things against the white man. In a strange way his standard of maleness is a Western standard of the male he most resents—the white man. Unable to judge the efficacy and value of black belief in and of itself, he determines its value from the starting point of white racism.

Eli sees Eula as "his" and the white man who raped her as taking what belongs to him. Nana Peazant has to remind him, "Eula don't belong to you. She marry you." In one moving scene, out of hurt and wounded male pride, disillusionment and anger, he smashes all of the glass bottles on the family "bottle tree."

Bottle trees are an African retention in African-American culture. They are still visible today in the Deep South. Elderly black people place pretty colored-glass bottles on tree branches until the tree is filled with sparkling multicolored bottles instead of leaves. The glass bottles are reminders of people who have passed on. They are understood as protection—not in the sense that the bottles themselves have any power to protect—because the memories of the old ones can help one remember the history and wisdom needed for survival.

The three strands of forgetfulness symbolized by these three characters ultimately revolve around the issues of protection, survival, and security of the African-American community. Hagar believes that money will protect her family. Viola believes that European-Christianity will protect her soul. Eli believes that brute force will protect his family. Of the three strands of forgetfulness, Hagar's materialism is the most virulent. Viola and Eli still love and respect Nana Peazant, even though they believe she is outdated and misguided. Hagar, however, is hostile and antagonistic, and Nana Peazant represents to her a threat to upward mobility.

In the film's final scene the entire family gathers on the beach before they board the small boats that will take them to the mainland on the first leg of their long journey North. They all pay homage to Nana Peazant, who will remain behind. Nana Peazant cautions them to appeal to the memories and recollections "we carry inside of we," the memories of the "old souls," the "old Africans." She advises her family, "Let them fill your head with wisdom not of this time…Celebrate our ways." She then ties roots and herbs over the top of a Bible and stands in front of her gathered family. She asks each one to kiss the Bible. In placing the two together, Dash symbolizes her vision of the salvation or the future strength of black culture–the joining together of the memory of the old ways and black Christianity. Only Hagar, consumed by materialism, refuses to kiss the Bible. She leaves the gathering, walking away in a huff. Viola bursts out crying, but she kisses it out of a profound respect for the elder that is more deeply ingrained than any imported religion. Eli is so moved that he decides to remain on Ibo Island with his family. His wife, Eula, is in apprenticeship to become the next generation's Nana Peazant.

The Piano Lesson

August Wilson's film, based on his play, takes place in the black community of Pittsburgh in 1955. Like the films of Gerima and Dash, the story has a circular, counterclockwise worldview and focuses on the concern for black memory as the way of survival for the black community.

The film opens as Boy Willie and his friend Lymon drive up from Sunflower County, Mississippi (Fannie Lou Hamer's home), with a truckload of watermelons. Boy Willie plans to sell the watermelons and his family's piano up North to raise a thousand dollars to buy cotton land from a white man in Sunflower County named James Sutter. Boy Willie is a sharecropper, as his family has been before him from after the Emancipation from slavery until the present day. He wants to own his own land. Boy Willie feels that the measure of a man lies in how much he owns. Like Eli and Hagar in *Daughters of the Dust,* he has adopted white values.

The family piano is in the home of his sister Berniece and his Uncle Doaker. Unwilling to sell the piano, Berniece and Doaker pull out guns and threaten to shoot Boy Willie if he tries to take it out of their house. They remind him that the piano represents the family history and heritage. Berniece tells Boy Willie, "Mama Ola polished this piano for seventeen years...She rubbed and cleaned and polished and prayed over it...She rubbed her blood and tears into this piano!...I can still hear her now saying, 'Play somethin' for me, Berniece. Won't you play somethin' for me, Berniece?'"

Berniece cannot convince Boy Willie of the piano's worth as a symbol of their ancestors and their family heritage. She says she has not played the piano in seven years: "I don't want to play on that piano because I don't want to wake them spirits." Boy Willie says he would understand if she gave piano lessons and needed the piano to make a living, but since it isn't bringing in any money, he is going to sell it. He cannot understand value except in dollars and cents.

So Uncle Doaker, African-*griot* style, tries to help Boy Willie understand why Berniece says there is not enough money in the world to pay the piano's worth. He recites the family's entire history as it is symbolized by the piano. The piano's history goes back to Robert Sutter (the present James Sutter's grandfather). Miss Ophelia, old Sutter's wife, wanted a piano. Old Sutter could not afford one, so he gave Mr. Nolander, the piano's original owner, one and one-half slaves for the piano. These slaves were Doaker's grandmother, Mama Berniece, and his father, Papa Boy Willie. After they were sold, they never saw their family again.

After some time passed, Miss Ophelia began to miss her slaves and wanted them back. Nolander refused to return them. Miss Ophelia took to her bed because she could not have what she wanted. Old Sutter asked Doaker's grandfather, Boy Charles, to carve pictures of Mama Berniece and Papa Boy Willie on the piano for Miss Ophelia. Not only did Boy Charles carve their likenesses on the piano, but, much to Old Sutter's anger and dismay, he also carved pictures–African-*griot* style– of *all* of his family's marriages, births, funerals, the selling of his wife and son, in fact, the whole family history. Ophelia was happy with the piano and played on it until the day she died.

On July 4, 1911, Boy Charles decided to set the piano free from Old Sutter because he felt it rightfully belonged to his family. After all, his wife and son were sold to buy it and he had carved the family history on it. While the Sutters were out, he stole the piano and hid it at his mother-in-law's house. Sutter became enraged when he found that it was gone and threatened to kill Boy Charles. Boy Charles hid in the boxcar of the #357 train (black people called it "the yellow dog" because the boxcars were painted yellow and it seemed to howl like a dog at night when the train's whistle blew) as he tried to flee town. Sutter found him and burned the boxcar to the ground with Boy Charles and a few hoboes still inside. From then on, black people called the train "The Ghost of the Yellow Dog." Shortly thereafter, Sutter fell down his well and died, and people said the "ghosts of the yellow dog killed him."

Boy Willie is still not convinced. He and Berniece begin to argue. All of a sudden they feel a presence in the house in the form of a rush of wind. Berniece screams. She says it is James Sutter's ghost upstairs in her house. Wilson uses the symbol of the ghost, familiar to black culture, to represent the way evil white materialistic values began to "haunt" their home when Boy Willie comes up from Sunflower County seeking to sell what money cannot buy—the family's memory.

Berniece asked Reverend Avery, her black pastor, to come and bless the house so that James Sutter's ghost will leave. Boy Willie says, "Avery ain't got no power to do nothin'." When Avery—saying prayers, sprinkling blessed water, and reading the Bible as he yells, "Sutter get out!"— tries to exorcise Sutter's ghost, he is almost killed. Sutter's ghost becomes more ferocious and attacks Reverend Avery.

Wilson used this scene to symbolize Christianity and the contemporary black church's ineffectiveness to protect black people or free them from white racism. For one thing, Reverend Avery is only interested in getting money to expand his church building. He is not against Berniece selling the piano and donating the money to the church. For another, he "toms" every day on his job as an elevator "boy," saying, "Yes, Suh!" and "Good morning, Suh!" to white men as he runs the elevator in their downtown office building. He could not obtain any other job. In the end, Reverend Avery (representing the contemporary black church) has no power to kill Sutter's ghost, because he too is basically interested in money.

At that point Boy Willie runs upstairs and tries to expel Sutter's ghost by brute force. The ghost starts killing him. Wilson makes it clear in this scene that violence cannot conquer white racism either. In desperation to save her brother, Berniece runs to the piano that she has not touched in seven years and begins to play. As she plays, she cries out, "I want you to help me! Mama Ola, Mama Berniece, Papa Charles, help me!" Sutter's ghost departs, peace and quiet return to the family, and Boy Willie is saved.

Boy Willie is saved by recognizing that his family history is more valuable than money and what it can purchase. In the end he finally understands and returns to Sunflower County without the piano. In the final scene Berniece is teaching her little daughter, Maretha, how to play the piano. The family's history is passed on to yet another generation, and the entire family is happy, reconciled and saved from the threat of racial extinction. Once again, salvation lies in preserving racial memory and in instilling a value system based on black culture.

CONCLUSION

Lerone Bennett advised the African-American community to resist "the assault on Black culture" and the black spirit by maintaining traditional black values that are not based on materialism:

> Can you believe it? There was a time in this country when you had to whip Black children to make them leave school...And one of the greatest crimes of this guilty country was the prolonged and systematic destruction of Black America's deep-seated love of learning and letters. This passionate and feverish pursuit of excellence continued in Black America for three or four generations. Old men and women sacrificed and worked in white folks' kitchens and in ditches and dives, they cleaned spittoons and outhouses, they bowed and scraped, they said "yes sir" "no ma'am" so their children would have a chance at the excellence denied them by American law and practice. And the children honored their mothers and fathers by studying day and night while holding two or three jobs on the side...[the] change was linked to fundamental changes in the material life of the people.[5]

Bennett suggests that black people return to "a great and holy beginning" by renewing black values. This involves caring as a community about the community's poor children. He writes, "If we cared, we would change the way they live by any means necessary." He states this as the "first precondition" for a revival of the spirit of excellence along with a "renewal of the values and structures of black America." He also maintains that the black community must "revive the spirit" of our fathers and mothers, where "*all* fathers and *all* mothers assumed responsibility for *all* children, and *all* mothers and *all* fathers had a right and a duty to exercise parental prerogatives whenever and wherever they saw black children getting out of line." There must be a "confrontation of love" with black youth on the part of responsible black adults who earned the right to confront them. Finally, there must be "the reeducation of black and white adults" to pursue excellence in struggle and excellence in life.[6]

And one other thing must happen. Contemporary African Americans must "beg the pardon" of the ancestors for the years of forgetfulness and neglect of black history, values, and cultural traditions undergirded by African-American spirituality. If the black community is to survive with a healthy identity, African Americans can no longer be ignorant of or afraid to bless their beginnings by recalling, remembering, and remolding their history as a way of begging the pardon of

all of the forgotten ones who have gone before. Jamaican-American
writer Paule Marshall symbolically describes the "beg pardon":

> Outside their kneeling circle the other guests had fallen silent. All
> movement had ceased in the yard. And in the silence, the stillness,
> Lebert Joseph slowly opened his arms, raised his tremulous head
> to the sky and, abruptly, like a shock wave on the air: *"Pa'doné*
> *mwê...! Si mwê mérite/Pini mwê/Si mwê ba mérite/Pa'doné mwê..."*–
> singing in his quavering yet piercing falsetto. "Is the 'Beg Pardon,'"
> Milda whispered and bowed her head...Arms opened, faces lifted
> to the darkness, the small band of supplicants endlessly repeated
> the few lines that comprised the Beg Pardon, pleading and peti-
> tioning not only for themselves and for the friends and neighbors
> present in the yard, but for all their far-flung kin as well–the sons
> and daughters, grands and great-grands in Trinidad, Toronto, New
> York, London... *"When you see me down on my knees...is not just for me*
> *one...Oh, no! Is for tout moun'."* And his little truncated arms had
> opened in a gesture wide enough to take in the world.[7]

Chapter 7

African-American Spirituality—A Definition

African-American spirituality can be defined from two key characteristics: (1) its essential nature as cultural resilience or the ability to bounce or spring back into shape or position after being stretched, bent, or compressed by cultural oppression; and (2) its "effects" or movement as it defines African-American values and cultural expression in the people's quest for identity and the building of community. These two characteristics or aspects of African-American spirituality are related to each other in the same way that ripples are related to the ocean. If a rock is thrown into the still waters of the ocean, the aspect or appearance of the water alters and we see ripples. When the "rock" of American racism encountered African-American spirituality in the form of the people's African legacy, it produced "ripples" in this resilient spirituality in its movement as the guiding and sustaining force beneath the people's formation of African-American religion, philosophy, theology, morals, and values. This formation governed the struggle for the people to establish their own sense of identity, their own culture, and their right to build and live in harmony in their own vision and ideal of community.

AFRICAN-AMERICAN SPIRITUALITY
AS CULTURAL RESILIENCE

African-American spirituality is defined in terms of its essence as its being or power independent of its existence, what Du Bois termed a "strife" or "warring" on both the physical and metaphysical planes experienced by African Americans in the conflict between racism in the outer world and a prior inner disposition, influenced by African-based values, that produced a fundamental tension at the heart of the African-American experience. In order to address this tension, the Africans and their descendants embraced a form of spirituality that bridged both the African heritage and the African-American experience. It was the underlying and guiding force that enabled the people to be resilient, to "spring back into shape" with courage and dignity in the face of the intense cultural oppression experienced during four hundred years of white racism. African-American spirituality, in this sense guided the people toward survival and the freedom of self-determination.

African-American spirituality as cultural resilience was operative first of all as *freedom*. While Africans in America and their descendants were not permitted to choose the frame of their destiny—whether to come to North America—they did choose the content of their destiny. What they chose to put into it, first and foremost, was their own spirituality. This spirituality, in turn, was the source of their resilience in their continual struggle for the freedom of self-determination. At its very heart, African-American spirituality is about freedom in the sense of the Yoruba concept of *ashe*, the power to make things happen through human choice. This freedom displayed itself in many ways.

First, African-American spirituality gave black people *the ability to transcend* the limitations imposed by racism. The central metaphor for this spiritual transcendence was the folktale of the flying Africans. Although constrained in almost every way, the enslaved people and their descendants did have the power to choose among alternative possibilities of action. They chose their own worship and ritual forms (such as the ring shout and the black alternative tradition), which were the religious antecedents of what C. Eric Lincoln called the "alert" black church. This church, derived from the legacy of Africa by way of slave religion, chose to interpret the Bible in its own way, celebrate God's goodness in its own way, sing and preach in its own way, and form its own values in its own way. The choice of these worship forms gave the people the strength they needed when the black church called for them to participate in the struggle for freedom from racism.

The enslaved and their descendants also chose the freedom to make decisions about who they were in accordance with the inner motives and ideals of black people. African-American spirituality helped black people define themselves as the antithesis of the false identity ascribed to them by white racism. Nancy Ambrose, Howard Thurman's grandmother, said that the slave preacher told them, "You are not slaves! You are not niggers! You are God's children!"

Second, African-American spirituality may be defined in its essential nature as cultural resilience as *the triumph of good—as it is occasioned by purpose and forgiveness—in the face of overwhelming evil.* The life of six-year-old Ruby Bridges illustrates this definition, as do the lives of any of the people discussed throughout this book.

Dr. Robert Coles said that he was constantly mystified by the *source* of the child's strength, dignity, and courage in the face of incredible hatred and danger embodied in the white mob waiting for her each day outside of the Frantz Elementary School. He was baffled by how such a young and "tiny" person could endure in the face of such cruel, vicious, and extreme hatred. "All this time I wondered what makes her so strong."[1] After many sessions of therapy he came to this important conclusion:

And so I learned that a family and a child under great stress and fear show exquisite dignity and courage because of their moral and religious values and because they had a definite purpose in what they were trying to accomplish. This purpose made them resilient. I couldn't figure out the *source* of this resilience because I had only worked with well-to-do children who really had nothing to work hard for; no reason driving them to accomplish anything. So now I see that the issue is not stress; but stress for what purpose? Having something to believe in protected Ruby from psychiatric symptoms and gave her a dignity and strength that is utterly remarkable.[2]

The source of Ruby's endurance and the bedrock of her hold on sanity was African-American spirituality and what it taught her, through her family, church, and community, to believe in. The purpose of her young life at that moment in history was self-sacrifice in service to her community. This identical spiritual perception informed and sustained the self-sacrificial life service of Tubman, Edmondson, Hamer, Thurman, King, and Malcolm X.

Not only did African-American spirituality allow these individuals to live a life of sacrifice for the sake of the community, with a strong sense of purpose, but it also made endurance possible through the power of forgiveness. This was revealed clearly in Ruby Bridges. In a particularly revealing therapy session, after watching Ruby turn around one day and appear to be speaking to the angry mob, Dr. Coles asked her, "What did you say to those people?" Ruby replied that she had been praying for them.

In order to understand the possibility of the power of forgiveness in such a young child, we must turn to the African unified worldview described earlier. Ruby's spirituality appears to have been rooted in a radical identification with God that did not separate God's experience from her own experience or God's presence from her own presence. This intimate, unified experience of God by the individual in service to the greater good of the community shows African-American spirituality as a resilience set in motion in the form of forgiveness.

Such capacity to forgive is made possible through the African-American religious belief in a circular, moral, and just universe. Dr. Coles asked Ruby what she did at school when a little white boy in her class persecuted her because of her race. She calmly said, "I used to do bad things. I heard at church that when someone does something bad, God makes that bad thing come back to them. I don't do bad things anymore." Fannie Lou Hamer expressed this identical religious belief after being horribly beaten in jail for helping to organize black people to vote. Malcolm X also expressed this spiritual sensibility when he said of America, after a period of great national grief and sorrow, "The chickens have come home to roost." African-American spirituality is not just the belief that "you reap whatever you sow" (Gal 6:7); rather, it is the action, informed by that belief, of the resilience of good in the face of overwhelming evil. Such resilience, or ability to forgive, is made possible because the individual, in radical identification of the experience of persecution stemming from being hated and misunderstood as simultaneously being God's experience, "steps back" from the injustice and pain of the experience and lets God deal with it. This "stepping back"–both emotionally and physically–and allowing forgiveness to take place is part of African-American spirituality. Its effect may be described as a refraining from returning in kind malevolence directed toward the undeserving. Thus, in African-American spirituality, the proper response to human suffering caused by injustice is to forgive; one "steps back" from evil by placing it within the realm of "God's business." In the face of blatant injustice black people often say, "I'll let God take care of it." To strike out against the innocent (those mistreated because of their race) is to strike out against God; therefore, God will "take care of it." In other words, God has created the universe in such a way that what a people do, for good or for evil, will return to them.

The other side of the coin is the belief that evil actions, in the same way, are perceived as intimately bound up in the spiritual realm as well as the material realm. The material and the spiritual, again, are not separate. Ruby's statement, and the statements of others described herein, reveal this belief. African-Americans believe that if people do evil things, evil returns to them. In African-American spirituality human action is believed to set in motion the circular, moral order of God's universe that responds, in like manner, to human choice—whether for good or for evil—as chosen by human beings. If human beings choose the evil of non-community, it will return to them and in the end they will suffer. If, on the other hand, they choose the good of community, it will return to them and they and the community will thrive.

Dr. Coles felt that the resilience or endurance and transcendence of racism by Ruby Bridges came about only because of the sense of purpose and accomplishment that was actualized in her experience of oppression. In other words, he had not experienced this same kind of resilience in his work with children of more prosperous lifestyles. African-American spirituality, though not identical with its context, is developed within the social context of the African-American experience of racial and cultural oppression. In this sense cultural resilience may be further defined as the growth of the human person's capacity for good that emerges from the tension between non-community and the struggle for community. It is like the spark of fire that results from the friction of sticks being rubbed together or a match being struck against a hard surface. The fire is neither the sticks nor the match nor the hard surface, but rather what emerges as a result of their interaction or conflict.

In conclusion, the spiritual origins of the African-American community closely resemble the traditional African worldview, where no event is seen to be without a spiritual/metaphysical cause. The earth is viewed as an essentially mysterious place ruled by spiritual forces of good and evil rooted in humans' choice either to remember, recall, and remold, or to neglect through forgetfulness their spiritual heritage. This heritage calls them to change from a way of being in the world characterized by radical selfishness to a way of being in the world characterized by radical compassion. It also calls them to protest societal values and norms that prohibit the possibility of the realization of community. African-American spirituality, in its essence, is the resilience of spirit that makes this conversion possible. It is this conversion that has helped black people to survive with sustained dignity, courage, and sanity throughout long years of perpetual racial and cultural assault.

THE EFFECTS OF AFRICAN-AMERICAN SPIRITUALITY

African-American spirituality may also be defined in terms of its effects on African-American culture. These effects are interwoven and dispersed throughout African-American philosophy, religion, theology, and morality—the values that governed the people's struggle for the freedom to establish their own sense of identity, their own culture, and their right to build and live in harmony with their own vision and ideal of community.

The Central Tenets of Black Theology

The following theological premises stem from the African legacy of a unified worldview:

God is the beginning of everything, radically related to everything, and binds everything together. Therefore,

1. The universe—with God as the beginning, and unendingly and indissolubly connected—is profoundly religious.

2. The ordinary and the extraordinary are linked as one; heaven and earth are not separate.

3. The universe is circular and moral, and what one does returns to one because God is not ignorant of the behavior of human beings. There will be a day of reckoning because God desires fair play, freedom, and forgiveness among human beings.

4. Time is a circle or a continuity without discrete moments; the past continually and eternally speaks to and either wreaks havoc in or empowers both the present and the future.

These central theological premises, in turn, informed African-American philosophy.

The African-American Philosophy of Life

The African-American philosophy of life is based on the community as expressed in the African-based philosophical tenet, I am because we are. This tenet, in turn, informs the African-American view of community, which is similar to the African view of community.

1. As in African belief, God is the most senior member of the community and guardian of the community.

2. God is radically in community through the concept of the family and the interrelated circle of God and the ancestors.

3. The community comprises the living and those who are dead. The past generations who are in the spirit world are ancestors of the individual and the individual is linked to all of them in a shared lineage.

4. The community is hierarchical from the oldest to the youngest. Therefore, elders are to be respected, and aging parents must be cared for by the family.

5. There is a special bond between grandparents (particularly grandmothers) and grandchildren.

6. Marriage is crucially important because it is the "meeting point" of the three layers of life: the departed, the living, and those to be born.

This conception of community then leads to a fundamentally African-based value system.

The Community's Morals and Values

1. Parents are obligated to care for and nurture their children. Husbands and wives are obligated to be responsible for each other (family morals as personal morals).

2. All are obligated to help to sustain the well-being of the community through service to the community by observing its morals and values (community morals as social morals).

3. All are obligated to be compassionate toward the poor. It is believed that God punishes those who break these moral laws. The end result of all of the above is a spiritually based culture highly invested in the moral domain by ideals of love, peace, justice, goodness, and optimism because God–in a circular fashion–is radically related to and cares about the community and all of Creation (morals of hospitality).

The African-American community expresses itself spiritually and religiously through a basically collective self-understanding that values and evaluates everything in terms of its capability to inspire loyalty to the community's primary concern of survival with human dignity and self-determination. African-American spirituality is the foundation of the embodied soul's ability to be centered or anchored in God and then stand for God in the community. When the individual stands in community, he or she simultaneously stands in the presence of the Source of ultimate meaning.

CONCLUSION

One late summer morning, I looked out from my podium at expectant young faces in a lecture hall at Spelman College. In characteristic fashion, in the first lecture of the new semester I informed the students that we would look at our past in slavery in order to chart the path for their future in freedom. In the corridor after class I overheard one of my brightest students, a religion major from Morehouse College, say, "Why does Dr. Bridges always talk about those old people? They were *slaves*." I am sure they all wondered this but were far too respectful to ask a white-haired, middle-aged professor why she was so passionate about "old-timey stuff." I simply smiled. My student neither realized the enormity of his question nor the vast "new-old" world I was obliged to open up to answer it. That class and subsequent classes on African-American spirituality grew to swell the classroom. Students filled the seats, lined the walls, and sat on the floor. They came to hear the simple stories of how God brought us through as a spiritual people.

Students enrolled in those classes, they brought friends along from other classes, and church members and others trekked with me to the Gullah Festival held every November for the celebration of Heritage Days on St. Helena Island. During the festival they sat in the island churches and heard elderly deacons lead the congregation in the singing of spirituals. They listened carefully as island elders spoke of the history of the illustrious dead in the island graveyard. They heard the history of the island's first black school, begun in one of the churches during slavery and continued throughout segregation. They wandered the back roads until they found Dr. Buzzard's trailer, hoping he would give them advice. At night they danced and listened to music at a huge, outdoor party given by the community as they stuffed themselves on traditional black food. They saw dirt roads, a modest black community, simple churches, and huge throngs of African Americans gathered from all over the United States. Each year I watched the Heritage Days festival grow larger and larger until an enormous caravan of cars stretched across the bridge from the mainland to the island in a seemingly unending pilgrimage.

The great Sioux chief Black Elk had a prophetic vision that the sacred hoop (or circle) of life for a deeply spiritual people—the native people of North America—would be broken in its life-and-death struggle with white racism. I believe the destiny of the circle spirituality of the African Americans is to remain unbroken. In its phoenix-like nature, it will never die because its essential nature is survival through transformation and resurrection as the people gather to hear the old, old stories of God's goodness to God's people in each generation. African-American spirituality will continue to empower black people to say to white racism, in the language of the community, "You can't break me because you didn't make me."

Notes

Introduction

1. C. Eric Lincoln, *The Black Church since Frazier* (New York: Schocken Books, 1974), see 103-10.

2. Calvin E. Bruce, "Black Spirituality, Language, and Faith," *Religious Education* 4 (July/August 1976): 63-76.

3. Ibid.

4. Ibid.

5. Ibid.

6. James Cone, *The Spirituals and the Blues: An Interpretation* (New York: Seabury Press, 1972; Maryknoll, N.Y.: Orbis Books, 1991).

7. These sources have been cited by the majority of African-American scholars researched for this study, including black theologians, musicologists, artists, writers, and so forth.

8. Joseph R. Washington Jr., "Are American Negro Churches Christian?" in *Black Theology: A Documentary History: Volume 1: 1966-1979*, ed. James H. Cone and Gayraud Wilmore (Maryknoll, N.Y.: Orbis Books, 1993), 92-100.

9. Ibid.

10. C. Eric Lincoln, *The Black Church since Frazier*, 105.

11. See Lawrence Levine's discussion of cultural marginality in *Black Culture and Black Consciousness: Afro-American Folk Thought from Slavery to Freedom* (New York: Oxford University Press, 1977).

12. See, for example, the work of musicologist John Lovell Jr., cultural historian Lawrence W. Levine, church historian C. Eric Lincoln, and many other scholars cited in this study.

13. Calvin E. Bruce, "Black Spirituality, Language, and Faith," *Religious Education* 4 (July/August 1976): 63-76.

14. Septima Clark was a prominent activist in the Civil Rights movement. See *Ready from Within: A First Person Narrative*, ed. Cynthia Stokes Brown (Trenton, N.J.: Africa World Press, 1990).

Chapter 1: The African Legacy—A Unified Worldview

1. Laurenti Magesa, *African Religion: The Moral Traditions of Abundant Life* (Maryknoll, N.Y.: Orbis Books, 1997).

2. Ibid., xi.

3. Temba J. Mafico, "The African Context for Theology," *The Journal of the Interdenominational Theological Center* 16, nos. 1-2 (Fall 1988/Spring 1989), 69-83.

4. Ibid.

5. Mary A. Twining and Keith E. Baird, eds., *Sea Island Roots: African Presence in the Carolinas and Georgia:* (Trenton, N.J.: Africa World Press, 1991), 1-3.

6. Mafico, "The African Context for Theology," 69.

7. Kwesi A. Dickson, *Theology in Africa* (Maryknoll, N.Y.: Orbis Books, 1984), 29.

8. Ibid.

9. Ibid., 30.

10. Ibid., 35.

11. Paulin J. Houtondji, *African Philosophy: Myth and Reality,* trans. Henri Evans with the collaboration of Jonathan Rée (Bloomington, Ind.: Indiana University Press, 1983), 20, 43.

12. Ibid., 44.

13. Ibid., 49.

14. W. E. B. Du Bois, *The Souls of Black Folk* (New York: Penguin Books, 1969), xi, xii.

15. Ibid., 45.

16. Houtondji, *African Philosophy,* 22.

17. Ibid., 24.

18. Ibid.

19. Ibid.

20. Mafico, "The African Context for Theology," 70.

21. Ibid.

22. John S. Mbiti, *Introduction to African Religion* (Portsmouth, N.H.: Heinemann, 1975), 35.

23. Ibid., 34.

24. Ibid., 32.

25. Ibid.

26. The Yoruba are a West African people from whom it is believed many African Americans are descended from the time of the Atlantic slave trade.

27. Wole Soyinka, *Myth, Literature and the African World* (Cambridge, England: Cambridge University Press, 1976), 10.

28. I purposely refrained from using the word *art,* because it carries a certain Western connotation (as does the word *religion*) that may be in tension with traditional African culture.

29. This symbol of the Ashanti bird is used in a contemporary Black film by the Ethiopian film maker Haile Gerima, entitled *"Sankofa." Sankofa* is an Akan word meaning "one must return to the past in order to move forward."

30. This point of view is expressed by Robert Farris Thompson, *Flash of the Spirit: African and Afro-American Art and Philosophy* (New York, N.Y.: Vintage Books, 1983), xiv.

31. Mafico, "The African Context for Theology," 71.

32. P. A. Talbot, quoted in J. Omosade Awolalu, *Yoruba Beliefs and Sacrificial Rites* (Essex, UK: Longman Group Limited, 1979), 53.

33. Ibid.

34. Ibid., 54.

35. Ibid., 54, 55.

36. Ibid., 57.

37. Ibid.

38. Ibid., 59.

39. Ibid., 60.

40. Soyinka, *Myth, Literature and the African World,* 10.

41. Ibid., 11.

42. Ibid.

43. John S. Mbiti, quoted in Awolalu, *Yoruba Beliefs and Sacrificial Rites*, 61.
44. Ibid.
45. Ibid., 66.
46. Mafico, "The African Context for Theology," 73.
47. Ibid.
48. Ibid.
49. Ibid., 74.
50. Mbiti, *Introduction to African Religion*, 44-64.
51. Ibid., 38.
52. Mafico, "The African Context for Theology," 74.
53. Ibid.
54. Ibid.
55. Awolalu, *Yoruba Beliefs and Sacrificial Rites*, 67.
56. Ibid.
57. Mafico, "The African Context for Theology," 74.
58. Ibid.
59. Ibid., 75.
60. Ibid.
61. Ibid.
62. Ibid., 75-76.
63. Mbiti, *Introduction to African Religion*, 65.
64. Ibid.
65. E. B. Idowu, quoted in Awolalu, *Yoruba Beliefs and Sacrificial Rites*, 80.
66. Ibid.
67. Margaret Field, quoted in ibid.
68. J. Middleton and E. H. Winter, quoted in ibid.
69. Ibid., 80
70. Ibid., 81.
71. Ibid.
72. Mafico, "The African Context for Theology," 76.
73. Ibid.
74. Ibid., 77.
75. A phrase used by the African scholar of religion Osadolor Imasogie. See *African Traditional Religion* (Ibadan, Nigeria: University Press Limited, 1982).
76. Chancellor Williams, *The Destruction of Black Civilization: Great Issues of a Race from 4500 B.C. to 2000 A.D.* (Chicago, Ill.: Third World Press, 1987), 56.
77. Mbiti, *Introduction to African Religion*, 82.
78. Ibid.
79. Ibid.
80. Ibid., 84-85.
81. Ibid., 86-87, italics added.
82. Imasogie, *African Traditional Religion*, 60-61.
83. Ibid., 61.
84. Ibid., 61-62.
85. Mbiti, *Introduction to African Religion*, 93.
86. Ibid.
87. Ibid., 94.
88. Imasogie, *African Traditional Religion*, 69.
89. Mbiti, *Introduction to African Religion*, 98.
90. Ibid.

91. Ibid., 99.

92. Imasogie, *African Traditional Religion*, 69.

93. Ibid., 70.

94. Mbiti, *Introduction to African Religion*, 104-6.

95. Imasogie, *African Traditional Religion*, 72.

96. Ibid., 73.

97. Ibid.

98. Ibid., 73-74.

99. Benjamin Ray, quoted in ibid., 59.

100. Imasogie, *African Traditional Religion*, 76.

101. Ibid.

102. Mbiti, *Introduction to African Religion*, 156.

103. Imasogie, *African Traditional Religion*, 77.

104. Ibid., 80.

105. Mbiti, *Introduction to African Religion*, 150.

106. Ibid., 157.

107. Ibid., 150.

108. Imasogie, *African Traditional Religion*, 83.

109. Ibid., 83.

110. Ibid., 86.

111. Ibid.

112. Mbiti, *Introduction to African Religion*, 175.

113. Ibid., 176.

114. Ibid., 177.

115. Imasogie, *African Traditional Religion*, 34.

116. See Fred Lee Hord and Jonathan Scott Lee, eds., *I Am Because We Are: Readings in Black Philosophy* (Amherst, Mass.: University of Massachusetts Press, 1995).

117. Idowu, quoted in Imasogie, *African Traditional Religion*, 44.

118. A review by Asa G. Hilliard III of Cheikh Anta Diop's article "The Cultural Unity of Black Africa: The Domains of Patriarchy and of Matriarchy in Cultural Antiquity," in *Great African Thinkers*, ed. Ivan Van Sertima, 102-9 (New Brunswick, N.J.: Transaction Books, 1987).

119. Ibid., 108. Hilliard emphasizes the importance of Diop's research revealing the African unified worldview.

Chapter 2: The Quest for Identity

1. Julie Dash, in her film *Daughters of the Dust*, uses a word play on "I own her" and the name "Iona" to demonstrate the name's designation of black parents owning their own child (as opposed to the slave master) in the black slave tradition.

2. G. D. Killam, ed., *Critical Perspectives on Ngugi Wa Thiong'O* (Washington, D.C.: Three Continents Press, 1984), 77.

3. Ngugi Wa Thiong'O, "Church, Culture, and Politics," in *Homecoming Essays on African and Caribbean Literature, Culture, and Politics* (London: Heinemann, 1986), 31.

4. Ibid., 32.

5. Sterling Stuckey, *Slave Culture: Nationalist Theory and the Foundations of Black America* (New York: Oxford University Press, 1987), 3.

6. Ibid., 10.

7. William Loren Katz, ed., *Narrative of Sojourner Truth* (New York: Arno Press and the New York Times, 1968), 17.

8. Georgia Writers' Project of the Work Projects Administration, *Drums and Shadows: Survival Studies among the Georgia Coastal Negroes* (Athens, Ga.: The University of Georgia Press, 1940), 79.

9. Stuckey, *Slave Culture*, 31.

10. Ibid., 15.

11. Melville and Frances Herskovits, quoted in ibid.

12. Ibid., 11.

13. Stuckey, *Slave Culture*, 18 ff., quoting from E. C. L. Adams, "Bur Rabbit in Red Hill Churchyard," *Nigger to Nigger* (New York: Scribner's, 1928), 171.

14. Ibid., 18.

15. William John Faulkner, quoted in ibid.

16. Melville and Frances Herskovits, quoted in Stuckey, *Slave Culture*, 19.

17. Melville and Frances Herskovits, quoted in ibid., 20.

18. Stuckey, *Slave Culture*, 16.

19. John Watson, *Methodist Error or Friendly Advice to Those Methodists Who Indulge in Extravagant Religious Emotions and Bodily Exercises* (1819), quoted in Albert J. Raboteau, *Slave Religion: The "Invisible Institution" in the Antebellum South* (New York: Oxford University Press, 1978), 67.

20. John and Alan Lomax, quoted in Raboteau, *Slave Religion*, 70.

21. John Watson, quoted in Stuckey, *Slave Culture*, 23.

22. Ibid.

23. Raboteau, *Slave Religion*, 72.

24. Daniel Alexander Payne, quoted in ibid., 68-69, italics added.

25. Ibid., 68.

26. Ibid., 74.

27. Georgia Writers' Project, *Drums and Shadows*, 71-72.

28. Al-Tony Gilmore, quoted in Gladys-Marie Fry, *Night Riders in Black Folk History* (Athens, Ga.: The University of Georgia Press, 1991), xi.

29. Fry, *Night Riders in Black Folk History*, xi-xii.

30. Ibid., 66.

31. Ibid., 70.

32. Yvonne Chireau, "Hidden Traditions: Black Religion, Magic, and Alternative Spiritual Beliefs in Womanist Perspective," in *Perspectives on Womanist Theology*, ed. Jacquelyn Grant (Atlanta, Ga.: The ITC Press, 1995), 68.

33. Howard Thurman, *Jesus and the Disinherited* (Richmond, Ind.: Friends United Press, 1981), 36-37.

34. Georgia Writers' Project, *Drums and Shadows*, 58-59.

35. Chireau, "Hidden Traditions," 79.

36. Ibid., 75.

37. Ibid., 76.

38. Fry, *Night Riders in Black Folk History*, 58.

39. Philip D. Curtin, *The Atlantic Slave Trade: A Census* (Madison, Wis.: The University of Wisconsin Press, 1975), 13.

40. See Peter J. Paris, *The Spirituality of African Peoples: The Search for a Common Moral Discourse* (Minneapolis, Minn.: Augsburg Fortress Press, 1995), 35ff.

41. Ibid.

42. C. Eric Lincoln, *The Black Church since Frazier* (New York: Schocken Books, 1974), 104.

43. Ibid.

44. Ibid., 105.

45. Ibid., 106-7.

46. Ibid., 106.

47. "Phoenix," in *Merriam-Webster's Collegiate Dictionary*, 3d ed. (1986).

48. Renita J. Weems, "Reading *Her Way* through the Struggle: African American Women and the Bible," in *Stony the Road We Trod: African American Biblical Interpretation,* ed. Cain Hope Felder (Minneapolis, Minn.: Fortress Press, 1991), 59.

49. See Friedrich Nietzsche, *The Will to Power*, trans. Walter Kaufmann and R. J. Hollingdale, ed. Walter Kaufmann (New York: Vintage Books, 1968).

50. Weems, "Reading *Her Way* through the Struggle," 59.

51. Jacquelyn Grant, *White Women's Christ and Black Women's Jesus: Feminist Christology and Womanist Response* (Atlanta, Ga.: Scholars Press, 1989), 211.

52. Howard Thurman, *Jesus and the Disinherited* (Richmond, Ind.: Friends United Press, 1981), 30-31.

53. Latta R. Thomas, *Biblical Faith and the Black American* (Valley Forge, Pa.: Judson Press, 1976), 13-14.

54. W. E. B. Du Bois, *The Souls of Black Folk* (New York: Penguin Books, 1969), 211.

55. Wyatt T. Walker, *"Somebody's Calling My Name": Black Sacred Music and Social Change* (Valley Forge, Pa.: Judson Press, 1979), 17.

56. Ibid., 16.

57. John Lovell Jr., *Black Song: The Forge and the Flame: The Story of How the Afro-American Spiritual Was Hammered Out* (New York: Macmillan, 1972), 198.

58. Du Bois, *The Souls of Black Folk*, 212.

59. C. Eric Lincoln, *The Black Church since Frazier* (New York: Schocken Books, 1974), 115.

60. Paris, *The Spirituality of African Peoples,* 106.

61. Ibid.

62. Stuckey, *Slave Culture*, 4.

63. Ibid., 4-5.

64. Thurman, *Jesus and the Disinherited*, 86.

65. Paris, *The Spirituality of African Peoples*, 149.

66. Ibid., 150.

Chapter 3: The Call to Protest

1. See Edward Wimberly, *Pastoral Counseling and Spiritual Values: A Black Point of View* (Nashville, Tenn.: Abingdon Press, 1982).

2. Harriet Tubman, *Scenes in the Life of Harriet Tubman*, transcribed by Sarah Hopkins Bradford (New York: Schomburg Library, 1869).

3. Ann Petry, *Harriet Tubman: Conductor on the Underground Railroad* (New York: Thomas Y. Crowell, 1955), 13.

4. Howard Thurman, *Jesus and the Disinherited* (Richmond, Ind.: Friends United Press, 1981), 54.

5. Petry, *Harriet Tubman*, 35.

6. Ibid., 45.

7. Ibid., 47.

8. Ibid., 65.

9. Ibid., 66.

10. Ibid., 241, italics added.

11. Ibid., 236, italics added.

12. William Edmondson, quoted in Edmund Fuller, *Visions in Stone: The Sculpture of William Edmondson* (Pittsburgh: University of Pittsburgh Press, 1973), cited in Georganne Fletcher, ed., *William Edmondson: A Retrospective* (Nashville, Tenn.: Southern Arts Federation, 1981), 12.

13. Ibid., 34.

14. Eugene D. Genovese, *Roll, Jordan, Roll: The World the Slaves Made* (New York: Vintage Books, 1976), 194.

15. John Michael Vlach, "From Gravestone to Miracle: Traditional Perspective and the Work of William Edmondson," cited in Fletcher, *William Edmondson*, 20.

16. Ibid.

17. Ibid.

18. Ibid., 21.

19. Ibid., 20.

20. Ibid., 8.

21. Kay Mills, *This Little Light of Mine: The Life of Fannie Lou Hamer* (New York: Dutton Books, 1993), 10.

22. Ibid., 9.

23. Ibid., 183. See Mills's photocopy of the newspaper story taken from documents preserved by the Mississippi Department of Archives and History.

24. My own mother, who was born in 1926, told her children stories when we were very young about how in her childhood black men were burned to death on occasion on Sunday afternoons in the town square by white people in Bainbridge, Georgia, where she was born. Thus she passed along black history in the form of oral tradition, which has always taken precedence among blacks over what white people have written down.

25. From the PBS documentary "The Africans in America."

26. Mills, *This Little Light of Mine*, 10-11.

27. Ibid., 13.

28. Ibid.

29. Ibid., 7-8.

30. James Weldon Johnson, quoted in William T. and Janice S. Dargan, "Toward a Critical Biography: The Singing Life of C. J. Johnson (1913–), Preliminary Considerations," *Black Music Research Journal* 7 (1987), 86.

31. Mills, *This Little Light of Mine*, 20.

32. Ibid., 21.

33. Ibid.

34. In the black community children had, and still often have, more than simply a biological mother. Mrs. Tucker took little Fannie to church, Sunday school, and home with her every Sunday because she herself had only one child.

35. Mills, *This Little Light of Mine*, 24.

36. Ibid.

37. Ibid.

38. Ibid., 43.

39. Ibid., 60.

40. Ibid.

41. Ibid., 17.

42. Ibid.

43. Ibid., 17-18.

44. Ibid., 18.

45. Ibid.

46. Robert Coles, *The Story of Ruby Bridges* (New York: Scholastic, 1995).

Chapter 4: The Community

1. Kenneth L. Smith and Ira Zepp Jr., *Search for the Beloved Community: The Thinking of Martin Luther King, Jr.* (Lanham, Md.: University Press of America, 1986), 120.

2. Lawrence Levine, *Black Culture and Black Consciousness: Afro-American Folk Thought from Slavery to Freedom* (New York: Oxford University Press, 1977), 4.

3. *Bainbridge Post Search Light,* June 28, 1917. Cited in Barbara R. Cotton, *Non Verba Opera: Not Words But Works: The Biography of Joseph Howard Griffin, M.D.* (Tallahassee, Fla.: Florida Agricultural and Mechanical University, 1981).

4. *Bainbridge Post Search Light,* May 9, 1918, and subsequent issues. Cited in Cotton, *Non Verba Opera.*

5. U.S. Department of Commerce, Bureau of the Census, *Negroes in the United States, 1920-1932* (Washington: U.S. Printing Office, 1935), 704. Cited in Cotton, *Non Verba Opera.*

6. Miss Harper and Miss Ida Mae. These are the only names by which my mother and everybody in Bainbridge ever called them. Both are recently deceased.

7. Interview with Dr. David Griffin conducted by Barbara R. Cotton, April 26, 1980.

8. Itabari Njeri, *Every Good-Bye Ain't Gone* (New York: Vintage Books, 1991).

9. Ibid., 16.

10. Georgia Department of Public Health, *Georgia 1950 Natality and Mortality Statistics* (Division of Vital Statistics, Department of Public Health, 1951), 11, 47. Cited in Cotton, *Non Verba Opera,* 37-38.

11. Ibid.

Chapter 5: Scaling the Mountain Peaks of Spirituality

1. Walter Fluker, *They Looked for a City: A Comparative Analysis of the Ideal of Community in the Thought of Howard Thurman and Martin Luther King, Jr.* (Lanham, Md.: University Press of America, 1989), 5.

2. Howard Thurman, *With Head and Heart: The Autobiography of Howard Thurman* (San Diego, Calif.: Harcourt Brace Jovanovich, 1979), 7.

3. N. A. Fadipe, *The Sociology of the Yoruba* (Ibadan, Nigeria: Ibadan University Press, 1970), 147.

4. Ibid., 148.

5. Fadipe, *The Sociology of the Yoruba.*

6. Howard Thurman, *Deep River and the Negro Spiritual Speaks of Life and Death* (Richmond, Ind.: Friends United Press, 1975), 24-25.

7. Ibid., 66.

8. Thurman, *With Head and Heart,* 9.

9. Ibid., 7.

10. Ibid., 8.

11. Howard Thurman, *The Search for Common Ground* (Richmond, Ind.: Friends United Press, 1986), 8-9.

12. Fluker, *They Looked for a City,* 5.

13. Thurman, *With Head and Heart,* 13.

14. Ibid., 11.

15. Ibid., 17.

16. Fluker, *They Looked for a City,* 22.

17. Ibid., 23.

18. Ibid., 26.

19. Ibid., 26-27.

20. Thurman, *The Search for Common Ground,* 9.

21. Ibid., 15.

22. Ibid., 76-104.

23. Howard Thurman, *The Creative Encounter* (Richmond, Ind.: Friends United Press, 1972 <1954>), 57-58.

24. Ibid., 124. This is the central thesis for the book.

25. Thurman, *With Head and Heart,* 144-45.

26. Thurman, quoted in Lerone Bennett Jr., "Howard Thurman: Twentieth Century Holy Man," *Ebony Magazine* (February 1978), 68.

27. Cited in James Washington, ed., *A Testament of Hope: The Essential Writings of Martin Luther King, Jr.* (San Francisco: Harper & Row, 1986).

28. Lewis Baldwin, *There Is a Balm in Gilead: The Cultural Roots of Martin Luther King, Jr.* (Minneapolis, Minn.: Fortress Press, 1991), 103.

29. Ibid.

30. Ibid., 104.

31. Ibid., 109.

32. Ibid., 110.

33. Ibid., 160.

34. Ibid., 161.

35. Ibid., 162.

36. The text of this essay is available at stanford.edu/group/King/papers/vol1/501122-An_Autobiography_of_Religious_Development.htm.

37. Ibid. See King's discussion of his religious development.

38. Baldwin, *There Is a Galm in Gilead,* 181.

39. Martin Luther King Jr., *Stride toward Freedom: The Montgomery Story* (San Francisco: Harper & Row, 1986), 36.

40. Ibid., 90.

41. Ibid., 84.

42. Martin Luther King Jr., quoted in Washington, *A Testament of Hope,* 9.

43. King, *Stride toward Freedom,* 134-35.

44. Kenneth L. Smith and Ira G. Zepp Jr., *Search for the Beloved Community: The Thinking of Martin Luther King, Jr.* (Lanham, Md.: University Press of America, 1986), 33.

45. Ibid., 120.

46. Martin Luther King Jr., cited in ibid.

47. Martin Luther King Jr., "Remaining Awake through a Great Revolution," in Washington, *A Testament of Hope,* 274.

48. Ibid.

49. Martin Luther King Jr., quoted in Washington, *A Testament of Hope,* 269.

50. Quoted in ibid., 636.

51. Noel Leo Erskine, *King among the Theologians* (Cleveland, Ohio: Pilgrim Press, 1994), xii-xiii.

52. Martin Luther King Jr., quoted in Baldwin, *There Is a Balm in Gilead,* 58.

53. Ibid.

54. James Cone, *Martin and Malcolm and America: A Dream or a Nightmare* (Maryknoll, N.Y.: Orbis Books, 1991).

55. Baldwin, *There Is a Balm in Gilead,* 3.

56. This view is based on my years of teaching young black and white college students at the Atlanta University Center as well as my general observations of Malcolm's current appeal to today's younger generation.

57. *The Autobiography of Malcolm X,* with the assistance of Alex Haley (New York: Ballantine Books, 1964).

58. Amy Jacques-Garvey, ed., *Philosophy and Opinions of Marcus Garvey* (New York: Atheneum Press, 1986), 6-7.

59. *The Autobiography of Malcolm X,* 4-5, italics added.

60. James W. Fowler and Robin W. Lovin, *Trajectories in Faith: Life Stories of Malcolm X, Anne Hutchinson, Blaise Pascal, Ludwig Wittgenstein, and Dietrich Bonhoeffer* (Nashville, Tenn.: Abingdon Press, 1980), 53.

61. *The Autobiography of Malcolm X,* 225.

62. Malcolm X, quoted in Fowler and Lovin, *Trajectories in Faith,* 56-57.

63. *The Autobiography of Malcolm X,* 341.

64. Ibid., 347. Malcolm believed it was crucial for African-American leaders to begin to think and become involved internationally.

65. Ibid., 340.

66. Ibid., 338.

67. Peter Paris, *Black Leaders in Conflict: Joseph H. Jackson, Martin Luther King, Jr., Malcolm X, Adam Clayton Powell, Jr.* (New York: Pilgrim Press, 1978), 140.

Chapter 6: Black Film as Theology

1. Lerone Bennett Jr., "The Crisis of the Black Spirit," *Ebony Magazine* (October 1977), 142-44.

2. Theophus H. Smith, "The Spirituality of Afro-American Traditions," in *Christian Spirituality Post Reformation and Modern,* ed. Louis Dupré and Don E. Saliers (New York: Crossroad, 1996), 372.

3. Ibid.

4. Bennett, "The Crisis of the Black Spirit," 142.

5. Ibid., 142-43.

6. Ibid.

7. Paule Marshall, *Praisesong for the Widow* (New York: Dutton, 1984), 236.

Chapter 7: African-American Spirituality—A Definition

1. Robert Coles, quoted from the Disney movie *Ruby Bridges.*

2. Ibid.

Bibliography

Abrahams, Roger D., ed. *Afro-American Folktales*. New York: Pantheon Books, 1985.

Achebe, Chinua. *African Short Stories*. Nairobi, Kenya: Heinemann Kenya, 1985.

——. *Things Fall Apart*. New York: Fawcett Crest, 1959.

Adegbola, E. A. Ade. *Traditional Religion in West Africa*. Ibadan, Nigeria: Daystar Press, 1978.

Allen, William F., Charles Pickard Ware, and Lucy Garrison, eds. *Slave Songs of the United States*. New York: Arno Press, 1971.

Andrews, William L., ed. *Sisters of the Spirit: Three Black Women's Autobiographies of the Nineteenth Century*. Bloomington, Ind.: Indiana University Press, 1986.

Ansa, Tina McElroy. *Baby of the Family*. San Diego, Calif.: Harcourt Brace Jovanovich, 1989.

——. *The Hand I Fan With*. New York: Doubleday, 1996.

Ansbro, John J. *Martin Luther King, Jr.: The Making of a Mind*. Maryknoll, N.Y.: Orbis Books, 1982.

Awolalu, J. Omosade. *Yoruba Beliefs and Sacrificial Rites*. Essex: Longman, 1979.

Baldwin, Lewis V. *There Is a Balm in Gilead: The Cultural Roots of Martin Luther King, Jr.* Minneapolis, Minn.: Fortress Press, 1991.

——. *Toward the Beloved Community: Martin Luther King, Jr. and South Africa*. Cleveland, Ohio: Pilgrim Press, 1995.

Bastide, Roger. *The African Religions of Brazil: Toward a Sociology of the Interpretation of Civilizations*. Translated by Helen Sebba. Baltimore, Md.: Johns Hopkins University Press, 1978.

Bennett, Lerone, Jr. "The Crisis of the Black Spirit." *Ebony Magazine* (October 1977).

——. "Howard Thurman: Twentieth Century Holy Man." *Ebony Magazine* (February 1978).

Berger Terry, ed. *Black Fairy Tales*. Fairfield, Pa.: Atheneum, 1969.

Billingsley, Andrew. *Climbing Jacob's Ladder: The Enduring Legacy of African American Families*. New York: Simon and Schuster, 1992.

Blassingame, John W. *The Slave Community*. New York: Oxford University Press, 1972.

Blassingame, John W., ed. *Slave Testimonies*. Baton Rouge, La.: Louisiana State University Press, 1977.

Bontemps, Arna. *Great Slave Narratives*. Boston, Mass.: Beacon Press, 1969.

Botkin, B. A. *Lay My Burden Down: A Folk History of Slavery*. Athens, Ga.: University of Georgia Press, 1945.

Branch, Taylor. *Parting the Waters: America in the King Years 1954-63*. New York: Simon and Schuster, 1988.

Brawley, Benjamin, ed. *Early Negro American Writers*. New York: Dover Publications, 1970.

Brent, Linda. *Incidents in the Life of a Slave Girl.* San Diego, Calif.: Harcourt Brace Jovanovich, 1973.

Brown, Cynthia Stokes. *Ready from Within: A First Person Narrative.* Trenton, N.J.: Africa World Press, 1990.

Bruce, Calvin E. "Black Spirituality, Language and Faith." *Religious Education* 4 (July/August 1976): 63-76.

——. "Black Spirituality and Theological Method." *The Journal of the Interdenominational Theological Center* 1 (Spring 1976): 65-76.

Bulhan, Hussein Abdilahi. *Frantz Fanon and the Psychology of Oppression.* New York: Plenum Press, 1985.

Cannon, Katie G. *Black Womanist Ethics.* Atlanta, Ga.: Scholars Press, 1988.

Carawan, Guy and Candie, eds. *Ain't You Got a Right to the Tree of Life?: The People of St. John's Island, South Carolina–Their Faces, Their Words, and Their Songs.* Athens, Ga.: University of Georgia Press, 1966.

Carter, Lawrence Edward, Sr. *Walking Integrity: Benjamin Elijah Mays, Mentor to Martin Luther King, Jr.* Macon, Ga.: Mercer University Press, 1998.

Chireau, Yvonne. "Hidden Traditions: Black Religion, Magic, and Alternative Spiritual Beliefs in Womanist Perspective." In *Perspectives on Womanist Theology,* ed. Jacquelyn Grant, 65-88. Atlanta: ITC Press, 1995.

Coles, Robert. *The Story of Ruby Bridges.* New York: Scholastic, 1995.

Cone, Cecil Wayne. *The Identity Crisis in Black Theology.* Nashville, Tenn.: African Methodist Episcopal Church, 1975.

Cone, James H. *Black Theology and Black Power.* New York: Seabury Press, 1969.

——. *God of the Oppressed.* New York: Seabury Press, 1969.

——. *Martin and Malcolm and America: A Dream or a Nightmare.* Maryknoll, N.Y.: Orbis Books, 1991.

——. *The Spirituals and the Blues: An Interpretation.* New York: Seabury Press, 1972.

——. *A Theology of Liberation.* Second ed. Maryknoll, N.Y.: Orbis Books, 1986.

Cone, James H., and Gayraud Wilmore, eds. *Black Theology: A Documentary History: Volume 1: 1966-1979.* Maryknoll, N.Y.: Orbis Books, 1993.

Cotton, Barbara R. *Non Verba Opera: Not Words But Works: The Biography of Joseph Howard Griffin, M.D.* Tallahassee, Fla.: Florida Agricultural and Mechanical University, 1981.

Courlander, Harold. *A Treasury of Afro-American Folklore.* New York: Crown, 1976.

Creel, Margaret Washington. *A Peculiar People: Slave Religion and Community–Culture among the Gullahs.* New York: New York University Press, 1988.

Crockett, Joseph V. *Teaching Scripture from an African-American Perspective.* Nashville, Tenn.: Discipleship Resources, 1990.

Cudjoe, Selwyn. *Resistance and Caribbean Literature.* Athens, Ohio: Ohio University Press, 1980.

Curtin, Philip D. *The Atlantic Slave Trade: A Census.* Madison, Wis.: University of Wisconsin Press, 1975.

Daise, Ronald. *Reminiscences of Sea Island Heritage: Legacy of Freedmen on St.Helena Island.* Orangeburg, S.C.: Sandlapper Publishing, 1986.

Dargon, William T. and Janice S. "Toward a Critical Biography: The Singing Life of C. J. Johnson (1913–), Preliminary Considerations." *Black Music Research Journal* 7 (1987).

David, Jay, ed. *Growing Up Black from Slave Days to the Present: 25 African-Americans Reveal the Trials and Triumphs of Their Childhoods.* New York: Avon Books, 1968.

Davis, Charles T., and Henry Louis Gates Jr., eds. *The Slave's Narratives.* New York: Oxford University Press, 1985.

Dickson, Kwesi A. *Theology in Africa.* Maryknoll, N.Y.: Orbis Books, 1984.

Diop, Cheikh Anta. *Great African Thinkers.* Edited by Ivan Van Sertima. New Brunswick, N.J.: Transaction Books, 1987.

Drake, St. Clair. *The Redemption of African and Black Religion.* Chicago, Ill.: Third World Press, 1970.

Du Bois, W. E. B. *The Souls of Black Folk.* New York: Penguin Books, 1969.

Dyson, Michael Eric. *Making Malcolm: The Myth and Meaning of Malcolm X.* New York: Oxford University Press, 1995.

Earl, Riggins R., Jr. *Dark Symbols, Obscure Signs: God, Self, and Community in the Slave Mind.* Maryknoll, N.Y.: Orbis Books, 1994.

Ellison, Ralph. *Invisible Man.* New York: Vintage Books, 1972.

Erskine, Noel L. *King among the Theologians.* Cleveland, Ohio: Pilgrim Press, 1994.

Fadipe, N. A. *The Sociology of the Yoruba.* Ibadan, Nigeria: Ibadan University Press, 1970.

Felder, Cain Hope, ed. *Stony the Road We Trod: African American Biblical Interpretation.* Minneapolis, Minn.: Fortress Press, 1991.

Fickling, Susan M. *Slave-Conversion in South Carolina, 1830-1860.* Columbia, S.C.: University of South Carolina Press, 1924.

Fields, Mamie Garvin, with Karen Fields. *Lemon Swamp and Other Places: A Carolina Memoir.* New York: Free Press, 1983.

Fletcher, Georganne, ed. *William Edmondson: A Retrospective.* Nashville, Tenn.: Southern Arts Federation, 1981.

Fluker, Walter E. *They Looked for a City: A Comparative Analysis of the Ideal of Community in the Thought of Howard Thurman and Martin Luther King, Jr.* Lanham, Md.: University Press of America, 1989.

Fluker, Walter Earl, ed. *The Stones that the Builders Rejected: The Development of Ethical Leadership from the Black Church Tradition.* Harrisburg, Pa.: Trinity Press International, 1998.

Fowler, James W., and Robin W. Lovin. *Trajectories in Faith: Life Stories of Malcolm X, Anne Hutchinson, Blaise Pascal, Ludwig Wittgenstein, and Dietrich Bonhoeffer.* Nashville, Tenn.: Abingdon, 1980.

Franklin, John Hope, and Alfred A. Moss Jr. *From Slavery to Freedom.* Sixth ed. New York: McGraw-Hill, 1988.

Frazier, E. Franklin. *The Negro Family in the United States.* Chicago, Ill.: University of Chicago Press, 1939.

Frazier, Thomas R. *Afro-American History: Primary Sources.* Second ed. Belmont, Calif.: Wadsworth Publishing Company, 1970.

Fry, Gladys-Marie. *Night Riders in Black Folk History.* Athens, Ga.: University of Georgia Press, 1991.

Gardiner, Patrick, ed. *Theories of History.* New York: The Free Press, 1959.

Genovese, Eugene D. *Roll, Jordan, Roll: The World the Slaves Made.* New York: Vintage Books, 1976.

Georgia Writers' Project of the Work Projects Administration. *Drums and Shadows: Survival Studies among the Georgia Coastal Negroes.* Athens, Ga.: University of Georgia Press, 1940.

Grant, Jacquelyn. *White Women's Christ and Black Women's Jesus: Feminist Christology and Womanist Response.* Atlanta, Ga.: Scholars Press, 1989.

Gutman, Herbert G. *The Black Family in Slavery and Freedom 1750-1925.* New York: Vintage Books, 1976.

Hale-Benson, Janice E. *Black Children: Their Roots, Culture, and Learning Styles.* Baltimore, Md.: Johns Hopkins University Press, 1982.

Hamilton, Virginia. *Her Stories: African-American Folktales, Fairy Tales and True Tales.* New York: The Blue Sky Press, 1995.

Harris, Joel Chandler. *The Complete Tales of Uncle Remus.* New York: Houghton Mifflin, 1955.

Haskins, Jim. *Voodoo and Hoodoo.* Chelsea, Mich.: Scarborough House, 1978.

Haynes, Leonard L. *The Negro Community within American Protestantism, 1619-1844.* Boston, Mass.: Christopher Publishing House, 1953.

Hodgson, Peter C. *Children of Freedom.* Philadelphia, Pa.: Fortress Press, 1974.

Holloway, Joseph E. "The Origins of African-American Culture." In *Africanisms in American Culture,* ed. Joseph Holloway. Bloomington, Ind.: Indiana University Press, 1990.

Hopkins, Dwight N., and George Cummings. *Cut Loose Your Stammering Tongue: Black Theology in the Slave Narratives.* Maryknoll, N.Y.: Orbis Books, 1991.

Hord, Fred Lee, and Jonathan Scott Lee, eds. *I Am Because We Are: Readings in Black Philosophy.* Amherst, Mass.: University of Massachusetts Press, 1995.

Hountondji, Paulin J. *African Philosophy: Myth and Reality.* Bloomington, Ind.: Indiana University, 1983.

Hurmence, Brenda, ed. *Before Freedom When I Just Can Remember.* Winston-Salem, N.C.: John F. Blair, 1989.

——. *My Folks Don't Want Me to Talk about Slavery.* Winston-Salem, N.C.: John F. Blair, 1984.

——. *We Lived in a Little Cabin in the Yard.* Winston-Salem, N.C.: John F. Blair, 1994.

Idowu, E. B. *African Traditional Religion.* London: SCM Press, 1973.

——. *Olodumare: God in Yoruba Belief.* London: Longman, 1962.

Imasogie, O. *African Traditional Religion.* Ibadan, Nigeria: University Press Limited, 1982.

Jackson, Bruce. *The Negro and His Folklore.* Austin, Tex.: University of Texas Press, 1967.

Jackson, John G. *Introduction to African Civilizations.* Secaucus, N.J.: Citadel Press, 1970.

Jacques-Garvey, Amy, ed. *Philosophy and Opinions of Marcus Garvey.* New York: Atheneum, 1986.

James, George G. M. *Stolen Legacy.* New York: Philosophical Library, 1954.

Jenkins, Ulysses Duke. *Ancient African Religion and the African American Church.* Jacksonville, N.C.: Flame International, 1978.

Johnson, Clifton H., ed. *God Struck Me Dead.* Philadelphia, Pa.: Pilgrim Press, 1969.

Jones-Jackson, Patricia. *When Roots Die: Endangered Traditions on the Sea Islands.* Athens, Ga.: University of Georgia Press, 1987.

Joyner, Charles. *Down by the Riverside: A South Carolina Slave Community.* Urbana, Ill.: University of Illinois Press, 1985.

Jumbam, Kenjo. *The White Man of God.* London: Heinemann, 1980.

Kahiga, Samuel. *The Girl from Abroad.* London: Heinemann, 1974.

Ki-Zerbo, J., ed. *General History of Africa,* Vol. 1: *Methodology and African Prehistory.* Berkeley and Los Angeles, Calif.: University of California Press, 1989.

King, John Owen III. *The Iron of Melancholy: Structures of Spiritual Conversion in America from the Puritan Conscience to Victorian Neurosis.* Middleton, Conn.: Wesleyan University Press, 1983.

King, Martin Luther, Jr. *Stride toward Freedom: The Montgomery Story.* San Francisco, Calif.: Harper & Row, 1986.

King, Noel Q. *African Cosmos: An Introduction to Religion in Africa.* Belmont, Calif.: Wadsworth Publishing, 1986.

Kofsky, Frank. *Black Nationalism and the Revolution in Music.* New York: Pathfinder Press, 1970.

Lakey, Othal Hawthorne, and Betty Beene Stephens. *God in My Mama's House: The Women's Movement in the CME Church.* Memphis, Tenn.: The CME Publishing House, 1994.

Lemann, Nicholas. *The Promised Land: The Great Black Migration and How It Changed America.* New York: Alfred A. Knopf, 1991.

Lester, Julius. *Black Folktales.* New York: Grove Weidenfeld, 1969.

Levine, Lawrence W. *Black Culture and Black Consciousness: Afro-American Folk Thought from Slavery to Freedom.* New York: Oxford University Press, 1977.

Lincoln, C. Eric. *The Black Church since Frazier.* New York: Schocken Books, 1974.

——. *The Black Experience in Religion.* Garden City, N.Y.: Doubleday/Anchor Books, 1974.

——. *Race, Religion, and the Continuing American Dilemma.* New York: Hill and Wang, 1984.

Litwack, Leon F. *North of Slavery.* Chicago, Ill.: University of Chicago Press, 1961.

Loewenberg, Bert James, and Ruth Bogin. *Black Women in Nineteenth-Century American Life.* University Park, Pa.: Pennsylvania State University Press, 1976.

Long, Charles H. *Signs, Symbols, and Images in the Interpretation of Religion.* Philadelphia, Pa.: Fortress Press, 1986.

Lovell, John, Jr. *Black Song: The Forge and the Flame: The Story of How the Afro-American Spiritual Was Hammered Out.* New York: Macmillan, 1972.

Mabee, Carleton. *Sojourner Truth: Slave, Prophet, Legend.* New York: New York University Press, 1993.

Mafico, Temba J. "The African Context for Theology." *The Journal of the Interdenominational Theological Center* 16, nos. 1-2 (Fall 1988/Spring 1989): 69-83.

Magesa, Laurenti. *African Religion: The Moral Traditions of Abundant Life.* Maryknoll, N.Y.: Orbis Books, 1997.

Malcolm X. *The Autobiography of Malcolm X.* With the assistance of Alex Haley. New York: Ballantine Books, 1964.

Mapson, Wendell J. *The Ministry of Music in the Black Church.* Valley Forge, Pa.: Judson Press, 1984.

Marshall, Hallie (adapted by). Teleplay by Roni Ann Johnson. *Ruby Bridges.* New York: Disney Press, 1997.

Marshall, Paule. *Praisesong for the Widow.* New York: E. P. Dutton, 1984.

Mazrui, Ali A. *The Africans: A Triple Heritage.* Boston, Mass.: Little Brown and Company, 1986.

Mbiti, John S. *African Religions and Philosophy.* Garden City, N.J.: Doubleday, 1970.

——. *Introduction to African Religion.* Portsmouth, N.H.: Heinemann, 1975.

Meltzer, Milton. *The Black Americans: A History in Their Own Words 1619-1983.* New York: Harper & Row, 1964.

Mills, Kay. *This Little Light of Mine: The Life of Fannie Lou Hamer.* New York: Dutton Books, 1993.

Mitchell, Henry H. *Black Religious Beliefs: Folk Beliefs of Blacks in America and West Africa.* New York: Harper & Row, 1975.

Mitchell, Mozella G. *Spiritual Dynamics of Howard Thurman's Theology.* Bristol, Ind.: Wyndham Hall Press, 1985.

Mitchell, Robert Cameron. *African Primal Religions.* Niles, Ill.: Argus Communications, 1977.

Morrison, Toni. *Beloved.* New York: Alfred A. Knopf, 1988.

Mosala, Itumeleng J. *Biblical Hermeneutics and Black Theology in South Africa.* Grand Rapids, Mich.: William B. Eerdmans, 1989.

Naylor, Gloria. *Mama Day.* New York: Vintage Books, 1988.

Nietzsche, Friedrich. *The Will to Power.* Translated by Walter Kaufmann and R. J. Hollingdale. Edited by Walter Kaufmann. New York: Vintage Books, 1968.

Njeri, Itabari. *Every Good-Bye Ain't Gone.* New York: Vintage Books, 1991.

Noll, Joyce Elaine. *Company of Prophets: African-American Psychics, Healers and Visionaries.* St. Paul, Minn.: Llewellyn Publications, 1991.

Paris, Peter J. *Black Leaders in Conflict: Joseph J. Jackson, Martin Luther King, Jr., Malcolm X, Adam Clayton Powell, Jr.* New York: Pilgrim Press, 1978.

——. *The Social Teaching of the Black Churches.* Philadelphia, Pa.: Fortress Press, 1985.

——. *The Spirituality of African Peoples: The Search for a Common Moral Discourse.* Minneapolis, Minn.: Augsburg Fortress Press, 1995.

Parrinder, E. G. *West African Religion.* London: Epworth Press, 1961.

Patterson, Orlando. *Freedom in the Making of Western Culture.* Vol. 1. New York: Basic Books, 1991.

Perry, Bruce, ed. *Malcolm X: The Last Speeches.* New York: Pathfinder, 1989.

Petry, Ann. *Harriet Tubman: Conductor on the Underground Railroad.* New York: Thomas Y. Crowell Company, 1955.

Raboteau, Albert J. *Slave Religion: The "Invisible Institution" in the Antebellum South.* New York: Oxford University Press. 1978.

Ray, Benjamin. *African Religion: Symbol, Ritual and Community.* New Jersey: Prentice-Hall, 1976.

Reagon, Bernice Johnson. "Let the Church Sing Freedom." *Black Music Research Journal.* Chicago, Ill.: Center for Black Music Research, Columbia College, Chicago, 1987.

Roberts, J. Deotis. *Black Theology in Dialogue.* Philadelphia, Pa.: Westminster Press, 1987.

Rooks, Charles Shelby. *Revolution in Zion: Reshaping African American Ministry, 1960-1974.* New York: Pilgrim Press, 1990.

Sanfield, Steve. *The Adventures of High John the Conqueror.* New York: Orchard Books, 1989.

Scherer, Lester B. *Slavery and the Churches in Early America, 1619-1818.* Grand Rapids, Mich.: Eerdmans Publishing Company, 1975.

Schomburg Library. *Homespun Heroines.* Edited by Hallie Q. Brown. New York: Oxford University Press, 1988.

——. *Six Women's Slave Narratives.* New York: Oxford University Press, 1988.

——. *Spiritual Narratives.* New York: Oxford University Press, 1988.

Scott, Charles. *The Language of Difference.* Atlantic Highlands, N.J.: Humanities Press International, 1987.

——. *The Work of the Afro-American Woman.* Edited by Mrs. N. F. Mossell. New York: Oxford University Press, 1988.

Shorter, Aylward. *African Christian Theology.* Maryknoll, N.Y.: Orbis Books, 1977.
———. *Christianity and the African Imagination.* Nairobi, Kenya: Paulines Publications Africa, 1996.
Smith, Kenneth L. and Ira G. Zepp Jr. *Search for the Beloved Community: The Thinking of Martin Luther King, Jr.* Lanham, Md.: University Press of America, 1986.
Smith, Luther E. *Howard Thurman: The Mystic as Prophet.* Lanham, Md.: University Press of America, 1981.
Smith, Theophus H. "The Spirituality of Afro-American Traditions." In *Christian Spirituality Post-Reformation and Modern,* ed. Louis Dupré and Don E. Saliers. New York: Crossroads, 1996.
Smith, Wallace Charles. *The Church in the Life of the Black Family.* Valley Forge, Pa.: Judson Press, 1985.
Sobel, Mechal. *Trabelin' on: The Slave Journey to an Afro-Baptist Faith.* Princeton, N.J.: Princeton University Press, 1979.
Southern, Eileen. *The Music of Black Americans: A History.* Second ed. New York: W. W. Norton, 1983.
Soyinka, Wole. *The Interpreters.* London: Andre Deutsch Ltd., 1965.
———. *Myth, Literature and the African World.* Cambridge: Cambridge University Press, 1976.
Starling, Marion Wilson. *The Slave Narrative.* Second ed. Washington, D.C.: Howard University Press, 1988.
Sterling, Dorothy, ed. "Some Old Acquaintances." In *We Are Your Sisters: Black Women in the Nineteenth Century,* 397-401. New York: W. W. Norton, 1984.
Stetson, Erlene. "Studying Slavery: Some Literary and Pedagogical Considerations on the Black Female Slave." In *All the Women Are White, All the Blacks Are Men, But Some of Us Are Brave,* ed. Gloria T. Hull, Patricia Bell Scott, and Barbara Smith, 61-84. New York: The Feminist Press, 1982.
Stuckey, Sterling. *Slave Culture: Nationalist Theory and the Foundations of Black America.* New York: Oxford University Press, 1987.
Tallant, Robert. *Voodoo in New Orleans.* New York: Pelican Publishing, 1946.
Thomas, Latta R. *Biblical Faith and the Black American.* Valley Forge, Pa.: Judson Press, 1976.
Thompson, Robert Farris. *Flash of the Spirit: African and Afro-American Art and Philosophy.* New York: Vintage Books, 1983.
Thompson, Rose, and Charles Beaumont, eds. *Hush Child! Can't You Hear the Music?* Athens, Ga.: University of Georgia Press, 1982.
Thurman, Howard. *The Centering Moment.* Richmond, Ind.: Friends United Press, 1969.
———. *The Creative Encounter: An Interpretation of Religion and the Social Witness.* New York: Harper and Brothers, 1954.
———. *Deep River and the Negro Spiritual Speaks of Life and Death.* Richmond, Ind.: Friends United Press, 1975.
———. *Jesus and the Disinherited.* Richmond, Ind.: Friends United Press, 1981.
———. *The Search for Common Ground: An Inquiry into the Basis of Man's Experience of Community.* Richmond, Ind.: Friends United Press, 1986.
———. *With Head and Heart: The Autobiography of Howard Thurman.* San Diego, Calif.: Harcourt Brace Jovanovich, 1979.
Truth, Sojourner, as narrated to Olive Gilbert. *Narrative and Book of Life.* New York: Arno Press, 1968.

——. *Narrative of Sojourner Truth.* Edited by William Loren Katz. New York: Arno Press and *The New York Times,* 1968

Tubman, Harriet, as narrated to Sarah Hopkins Bradford. *Scenes in the Life of Harriet Tubman.* New York and Auburn: Schomburg Library, 1869.

Twining, Mary A., and Keith E. Baird. *Sea Island Roots: African Presence in the Carolinas and Georgia.* Trenton, N.J.: Africa World Press, 1991.

Wa Thiong'O, Ngugi. "Church, Culture and Politics." In *Homecoming Essays on African and Caribbean Literature, Culture, and Politics,* 31-36. London: Heinemann, 1986.

——. *Critical Perspectives on Ngugi Wa Thiong'O.* Edited by G. D. Killian. Washington, D.C.: Three Continents Press, 1984.

Wade-Gayles, Gloria, ed. *Father Songs: Testimonies by African-American Sons and Daughters.* Boston: Beacon Press, 1997.

Walker, Wyatt Tee. *"Somebody's Calling My Name": Black Sacred Music and Social Change.* Valley Forge, Pa.: Judson Press, 1979.

Washington, James M., ed. *A Testament of Hope: The Essential Writings of Martin Luther King, Jr.* San Francisco, Calif.: Harper & Row, 1986.

Watley, William D. *Roots of Resistance: The Nonviolent Ethic of Martin Luther King, Jr.* Valley Forge, Pa.: Judson Press, 1985.

White, Joseph L., and Thomas A. Parham. *The Psychology of Blacks: An African-American Perspective.* Second ed. Englewood Cliffs, N.J.: Prentice-Hall, 1990.

Williams, Chancellor. *The Destruction of Black Civilization: Great Issues of a Race from 4500 B.C. to 2000 A.D.* Chicago, Ill.: Third World Press, 1987.

Williams, Juan. *Eyes on the Prize: America's Civil Rights Years 1954-1965.* New York: Viking Penguin, 1987.

Williams, Patricia J. *The Alchemy of Race and Rights.* Cambridge, Mass.: Harvard University Press, 1991.

Wilmore, Gayraud S. *Black Religion and Black Radicalism: An Interpretation of the Religious History of Afro-American People.* Second ed. Maryknoll, N.Y.: Orbis Books, 1986.

Wilson, Emily Herring, ed. *Hope and Dignity: Older Black Women of the South.* Philadelphia, Pa.: Temple University Press, 1983.

Wimberly, Edward P. *Counseling African-American Marriages and Families.* Louisville, Ky.: Westminster John Knox Press, 1997.

——. *Pastoral Counseling and Spiritual Values: A Black Point of View.* Nashville, Tenn.: Abingdon, 1982.

Wimberly, Edward P., and Anne Streaty. *Liberation and Human Wholeness: The Conversion Experiences of Black People in Slavery and Freedom.* Nashville, Tenn.: Abingdon, 1986.

Witvliet, Theo. *The Way of the Black Messiah: Theology as a Theology of Liberation.* Translated by John Bowden. Oak Park, Ill.: Meyer Stone Books, 1987.

Woodson, Carter G. *The History of the Negro Church.* Third ed. Washington, D.C.: The Associated Publishers, 1921.

Work, John W., ed. *American Negro Songs and Spirituals.* New York: Bonanza Books, 1940.

Index